Penguin Books
Apartheid in Crisis

D0615763

Apartheid in Crisis

Edited by Mark A. Uhlig

Penguin Books

Penguin Books Ltd, Harmondsworth, Middlesex, England
Viking Penguin Inc., 40 West 23rd Street, New York, New York 10010, U.S.A.
Penguin Books Australia Ltd, Ringwood, Victoria, Australia
Penguin Books Canada Limited, 2801 John Street, Markham, Ontario, Canada L3R 1B4
Penguin Books (N.Z.) Ltd, 182–190 Wairau Road, Auckland 10, New Zealand

First published in the U.S.A. by Random House, Inc., 1986, and
simultaneously in Canada by Random House of Canada Limited
First published in Great Britain by Penguin Books 1986

Copyright © Mark A. Uhlig, 1986
All rights reserved

Made and printed in Great Britain by
Richard Clay (The Chaucer Press) Ltd, Bungay, Suffolk

ACKNOWLEDGMENTS

My work on this book has benefited from the advice and assistance of many people, experts and non-experts, both in the United States and in Africa.

First among them is James Chace, my colleague first at *Foreign Affairs* and now at *The New York Times,* who helped make the book possible, and who has helped immeasurably in its completion.

I also owe a special debt to Tom and Mary Karis, whose concern for and dedication to the people of South Africa is complete.

In my initial work on the subject, I received valuable assistance and encouragement from Susan I. Williams, Jennifer Whitaker at the Council on Foreign Relations, Robert Silvers and Mark Danner at *The New York Review of Books,* and Ina Perlman at the South African Institute of Race Relations in Johannesburg. And I have benefited from the knowledge and skills of many of my colleagues at *The New York Times,* including Ed Klein, Martin Arnold, Michaela Williams, Harvey Shapiro, Ken Emerson, Peter Howe, Alice Weil, Audrey Razgaitis, and Natasha Perkel.

At Random House, my editor, Anne Freedgood, has been wise and very patient. I am also indebted to Becky Saletan and Kate Trueblood for all of their help on this project, and to Philip Gordon for his precise and insightful critique of the final manuscript.

Finally, I would like to thank my parents for their unflagging support, and Martine Singer, who has been a source of constant encouragement and help.

Mark A. Uhlig
New York City
May 1986

CONTENTS

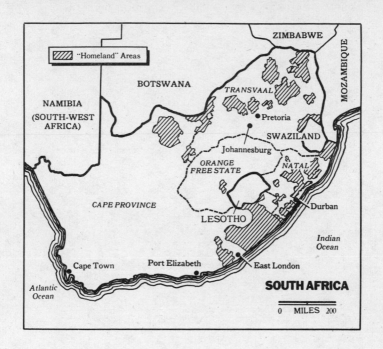

"Homeland" Areas

ZIMBABWE

MOZAMBIQUE

NAMIBIA
(SOUTH-WEST
AFRICA)

BOTSWANA

TRANSVAAL

●Pretoria

SWAZILAND

Johannesburg

ORANGE
FREE STATE

NATAL

CAPE PROVINCE

Durban

LESOTHO

Indian
Ocean

Cape Town

Port Elizabeth

East London

SOUTH AFRICA

Atlantic
Ocean

0   MILES 200

INTRODUCTION

THE COMING BATTLE FOR SOUTH AFRICA

Mark A. Uhlig

Mark A. Uhlig is an editor of The New York Times Magazine. *He was formerly the associate editor of* Foreign Affairs *quarterly.*

On February 17, 1986, a crowd of black protestors surged through the dirt streets of Alexandra, a black township just north of South Africa's largest city, Johannesburg. Pressing against the high wall surrounding a white-owned factory, the demonstrators hurled rocks and gasoline bombs toward the factory walls.

Armed with pistols and shotguns, the white men inside opened fire on the crowd.

"We thought they were trying to outflank us, so I took one side and my father took the other and we opened up on them," one white defender told *New York Times* reporter Alan Cowell.

"Just let them come back," said another white defender, gesturing with his shotgun toward the black crowd in the distance. "We're waiting."

The seeds of such violent conflict in South Africa were sown more than 300 years ago, with the first meetings of white settlers and indigenous black tribes in an unequal relationship that was destined one day to become unsustainable. The final costs, both human and economic, of reconciling that historic inequity are likely to be enormous. But perhaps even more tragic has been the sheer predictability of the event: it has been in full view for decades—for centuries, if early reformers are to be remembered fairly.

South Africa's crisis is thus far more than simply a conflict about race, or power, or even human rights. It is a failure of human foresight. It is a failure of white South Africa to accept, even within the narrowest terms of self-interest, the benefits of mutual accommodation and conciliation and to plan for the day when a house built on sand must be rebuilt on firmer ground.

In some senses, the events at the factory in Alexandra can be viewed as just another episode in an inconclusive drama of racial confrontation that holds little larger meaning for the future of South Africa. White South Africans in particular are fond of pointing out that their regime has weathered worse storms—including two major crises in the last twenty-five years. In March 1960, when police at Sharpeville killed sixty-nine unarmed blacks at a peaceful protest against the pass laws, the nation went into a kind of political shock. The major black political organizations were banned, harsh new security laws were enacted, and the economy was shaken by a serious loss of investor confidence. But the nation emerged intact, with white rule arguably strengthened by the experience.

The cycle was repeated in 1976–77, when a protest by schoolchildren in the black township of Soweto, outside Johannesburg, exploded in a nationwide paroxysm of racial violence that claimed over 700 lives. Then, too, doomsayers predicted the end of white domination, the onset of a final, fatal confrontation between the nation's white minority and its newly assertive black majority. A new set of black opposition groups was crushed by police repression, the stock market plunged—but the country again survived and indeed flourished, entering a period of sustained growth and renewed domestic order.

It is tempting to predict, on the basis of this record, that current and future crises will follow the same pattern—that white rule is resilient enough to withstand still further shocks and emerge stronger as a result. Yet such a view underestimates the important changes that have occurred beneath the surface of racial relationships in South Africa. It ignores the facts that the black opponents of the regime have also learned from the past and grown stronger, and that every successful effort to frustrate black political demands has fueled a new round of anger and confrontation.

Ironically, one of the most important changes that has worked to undermine white rule has been the regime's own attempt to consolidate its position through the promulgation of a new constitution. This change, which has sought to divide black opinion by co-opting so-called Coloured and Indian voters in a new tricameral Parliament, has failed to attract significant support from members of those two racial groups.[1] More important, it has sparked unprecedented hostility from the country's African population, which has interpreted the new arrangement as formal proof of the regime's intention to avoid any kind of franchise or dispensation that might include Africans in the country's central government.

Aided by the anger and controversy engendered by the new constitutional plan, black opposition groups both inside South Africa and in exile have grown stronger than ever before. Unlike 1960, when there was no significant exile opposition, or 1976, when the exiled African National Congress was competing for popularity with the various groups of the Black Consciousness Movement inside South Africa, current opposition to the white regime is increasingly unified and well organized. Having survived a grueling period of adjustment to life in exile after its banning in 1960, the ANC has regained its status as the principal leader of black opposition to apartheid and built an extensive network of international diplomatic and military contacts in support of its efforts against the white regime.

Inside South Africa, aboveground organizations opposed to white rule have also gained strength, benefiting from hard lessons learned during previous periods of police repression. In contrast to the centralized structure of opposition groups in the late 1950s or of the Black Consciousness Movement in the mid-1970s, both of the major organizations now opposing the regime—the United Democratic Front (UDF) and the National Forum—are highly decentralized and have taken other important steps aimed at reducing their vulnerability to police action.

Although rivalries among the various groups remain strong, the relative strength of the largest organization, the United Democratic Front, has reduced the importance of internecine struggles within the opposition. The same has been true of the labor movement, which has overcome many long-standing differences in forming the Congress of South African Trade Unions (COSATU). That federation now looms as a major additional source of pressure upon the government.

Finally, the established sympathies between the major exile and internal groups have permitted the growth of a united opposition on a scale that has never before existed. The connections, however informal, that tie the ANC, UDF and COSATU together have allowed each organization to expand its own influence. They have also provided an opportunity for coordination and consultation that in itself represents a qualitatively new challenge to a regime that has traditionally spared no effort to divide its enemies.

There can be no doubt that the obstacles to any change in South Africa's political structure remain formidable and have in many ways been strengthened over time.

Perhaps the most important obstacle, now as in the past, is the enormous economic cost that any meaningful program of reform will imply for whites. As a small privileged enclave in a vast country whose black majority is largely landless and impoverished, whites cannot expect to retain their current standard of living in any significant program of reform—even one that does not involve wholesale redistribution of wealth. Although an elimination of racial barriers within the South African marketplace could eventually be expected to encourage overall national economic growth and development, that growth is hardly likely to compensate for the economic losses suffered by whites through the elimination of existing legal privileges—still less when the short-term costs of the transition period are considered. Strictly in economic terms, then, this high relative cost continues to suggest that change will come only when the costs of violence and national unrest loom larger than the costs of reform—and, by that time, the opportunity for reform is likely to have passed.

Another important obstacle to change has been Pretoria's increasing efforts to assert the prerogatives of a regional superpower in protecting itself against its internal and external enemies. Employing the full range of military and diplomatic means at its command, the white government has been able to use its regional hegemony as an instrument of domestic policy, cutting off support for ANC insurgents and establishing a *cordon sanitaire* of dependent buffer states to protect it from direct ANC military action.

Finally, the unique and insular Afrikaner world view remains as defiant and fiercely independent as ever. The electoral divisions between Afrikaner and English political parties show no sign of eroding, compounding the difficulty of reform by making it contingent on a bridging of deep-seated Afrikaner-English differences.

These obstacles to reform should not be mistaken for elements of strength. Rather, the contrary is true. Like a brittle tree that cannot bend in the winds, the internal rigidities of white South African politics make the current regime more, not less, susceptible to destruction. By postponing an eventual reconciliation of the nation's fundamental political conflicts, they can work only to encourage polarization and insure that the terms of a final settlement are as harsh as possible for whites. A settlement reached today will be less advantageous for whites than one that might have been possible in the late 1950s. A settlement that is reached tomorrow will be harsher still.

As the need for compromise has grown more urgent, the process of polarization has proceeded at an unprecedented rate. Whites, seeking to protect their property and privileges, have moved increasingly to the right. Right-wing groups such as Andries Treurnicht's Conservative Party have grown rapidly in membership and electoral support, and liberal alternatives such as the Progressive Federal Party have lost strength and leadership as the limits of reform under any white government have become apparent.

Blacks, rebuffing moderates in their midst, have lashed out with ever-increasing ferocity—not only at the white government, but at anyone associated with it. Black policemen, have become special targets of popular rage and have been singled out for such grisly weapons of mob vengeance as the "necklace," a gasoline-filled tire that is placed upon the victim's shoulders and then set afire. Rebel organizations such as the African National Congress, which have long sought to encourage armed resistance to the regime, have found themselves hard pressed to keep pace with such violence and anger. Spontaneous uprisings have occurred in nearly all of South Africa's major black townships, and violence has spread for the first time to those areas of the country now reserved for whites.

A striking feature of this quickening confrontation has been the degree to which it has remained a South African affair. Despite the growing outrage of apartheid's foreign critics and Pretoria's loud assertions that it is the target of a Soviet-led "total onslaught," South Africa's crisis has shown itself to be remarkably immune to outside manipulation. Unlike other countries whose internal conflicts have been deeply affected—if not inspired—by external pressures, South Africa, with its enormous natural resources and unchallenged regional hegemony, has been able to isolate itself from foreign masters and, regrettably, from foreign mediators.

The coming battle for South Africa thus promises to be fought out by South Africans themselves, marching toward a collision of interests and lives that has been foreseeable for generations, paralyzed in the face of a mutual tragedy that is as obvious as it is inexorable.

Oliver Tambo, president of the African National Congress, put it to me in perhaps the simplest terms of all: "What the blacks want more than anything else is to be free in our country—more than anything else. We are dying under the system. We are treated like foreigners in our own country. At best, we are sent to small little barren areas, and we die there. The system itself is an act of violence, because it subjects you to Draconian laws, to impossible laws, which must be obeyed for fear of arrest and being shot down. Your life is defined by these laws, and by the police who are standing around, and by the law courts who are waiting to sentence you. And you have nowhere to go.

"And we say we can't allow this. We say: End that system. We will fight, and we will sacrifice to that end. We want to live in our country—we want to govern our country. It's true we have various racial groups and must govern together. We don't want anybody to leave—everybody's welcome here. But let's learn to regard ourselves as human beings. And until we have reached that position there will be no peace. There can be no peace."

NOTES

1. Here and throughout this book, the term "black" is used to include all three of South Africa's official "nonwhite" racial categories: Africans, Indians and mixed-race "Coloureds."

OVERVIEWS

THE EDUCATION OF FREE MEN

Desmond M. Tutu

Bishop Desmond M. Tutu, the 1984 recipient of the Nobel Peace Prize, is the Anglican Bishop of Johannesburg.

We are passing through a critical, quite traumatic period in the history of our land. That is surely a trite observation, but it is worth making: We are experiencing a virtual breakdown of order, when normal values are overturned.

The very fact that a state of emergency has been declared—even if it be a limited one, since, as government apologists are always at pains to point out, it is not countrywide—is an acknowledgement by the authorities that they have failed to maintain normality, when the usual conventions of a civilized people are observed. Under normal circumstances, people do not expect to have their homes petrol-bombed. Nor do we expect that people will disappear mysteriously, only to be found as gruesomely murdered corpses in burned-out cars. Nor do we expect people who are critical of a particular sociopolitical dispensation to be gunned down in front of their children as they try to reach the safety of their homes. Nor do we expect those who are condemned as collaborators to be burned to death in such horrible fashion as has been happening with such frequency.

There are those who believe that what we want is the restoration of law and order, even if this has to happen with the application of force in the severest form possible.

Somehow people are persuaded that the breakdown in order must ultimately be laid at the door of those whom the State President, in his widely publicized Durban speech, described as "Communists and murderers"—possibly giving a slight variation on the well-known theme of the "agitators" who seem to be so active in persuading blacks to believe that they are unhappy in the best of all possible African worlds.

Why, as the State President asked in that speech, do blacks from other countries stream to South Africa? Do you rush to go to hell? The party faithful answer "No"— South Africa is not hell. Any who believe it to be less than paradise are maligning a great country or have been put up to it by people who are less than scrupulous, as if blacks had to wait until someone said, "Hey, you have a toothache," and they would say, "Ah, yes, I do have a toothache."

And so there is an obsession with law and order, and tough measures leading to the arrest of children as young as seven years old, and to the detention of an eleven-year-old boy for weeks at a time. When people get obstreperous, just knock them one in the head and you will have sorted them out properly!

We do not seem to realize that we will not have dealt with the underlying causes of the unrest merely because we have bludgeoned people into a sullen submission. We seem not to realize that the condition described as law and order is not an absolute good, because if it were then it would be commendable wherever it occurred. But we know that there is law and order in Russia and other repressive and totalitarian countries. And we do not normally find the conditions in those countries, where dissent and discussion are suppressed, attractive and something to want to emulate.

Repressive measures seem to deal with disorder in an efficient way that brooks no nonsense, and this is often attractive to those who fear the invigorating uncertainties that occur when different points of view are vying for the patronage of the public. Disagreement and debate can sometimes appear to be an encouragement to anarchy. People do not seem to want to be bothered to think for themselves, and to have to engage in the disturbing albeit exhilarating enterprise of having to choose between the options that are on offer—having to decide on which conclusion to accept as being most consistent with the evidence available.

In our beloved country we are too prone to think we have dealt with the problem of unrest—which appears to be becoming endemic—by blaming it all on the universal scapegoat—the agitator—and thinking we have done all that really needs to be done to have restored whatever semblance of order we might manage through the exercise of the might of the state.

We sometimes deal with the symptoms of the malaise of the body politic with superficial panaceas and leave the real disease unattended. And all that happens is that we have a false and superficial calm which will be shattered in the short run or the long run. And so we have a cycle that repeats itself—Sharpeville 1960, Soweto 1976 and 1985. And we delude ourselves into believing that the problem will go away for a little while.

We seem unaware of the law of diminishing returns: we will have to apply greater and greater police and military power in return for a reducing degree of order, calm and stability. We seem to have forgotten, too, that increasing force merely gets those against whom it is applied to say, "We might just as well be hanged for a sheep as for a lamb," which has formidable, actually frightening, consequences for our beloved land.

White people by and large are unaware of what can only be called the recklessness of increasing numbers of young blacks who believe that there is no other option for changing the oppressive and evil system of apartheid than violence and who, more shatteringly, believe that they are going to die and do not care any longer.

None of them, for instance, can guarantee that, when they go to one of the funerals which are becoming an almost permanent feature of our lives in the black community, they will return home alive. I have not been so scared as I was at a recent funeral when I intervened and negotiated with the police. Mercifully, there were reasonable police officers who arranged transport for the mourners. Those children said, with quiet determination, "Bishop, we have come to bury our comrade. We intend to go to the graveyard." If the police had not arranged transport, I shudder to think what would have happened if those children had marched.

This is why I have been saying that we are on the verge of a catastrophe of tragic proportions unless a miracle intervenes.

Any student of the South African situation who is worth his salt will point out that our trouble really stems from apartheid, this sociopolitical and economic dispensation which makes no pretense of being democratic. After all, every sane person with just a modicum of intelligence is climbing the bandwagon to call for the demise of this vicious, immoral and unjust policy.

So it is common cause that the villain of the piece is apartheid. But I want to put forward my favorite thesis, which is that we have reached this sad state of affairs because of our appalling educational system. Now one

would think, of course, that I am referring to Bantu education. No, that is only the worst example of a thoroughly
bad lot. I am, sadly, referring to the entire South African
educational system.

With only a very few remarkable exceptions, our educational system is geared to satisfy the examiner. Fundamentally, therefore, the purpose of teaching, if it can be called
that, is to drill the candidate in remembering the right
answer. Consequèntly, we discover our educational system is designed to teach people what to think rather than
how to think. It is designed to produce docile, unquestion-
ing, quiescent creatures who are taught that the best way
to survive is by toeing the line and keeping in with the herd
—goals totally at variance with the ideals of true liberalism (which, do note, is close to liberation).

True and authentic education is not so much concerned
with stuffing people with predigested "facts" and ready-
made, shop-soiled, flyblown, hackneyed responses. Authentic education is intended to help people grow in the
realization of their God-given potential so that they will
develop to become more fully human, with a humanity
which for Christians is to be measured by nothing less
than the humanity of Christ Himself.

Good education is meant to help us become truly
human, and the attribute that is most distinctive about us
is that we are decision-making animals. We are created
freely by God for freedom. In a real sense, an unfree
human being is a contradiction in terms, because we are
created to be morally responsible creatures, those who can
be blamed or praised for vice or for virtue, and you cannot
have moral responsibility without the freedom to choose
between two contrary options—to obey or to refuse to
obey, to love or to refuse to love. And God, who alone has
the perfect right to be a totalitarian, has such a deep

respect for our freedom that He had much rather see us go to hell freely than compel us to go to heaven.

Sadly, our educational system is not designed to develop that embarrassing thing, a questioning mind that will be ready to pose the awkward question, "But why?" And yet we know that any worthwhile advances in human knowledge have happened when a person has refused to be browbeaten into conformity and has called into question the accepted conventions—often at some risk to himself, since those who have a vested interest in maintaining the old parameters of knowledge will not usually regard these others as their blue-eyed boys.

The Church was not exactly enamored of the work of such men as Copernicus and Galileo, who, on the basis of their studies, called into question the tenaciously held view that we lived in a geocentric rather than a heliocentric universe. That gentleman who lay under an apple tree did not, when an apple bonked him one on the head, just shrug his shoulders and say, "Tough luck." He asked, "But why do things fall downwards and never upwards?" and so we got the law of gravity. We could multiply examples to support my thesis.

In this beautiful but sad land we have not, it seems to me, been able to distinguish between authoritative and authoritarian. Someone is authoritative when experience has shown that his or her pronouncements have the capacity of being consistent with the available evidence and of helping to make sense of the situation to which the evidence applies.

He or she tells you that tuberculosis is due to a particular germ which plays havoc with the body when its resistance is low, and that explanation makes sense of a lot of situations to which the relevant evidence applies. If he were to say that TB is due to the evil eye, it would soon be clear that the conclusion could not be sustained by the available evidence. The authoritative person is usually not prone to dogmatism and browbeating, for he knows that the truth is its own justification in the end, because truth will out.

The authoritarian relies not so much on the congruence between his suggested conclusion and the evidence, but on something quite extraneous: his supposed authority, which he does not delight in having questioned. He cannot usually bear to be contradicted or questioned about the grounds on which his conclusion is based. "This is so because I say so"; but too often what he declares to be the case tends to fly in the face of facts. He does not trust that truth is ultimately self-authenticating and has an authority that is in the final analysis unassailable, morally speaking.

When you look at the mess in which we have been landed by those who were guiding the ship of state, you will see that most if not all of their policies just do not make moral, political or even social and economic sense. And yet very few of those who could speak up did in fact do so. On the contrary, there was an extraordinary acquiescence in all the disgraceful erosion of even the minimal rights and freedom that black South Africans enjoyed.

We are the only country in the world where it is actually a crime to want to sell your labor—to be so responsible socially as to want to find work. Under the iniquitous influx control system—which we are told is to be repealed —a person, just because he or she is black, would be committing a crime if they looked for work when their *dompas* (passbook) was not in order. And yet those who claim to believe in free enterprise, one of whose cardinal tenets is that everyone should be free to sell his or her commodity in the open market, have been conspicuous by their remarkable silence at such an aberration in the free enterprise system.

People are not allowed to move freely in the land of their birth. South Africa is the only country I know of in the world which makes it a crime for a man to sleep with his wife. If you are a migrant laborer, perfectly legally married to your wife (that is why she is your wife!), you must for eleven months of the year live in a single-sex hostel. Should your wife visit you and want to sleep with you—you who, together with her, were told in your wedding that "What God has joined let no man put asunder" —she would be committing a statutory offense.

We saw how the authorities dealt with the women at a camp near Cape Town: The police tore down their plastic shelters and let them sit with whimpering babies on their thighs in the cold Cape winter rain, with their household effects a pathetic pile around their feet. And their heinous crime was that these mothers wanted to be with their husbands and the fathers with their children. Their family life was being grossly undermined not just accidentally but by deliberate government policy—and this in a country which quite remarkably has a public holiday, Family Day, dedicated to the sanctity of family life!

We have come to a sad pass in our beautiful land. Many of us do not any longer know the difference between what is morally right and what is legal. Many think that these concepts are identical, and that what is legal—that is, decreed by the law—must also be morally right and virtuous. But this is not the case when the law of the land demands, as in the case of migratory labor, something that contravenes God's law—that a husband and wife must be together.

People in South Africa, therefore, get very hot under the collar when others in conscience disobey unjust or immoral laws which in the Christian tradition do not oblige obedience, for Christians follow the example of the Apostles, who declared that they had much rather obey God than man. This venerable tradition in South Africa is looked at askance because many believe that what is illegal is necessarily also morally reprehensible; hence the strictures against so-called civil disobedience.

But let us give a few more examples of some of the things in this land which make little sense, and yet which have hardly been challenged by anyone who has been educated to ask the awkward question, "But why?"

The government of this land thought they had found a morally defensible method of implementing an obnoxious policy of racial discrimination, this through the notorious Bantustan policy. They flew in the face of quite obvious facts. They spoke about how South Africa was made up of racial minorities—fairly plausible, except that the way they determined what composed a minority did not make much sense. They decided that the whites cohered to make up one nation: English, Afrikaners, Germans, French—you name them, and we have got them. And we said, "Ah ha, yes!" But the blacks, we were told, split up into distinct nations: Xhosa, Zulu, Tswana, etc.

We then asked by what tour de force, by what alchemy, was it possible for the whites, so disparate, to cohere into one group, whereas this failed so dismally with the blacks? And remarkably we had that extraordinary phenomenon whereby the Xhosas did not form one nation—they actually split up into two nations, Ciskeian Xhosa and Transkeian Xhosa, and never the twain shall meet. All this was certainly too subtle for us, not surprisingly given that we were congenitally slow thinkers.

Another example can be found in my own case. Most would agree that I am as South African as *biltong*. [1] (I was going to say the rand, but it is in somewhat troubled waters at present.) But until recently I have had to use not a South African passport, but a travel document which described my nationality as undeterminable at present. I do not take umbrage at others who infringe our copyright on slow thinking.

Now we hear that the government will restore our birthright, our South African citizenship. They have found out that we are South Africans, as if it were a major scientific discovery. But just as we were about to celebrate this epoch-making discovery by the State President, his minister responsible for constitution-making poured cold water on our fervor. This citizenship does not involve political rights, so we shouldn't get excited. And then our ambassador in Washington joins South Africa's favorite pastime, semantic games in politics, and declares that the government does intend to dismantle apartheid and involve blacks in political decision-making. Who are we supposed to believe?

Many South Africans are overawed when someone in authority stands up to speak. And so the Minister of Foreign Affairs tells us solemnly that South African troops have been withdrawn from Angola. But very soon thereafter there is the Cabinda affair, in which South African soldiers are caught in the act of trying to sabotage Angolan oil facilities. Our Minister of Foreign Affairs is shown to have lied. In a free world he would have had to resign from public office. Not in South Africa.

The minister tells us that South Africa, in accordance with the Nkomati accord, has not been assisting the Renamo guerrillas in Mozambique. And then evidence irrefutably shows that this has in fact been taking place. The same minister, without one word of apology for misleading the public, stands up to say the opposite of what

he had declared so solemnly to be the case. Again there
is no uproar. In South Africa the sun still rises in the east,
the birds are twittering in the trees, and the minister remains in office with hardly anyone taking him to task.

Public morality is not maintained when good people
keep silent. Rome, the historians tell us, fell not because
of the attacks of the barbarians. Rome fell because she was
rotten morally. But of course, as a cynic has pointed out,
we learn from history that we don't learn from history.

We live under a racist dispensation which is totally evil,
immoral and unchristian. Its opponents have sought to
oppose it nonviolently, and they have got it in the neck for
their pains.

Let me make this point categorically. The situation in
South Africa is violent, and the primary violence is the
violence of apartheid. It is the violence of forced population removals. It is the violence of detention without trial.
It is the violence of mysterious deaths in detention. It is
the violence that forces children to be stunted through a
deliberately inferior educational system. It is the violence
of the migratory labor system which purposely destroys
black family life. The catalogue is endless.

I have declared myself opposed to all forms of violence.
I have condemned all violence repeatedly.

This government does not know how to handle dissent
because South Africa has only a very weak tradition of
dissent, carried out so nobly by such as the Black Sash and
one or two newspapers. The government almost always
responds with the iron fist, and so we have a state of
emergency that makes de jure what has been the case for
many years—that we have been living under a de facto
state of emergency, given the draconian powers that have
been available to the police.

Now they can do some even more bizarre things, so that my son can be detained under the emergency regulations for fourteen days because he swore at the police, telling them what many of us believe about their actions even though we might not have used equally picturesque language. How, I must ask, does swearing at the police constitute a threat to the security of the state? After fourteen days in Deipkloof jail, Trevor has not changed his views. Does he remain a threat to the security of the state?

Hundreds of children are arrested from the age of seven, and many are kept overnight in jail, and there is hardly a squeak, not a semblance of outrage, in the white community. A boy of eleven years is kept in jail with hardened criminals for fifty-seven days, and not too many are concerned. At a funeral in Bethal, a teenager has her teeth kicked out by the police, and our people are killed as if their deaths amounted to little more than the swatting of flies.

Yet all of this elicits not more than a whimper of protest from those altruists who are concerned that blacks will suffer most if economic sanctions are applied against South Africa. They are concerned apparently about possible future suffering and do not care a bean about our suffering now, which is all too real. In the old style, they know what is best for us. I do not know what they will make of the recent surveys that indicate that an overwhelming majority of blacks favors sanctions.

Our white fellow South Africans live in their affluent ghettos, cut off from their black compatriots who inhabit their squalid ghettos. And white South Africans could well ask, "What state of emergency? What curfew?" What do whites know of the roadblocks whose gauntlet we run regularly en route to our black townships, state of emergency or no state of emergency?

I am the Bishop of Johannesburg. I am a Nobel Laureate. Any policeman who says he does not know me does not deserve to be in the police force. I am stopped at a roadblock and my car is searched, and the police want to body-search my wife and daughters. This eventually happens at a police station, where my wife and daughters are stripped to be searched. A whippersnapper of a policeman asks for some identification from me. It is not just that your dignity as a human being is rubbed in the dust. It is trampled underfoot to boot. If they treat me like that, what do they do to so-called ordinary people?

What do whites know about tear gas, about police dogs, about Casspir armored cars rumbling through the streets of their suburbs, about rubber bullets which kill three year olds playing innocently in the street? What do they know about having the Defense Force quartered on a defenseless civilian population?

When you are in the army you are taught to kill the enemy. Who is the enemy? Is it possible that someone who has been your classmate will be at the other end of your gun barrel because you are white and he is black? What are we doing to our children, what are we doing to our beautiful, beautiful land? What ghastly legacy are we building up for posterity? No country can afford to bleed as much as ours is doing when black lives are dirt cheap. No country can afford to lose property so wantonly.

We cannot protest peacefully against apartheid. We cannot organize a peaceful demonstration march without being taken into custody, as has happened with Allan Boesak. We cannot be an effective opposition to apartheid without being charged with high treason, as has happened especially with members of the United Democratic Front. We cannot even organize a consumer boycott without the police harassing and arresting black traders. And this in a free-enterprise system! We have reached the stage where a peace lecture is thought to endanger public safety and state security. We cannot now even talk about peace!

Like most blacks, I have no confidence in the police. I do not regard them as my friends. I do not regard them as upholders of law and order. For me they are defenders of an indefensible system. Someone broke down part of our wall in Soweto. I did not think it worth any of my time to report it to the police, for I believe the damage was perpetrated by those who support the system, and the police also support the system. Otherwise how is it that antiapartheid activists almost always come to grief, that they are shot dead in front of their children, that their charred bodies are found in burnt-out cars and that, almost invariably, their killers are never apprehended? Someone with a mug inscribed with ANC slogans gets a stiff prison sentence, while a man who kicked to death a so-called Coloured for walking with a white girl is fined thirty rand.

I also have very little confidence in the South African judicial system. The judges, with a few very splendid and outstanding exceptions, are political appointees who are promoted for heading government-appointed commissions that produce reports which favor the government.

The courts have to dispense justice through laws that are fundamentally unjust, lacking the assent of the bulk of the governed. The rule of law has been seriously abrogated. Habeas corpus is a museum oddity in our land. Often the onus is on the accused to prove that he is innocent—a damaging reversal of a time-honored legal canon that a person is deemed innocent until he is proved guilty beyond a shadow of doubt, and the onus is on the prosecution to do this.

I want to ask why our judges and lawyers still participate in a system that is so patently unjust, and by doing
so give the impression that we do in South Africa have an
honorable system of justice—as once, to a large extent,
was the case?

We are constantly regaled with accounts of how South
Africa is changing. We have crossed the Rubicon, we are
told. Where to? How? No one seems to want to enlighten
us.

Those who claim that there is change are almost always
whites. Very few blacks say so. When someone has been
choking you, he cannot tell you, "Hey, things are better
now, I am not choking you quite so hard." It surely will
be the victims who will say, "Ya, you have eased the
pressure." The world will not hear businessmen such as
those before the United Nations. They are white. They
have benefited from this vicious policy. They will not
suffer, even if this whole business of change were to be long
drawn out and protracted. The world will believe only
when we, the victims, say, "Ya, things are changing at
last."

South Africa is a great country. It is richly endowed
with natural resources, and even more richly endowed
with truly great people. We must work for our liberation,
blacks and whites together. Black and white, we shall be
free—and only when blacks are free will whites be free
too.

We must call on the government to sit down and talk
with those whom each community regards as its authentic
leaders and representatives, to work out a blueprint for the
new South Africa where all of us—black and white together—will count. Because all of us—black and white
together—are of infinite worth, since we are made in the

image of God. And all of us—black and white together—
are made for freedom.

NOTES

1. *Biltong* is a traditional South African foodstuff made from
   sun-dried strips of meat.

A LETTER FROM JOHANNESBURG

Nadine Gordimer

Nadine Gordimer is the author of many novels and short-story collections including, most recently, "Something Out There."

Dear ———,

What is it you need to know about us that you cannot read as plain reportage, I wonder?

Well, maybe there is an indication in the ambiguity of the pronoun "us." When I, as a white English-speaking South African, employ it in this context, of whom do I speak? Of whom do you Americans understand me to be speaking? For you ask about the "position that non-Afrikaners find themselves in after the declaration of the state of emergency in South Africa," and doubtless you would assume it is from that position that I respond because I am white, English-speaking, etc. But your question at once reveals that an old misconception is still current abroad: the Afrikaners are the baddies and the English-speakers the goodies among whites in our country; all Afrikaners support the state of emergency and the sadistic police and army actions that led up to it, and all English-speakers would implode apartheid tomorrow if it were possible to prevail against the Afrikaner army that mans the Afrikaner fortress.

This surprises me because anyone who follows the reports of foreign press correspondents in South Africa must be aware that in November 1983 the then-Prime Minister,

Mr. P. W. Botha, received an overwhelming "Yes" vote for his new constitution with its tricameral Parliament for whites, Indians, and so-called Coloureds, and total exclusion of the black majority. The referendum held was open to whites only, Afrikaans- and English-speaking; Mr. Botha could not have received a mandate if the English-speakers had voted "no." "Yes," they said, voting along with Mr. Botha's supporters in the National Party. "Yes," they said, twenty-three and a half million black people shall have no say in the central government of South Africa. And "yes," said the Reagan government, entering into constructive engagement with a policy destructive of justice and human dignity, while mumbling obeisance to abhorrence of apartheid like those lapsed believers who cross themselves when entering a church.

There is no such special position as "one in which non-Afrikaners find themselves" now, nor has there been for a very long time. The categories do not fall so neatly into place. The actual division among whites falls between those—the majority—Afrikaner and English-speaking who support, whether directly or circuitously, the new constitution as a valid move toward "accommodating black aspirations" (let us not invoke justice), and those—the minority—English-speaking and Afrikaner who oppose the constitution as irremediably unjust and unjustifiable. There are fewer Afrikaners than English-speakers in the latter category, but the support of English-speakers in the former represents a majority in their language group. When blacks speak about the "Boer" these days, the term has become a generic rather than an ethnic one: it is likely to refer to a mode of behavior, an attitude of mind, a *position* in which the nomenclature encompasses all whites who voluntarily and knowingly collaborate in oppression of blacks. Not all Afrikaners are "Boer," and many English-speakers with pedigrees dating back to the 1820 settlers are.

States of mind and ways of life under crisis would be expected more or less to follow the lines of division, and I believe that states of mind do. Everywhere I go I sense a relaxation of the facial muscles among whites who had appeared to be tasting the ashes of the good life when Soweto was on fire in the week before the state of emergency was declared. Approval of the state's action is not often explicit in my company because it is known that I belong to the minority-within-the-white-minority that opposes the constitution as a new order of oppression in contempt of justice and sees the state of emergency as an act of desperation: a demonstration of the failure of the government's atrocious "new deal" only a few months after it was instituted.

The general feeling among whites is that fear has been staved off—at least for a while. The police dogs are guarding the gates of paradise. Keep away from roads that pass where the blacks and the police/army are contained in their vortex of violence, and life can go on as usual. One can turn one's attention to matters that affect one directly and can be dealt with without bloodying one's hands: lobbying all over the world against disinvestment and sports boycotts—an area where sophisticated people understand one another in economic and leisure self-interests; for many, the only brotherhood that transcends nation and race. There is a physical and mental cordoning-off of "areas of unrest." The police and army take care of the first, and that extraordinary sense of whiteness, of having always been different, always favored, always shielded from the vulnerabilities of poverty and powerlessness, takes care of the second.

We whites in South Africa present an updated version

of the tale of the Emperor's clothes; we are not aware of our nakedness—ethical, moral, and fatal—clothed as we are, in our own skin. This morning on the radio, the news of the withdrawal of more foreign diplomats from South Africa and the continuing threat of the withdrawal by foreign banks was followed by a burst of pop-music defiance by the state-owned South African Broadcasting Corporation, on behalf of Afrikaner and English-speaking whites. "Allies," yelled a disco idol, "We're allies, with our backs against the w-a-ll . . ."

As for the less worldly among the white majority, they express openly their approval of government violence in the last few months, and there is a group that believes there has not been enough of it. "The government should shoot the lot." This remark was offered to my friend, the photographer David Goldblatt, in all crazy seriousness, not as a manner of speaking: there are whites in whose subconscious the power of the gun in a white man's hand is magical (like his skin?) and could wipe out an entire population more than five times as large as that of the whites. This, in bizarre historical twinship, is the obverse of the belief of the mid-nineteenth-century Xhosa prophetess, Nongquase, who told her people that by following her instructions they could cause all those who wore trousers (the white men) to be swept away by a whirlwind.

It is not true that the South African government is bent on genocide, as some black demagogues have averred (the black man is too useful for that), but it is true that the unconscious will to genocide is there, in some whites. So is belief in the old biblical justification for apartheid that has been embarrassedly repudiated by even the Dutch Reformed Church. Over lunch on his father's Transvaal farm recently, I met a handsome young Afrikaner on leave from military service. Grace was said. When the young man lifted his bowed head he began an exposition of biblical justification that was all his own, I think: blacks are the descendants of Cain and a curse on humankind. I did not rise to the bait, but my eyes must have betrayed that I could scarcely believe my ears. When, among the women of the family, I was being shown their new acquisition, a pristine white dishwasher that had replaced the black maid, he took the opportunity to fire at me: "Yes, it's a good white kaffir girl."

During the weeks that led up to the state of emergency, the eastern Cape black townships had become ungovernable—even in the streets of Grahamstown, the English 1820 Settlers' Association showpiece answer to the Afrikaner Voortrekker Monument at Pretoria, soldiers and armored vehicles had taken the place of festival visitors. Most whites in South Africa were in a state of anguish—over the outcome of the New Zealand government's determination to stop the All Blacks' rugby tour of South Africa. It was only when Soweto became a hell to which Johannesburg's black workers returned each night as best they could (buses would not venture farther than Soweto boundaries) that white faces in Johannesburg became strained.

But the state of mind of the minority-within-the-white-minority did not have to wait for any declaration to be aware of an emergency beyond the national rugby fields. People like Bishop Tutu, Reverend Beyers Naudé, Reverend Allan Boesak, and Sheena Duncan of the Black Sash —a women's organization that has done more than any other source to expose the appalling forced removals of black rural people—had been warning for months that an uprising was inevitable, built into the new constitution as its own consequence.

The government was arresting trade union leaders and

leaders of the nonracial United Democratic Front. Just as, abroad, one may mutter abhorrence of apartheid and go on funding it morally and materially, so the government continued (as it continues) to reiterate a litany of dedication to consultation and change while arresting almost every black leader with any claim to be consulted about change. On the minority side of the dividing line between white and white, a new organization had grown in urgent response to the use of army recruits against the people of the black township of Sebokeng last October.

Resistance to conscription was suddenly no longer some fringe defection on religious grounds by a handful of Seventh Day Adventist, but a wave of revulsion against "defending one's country" by maiming, killing, and breaking into the humble homes of black people. In this horrifying domestic context, the End Conscription Campaign held a three-day gathering in Johannesburg where a large crowd of young men and their families debated the moral issues of conscientious objection and defined their position not as pacifist but as a refusal to defend apartheid. I gave a reading there of poetry by South African writers, black and white, in whose work, like that of playwrights lately, this has been the theme. The subject has to be handled gingerly, whether in poetry or platform prose; it is a treasonable offense, in South Africa, to incite anyone to refuse military service. The ECC is not yet a mass movement and maybe will not be, but the government is sufficiently alarmed by it to have detained several members.

Again, there is a strange historical twinship. Even after 1960, when the South African revolution may be said to have begun, the sons of liberal and left-wing families docilely accepted, *force majeure,* the obligation to do military service, if with a sense of resentment and shame. At the same time, whites who support black liberation have long wondered why blacks have not turned significantly against the informers and collaborators among their own people. Now, young whites have at last found the courage to fulfill the chief provision blacks demand of them if they are to prove their commitment to the black cause: to refuse to fight to protect racism. Young blacks themselves have reached the stage of desperation that leads them to hunt down and destroy those who are their own people in terms of skin but not loyalty. Both developments—the first positive, the second tragic—are the direct result of the new constitution. The blacks were not consulted about it, they rejected it and they are now in a continuous state of rebellion out of bottomless frustration at finding themselves finally cast out, in civic and even physical terms, from their own country. The government deals with this rebellion by sending in white soldiers to terrorize them into temporary submission; young whites are confronted with the loathsome "duty" it was surely always clear racism eventually would demand.

For years, when one asked blacks why they allowed black police to raid and arrest them, they would answer: "Our brothers have to do what whites tell them. We are all victims together." Now, black youths are confronted with what surely always was clear would be the ultimate distortion of their lives by apartheid: brothers, co-opted as police informers and City Fathers by white power, becoming enemies.

Many of us who belong to the minority-within-the-white-minority already were accustomed, before the state of emergency, to using the telephone for the kind of call not made outside thriller movies in your country. When the South African Defence Force raided the capital of one of our neighboring countries, Botswana, earlier this year, we feared for the lives of friends living in exile there. For some days, we could piece together their fate only by exchanging guarded word-of-mouth news. For my fellow writer, Sipho Sepamla, the news was bad; he traveled across the border to Botswana to the funeral of a relative murdered in the raid, and we were nervous about his doing so, since the brutal raid—which resulted in indiscriminate killing, so that even children died—was purportedly against African National Congress revolutionaries, and the demonstration of any connection with even random victims could rub off as guilt by association. With the beginning of the state of emergency there came mass arrests and severe penalties for revealing without authority the identity of any detainee. The names we know are confined to those permitted by the police to be published. Who can say how many others there are? So our ominous kind of morning gossip has increased—and there remains the fear that the individual one calls may not answer because he or she has been taken.

Some of us have friends among those who are the accused in the treason trials, mainly trade unionists and leaders of the United Democratic Front, in session or about to commence. I telephone my old friend, Cassim Saloojee, a social worker and an office holder in the United Democratic Front. He is at home on bail after many weeks of detention before being formally charged with treason. One discovers, these days, that genuine cheerfulness exists, and it is a by-product of courage. He has only one complaint, which is expressed in a way that catches me out: "I've been spending my time watching pornographic films." I give my tactfully unshockable laugh; then I remember that active resistance to apartheid is political pornography in South Africa. The state has seized video cassettes of public meetings made by the United Democratic Front as records of their activities.

For the purpose of their defense, the accused must study what may now be used as evidence against them, "ninety hours of viewing . . ."

The case is *sub judice,* so I suppose I cannot give here my version of whether the particular meetings I attended (the UDF is a nonracial, nonviolent and legally constituted movement) could possibly be construed as violent and treasonous, but I hope that among all that footage there is at least recorded the time when the crowd in a Johannesburg hall heard that there was police harassment of some supporters in the foyer, and from the platform Cassim Saloojee succeeded in preventing the crowd from streaming out to seek a confrontation that doubtless would have resulted in police violence.

While writing this letter I have had a call from a young white student at the University of the Witwatersrand, down the road, who himself is a veteran of detention and whose brother is now in detention for the second time. At last, after more than two weeks, Colin Coleman's parents have managed to get permission to visit Neil Coleman in prison—like well over a thousand others, he has not been charged. The parents are founder-members of the well-established Detainees' Parents Committee, a title and status that indicate the enduring state of mind, stoic but unintimidatedly active, on the part of all prisoners of conscience, black and white, whether or not in the family, that prevails among white people like these.

Colin has called to ask me to take part in a panel discussion on South African culture to be held by the students' Academic Freedom Committee. Irrelevant while we are in a state of emergency? Concurrently with engagement in the political struggle for the end of apartheid, there exists an awareness of the need for a new conception of culture, particularly among whites. Young people like these are

aware that a *change of consciousness,* of the white sense of
self, has to be achieved along with a change of regime, if,
when blacks do sit down to consult with whites, there is
to be anything to talk about. The arts in South Africa
sometimes do bear relation to the real entities of South
African life in the way that the euphemisms and evasions
of white politics do not.

These are the *states of mind* of the majority of white
South Africans and of the minority within the white population. In the first, the preoccupations of the second are no
more than newspaper stories you, too, read thousands of
miles away: so long as the Casspir armored monsters patrol the black townships and even mass funerals are
banned, the majority feel safe, since there is no possibility
that they may be imprisoned for a too-active sense of
justice or find any member of their families or their friends
in detention, on trial or in danger of losing a life in right-
wing terrorist attacks. Nor is there any possibility that one
of their lawyers might be gunned down, as was a member
of a treason trial defense team outside her home a few
nights ago.

The conditions of life, for whites, are a different matter.
Even those few whites who have members of their families
in prison themselves continue to wake up every morning
as I do, to the song of weaverbirds and the mechanical-
sounding whirr of crested barbets in a white suburb.
Soweto is only eight miles from my house; if I did not have
friends living there, I should not be aware of the battles
of stones against guns and tear gas that are going on in its
streets, for images on a TV screen come by satellite as
easily from the other side of the world as from eight miles
away and may be comprehended as equally distanced
from the viewer. How is it possible that the winter sun is
shining, the randy doves are announcing spring, the do-

mestic workers from the backyards are placing bets on the numbers game, Fah-Fee, with the Chinese runner, as usual every afternoon?

In terms of ways of life, conditions of daily living are sinisterly much the same for all whites, those who manage to ignore the crisis in our country, and those for whom it is the determining state of mind. Some go to protest meetings, others play golf. All of us go home to quiet streets, outings to the theater and cinema, good meals and secure shelter for the night, while in the black townships thousands of children no longer go to school, fathers and sons disappear into police vans or lie shot in the dark streets, social gatherings are around coffins and social intercourse is confined to mourning.

The night the state of emergency was declared I was at a party held at an alternative education center, the Open School, in the downtown area where banks and the glass palaces of mining companies run down into Indian stores and black bus queues. The school is directed by Colin and Dolphine Smuts (black, despite their Afrikaans surname) for black youths and children who study drama, painting, dance and music there—subjects not offered by government "Bantu" education. The occasion was a celebration: the school, which had been in danger of closure for lack of funds, had received a Ford Foundation grant. Colin had not known until the evening began whether the new ban on gatherings might not be served on the celebration; Dolphine had gone ahead and prepared food. There were polite speeches, music, drumming and the declamatory performance of poetry that has been part of resistance rhetoric since young people began to compose in prison in 1976 and which sets such gatherings apart from their counterparts in other countries.

Soweto was sealed off by military roadblocks. Yet the

black guests had come through somehow, thoroughly frisked in the "elegantly casual" clothes we all, black and white, wear to honor this kind of occasion. I asked a couple I had not met before what it was like to be in Soweto now, looking at them in the inhibited, slightly awed way one tries not to reveal to people who have emerged alive from some unimaginable ordeal. The man took a bite from a leg of chicken and washed it down with his drink. "In your street, one day it's all right. The next day, you can cross the street when a Casspir comes round the corner, and you'll die. It's like Beirut."

Yes, if you want to know what it's like here, it's more like Beirut than he knew. I remember a film I once saw, where the camera moved from destruction and its hateful cacophony in the streets to a villa where people were lunching on a terrace, and there were birds and flowers. That's what it's like. I also remember something said by a character in a novel I wrote ten years ago: "How long can we go on getting away scot-free?"

Sincerely,
Nadine Gordimer

A LETTER FROM SOWETO

Mothobi Mutloatse

Mothobi Mutloatse is a South African novelist. He also serves as editor and managing director of Skotaville Publishers in Braamfontein, South Africa.

Dear ———,

As I write these notes, Mama Winnie Mandela is in jail, having been forcibly dragged from her Soweto home by armed policemen and soldiers when she insisted on returning there instead of to the house in Brandfort, Orange Free State, to which she had been banished.

What do we black South Africans make out of Mama Winnie's arrest? We watch quietly, pondering—not wondering—how to avenge it. One day, perhaps tomorrow. Somehow, maybe aggressively. And spilling blood, somebody's blood—perhaps that of a "collaborator" who may happen to be black. It is unfortunate that black has to attack black. But then, anger is no respecter of traditional ties. So say the comrades, for these informers (*impipis,* in the local patois) are responsible for the arrest and killing of many of our brothers in the struggle against the system —the apartheid system, to be exact. Justifiable? Perhaps not, but then the heat is on, and the people have seemingly lost all sense of caution, of mercy.

We are a country that is at war with itself, a nation in the throes of a protracted civil war. If that were not so, there would have been no need for the army to intervene in the black ghettos. And, as in Namibia, the army is there to stay: as the military *fundis* will tell you, it is easier to send army troops into trouble-torn areas than it is to remove them. In Soweto, the army will be spending Christmas with us, not by our invitation, but because it has occupied ghettos like Soweto since the official declaration of the state of emergency by P. W. Botha in July 1985.

So it was inevitable that apartheid would politicize the members of the voteless majority, who happen to be black, and turn them into reluctant guerrillas. Yes, every black South African is, one way or another, a guerrilla. Either an armed one, on that side of the border, or an unarmed one, on this side.

That is where we are today. South African blacks are no longer looking for outside help or a messiah to liberate them. They are doing it themselves. The people have risen, the people are in revolt. The people have had enough of the apartheid poison, of the apartheid lie that "*alles sal regkom* (all will come right)." The people won't take another *sjambokking*[1]—they are hitting back, they are shooting back. They are hurling hand grenades, they are making their own Molotov cocktails. They are getting adept at it from as early as eight years of age. Yes, a guerrilla has no age. He has been getting younger since the 1976 Students' Revolt.

Even my three-year-old daughter speaks revolution, sleeps revolution and lives revolution at her kindergarten age. She and her mates chant:

We want Mandela
We don't want *motoho* [porridge]
We want Mandela
We're tired of *motoho*.

The other day I overheard the following dialogue between my wife and our revolutionary daughter:

"Mama, will you buy me . . ."

"What now?"

"Will you buy me a gun?"

"But toy guns are for boys."

"No, mama. I want to shoot the hippos [armored riot-control vehicles]."

There was silence. My wife was tongue-tied.

The authorities claim that revolutionaries are behind the seemingly endless revolts in the ghettos which were ignited by the abortive tricameral parliamentary system and by the school boycotts of 1984. Perhaps my three-year-old daughter is one of these revolutionaries responsible for the mess in which South Africa finds itself today. Yes, guerrillas come in all shapes and ages.

And myself? I have become what you could call a guerrilla with a literary bent. Bishop Tutu and Allan Boesak are guerrillas with a theological bent. Cyril Ramaphosa could be likened to a guerrilla with a trade unionist bent. Yes, even people who call themselves moderates—that is, black people who would rather tell the white man what he wants to hear than what the black person deeply feels—even they are guerrillas who are too frightened to stand up and be counted.

Which implies that there are in fact no moderates in black South Africa. Only slaves, devising ways and means of liberating themselves—some openly, some quietly, some loudly, some aggressively, some half-heartedly, some using the Judas Iscariot method, some using the same methods of the oppressor, some through the arts, through the spoken word, through the written word, through song (like Mama Zenzi Miriam Makeba), some from home, some from away from home.

But always somehow, be it in America, south or north,

east or far east, north or far north. Always somehow, never having renounced one's ties with home. Always hankering for a home without apartheid, dreaming of a return to a humanist home. It is no longer South Africa —the word has become a swearword. Perhaps it is "Azania," at least for the time being as a rallying point. But after that, after we attain our freedom and regain our humanity—and about that we are emphatic, even if we have to die to be free—we will rename South Africa. Democratically.

Obviously, the question remains: Will we regain our humanity peacefully or . . . otherwise? We can't use the word "violently," as it has a bad connotation, implying that some forms of resistance are reprehensible, too extreme. But by the same measure I won't use the word "nonviolence" either, as it too is a word that ensnares the user.

Slaves are not concerned with semantics. All they want is to get their humanity back—and to get the oppressor off their backs. How? That's not the point. To use an African idiom, you don't ask a man whose house is burning to use restraint in putting out the fire. And our house is ablaze.

We will use our own methods of arresting this problem, and the West will have to play its part too, since it is embroiled in our oppression, having always benefited from the cheap labor that apartheid and its partner, capitalism, have afforded at the expense of our human rights. Now the West must prove its bona fides to the oppressed. It must show that it means business, that it is committed to the fundamentals of human rights as enshrined in the Universal Declaration of Human Rights of the United Nations.

Am I advocating punitive action? Sanctions? For me, it's an academic question. You and I know quite well what language Pretoria will understand, since it has steadfastly maintained that it won't be steamrollered into "humanizing" South Africa—that it shouldn't be pushed too far, that it has nothing to be ashamed of, nothing to be sorry for. That there is no earthly reason why it has to apologize to blacks. That the world must stop meddling in its apartheid policies. That it won't give up its white supremacist ideals. That it won't yield to Black Power. That it won't go the way of former Rhodesian Prime Minister Ian Smith. That it will fight a pitched battle against the mythical "commies" claiming to be freedom fighters. Until the last drop of blood—their own and ours and everybody's.

My instincts tell me that only when the privileged electorate, which happens to be white, feels the pinch in its pockets, thereby drastically affecting its affluent lifestyle, its indecent splendor among the horrid squalor, can there be a reasonable chance for a less volatile atmosphere or a situation that culminates in discussions about returning the country—the land and all that goes with it—to the people. To the indigenous people, the natives of this country.

Nothing short of that will appease us. And, even then, genuine change is going to be a painful exercise. For all of us, guerrillas and privileged alike, there is no escape. All we can humanly do is try to minimize the pain. There is no escape from the hell that apartheid built.

Yes, the African giant has awakened. And that giant may have to flatten South Africa to regain its traditional position on this continent, as master of its own destiny. The West owes us billions of dollars for having abetted and connived with apartheid without flinching, and that is why we are primarily addressing ourselves to the West. We were first colonized by them. They took away our religions and imposed their own. They took away our customs, replacing them with their own civilizing European ideals, and tried to make little Europeans out of us. But, worst of all, they cut up our land as if it were a birthday cake for everyone, demarcating large chunks for themselves and crumbs for us. And massacring us along the way.

We have not forgotten how we were robbed of Umhlaba Wethu. Our Land. We know that a people without land is like a person without a soul. And we are still without a soul. Even those who died fighting for their land are still without a soul—and want it back. That's why we are in revolt today. Resisting, resisting and resisting. The African gods are angry. They too have had enough. We will not be ruled by other people a day longer!

We want more than just political and economic power. We want the soil too, for we are people of the soil. That is whence we came. Where we go when we die. That is why we regard the forced removals, relocations, resettlements as sacrilege, as violence to the African soil. It is even worse when our dead are tampered with, uprooted, and dumped elsewhere, much against our will and much against simple human decency. That is how guerrillas are born.

Hector Petersen would have been twenty-three years old had his young life not been snuffed out by the police on June 16, 1976, on a Soweto street as he protested an obscene educational system concocted by madmen to render us impotent, docile, zombies. We remember all the Hector Petersens who died in the tragic eighteen months that followed—more than 700 black South Africans who were murdered by the police and army. This year, 1986, is the year of remembrance: the tenth anniversary of the Students' Revolt against Human Indignity to the African Soul.

It is certainly going to be a watershed year, a point of no return. This far and no farther with apartheid, with white domination. So we have all decided, internal and external guerrillas, armed and unarmed. The African giant is on the warpath. Total onslaught? Maybe. But this time the heat is being generated from within. Within our hearts. Within the country. And we aren't looking back, afraid of the dark or of our own shadows. *"Phambili masoja, hayi, hayi*—forward, warriors, *hayi, hayi!"*

The year 1986 might mean no schooling for black South African children until we have control over the kind of educational system we want for ourselves as a people—and political and economic power. But first, education cannot be allowed to decay in the hands of people who do not understand the nuances of African culture or care a damn about our sense of being—*botho ba rona,* our humanity.

The culture of our oppressors has never taught them to respect our people's values and culture. That is why it is difficult for the majority of the white electorate to accept the self-evident truth that one day blacks are going to govern South Africa, their motherland. Not because of any "communist" connection. But naturally, because history has so decided. And because the black majority won't allow itself to be bullied, terrorized and brutalized into submission anymore without rising up in revolt. Because no apartheid lie can live forever. No oppression can go on indefinitely—human nature does not allow that.

The people are on the march to freedom. And they know it. They know it as well as they know the consequences for daring to stand up against the regime. That is why the Young Warriors are chanting: "We are going to Pretoria, *hayi, hayi!"* And not to play marbles there.

Today, in our lives, tear gas is everywhere. *Sjambokking.* Detention without trial. Emergency laws. The soldiers are in the ghetto to stay, having been sent "in support of the police force" as a temporary measure. That was months ago.

Yet the people are winning the war, psychologically. They are winning because they are no longer afraid. They can now impose their own brand of sanctions, such as consumer sanctions against white businesses, in order to elicit specific, sometimes short-term solutions to black suffering. Today, three-year-old revolutionaries have been hardened, politicized, militarized. They no longer flee at the sight of the police, the army, the maintainers of "law and order." They take as their models such heroes as the legendary Makhanda, who took on the British settler forces at Grahamstown and after his capture became one of the first political prisoners on Robben Island prison. He was to be followed there generations later by Robert Mangaliso Sobukwe, and by Nelson Mandela, just to name two.

The spirit of Makhanda, of resisting until the end, burns in the breasts of the Young Warriors. They will not rest until Mandela, who symbolizes all political prisoners, is released unconditionally so he can return home a free man, in a free country, among a free and undivided people.

Why are they who rule us—but who don't govern us—afraid of Mandela, an old man? As the Young Warriors say, the guilty are always afraid. Afraid even of defenseless Mama Winnie just because she is his wife. Ironically, by their fear they have reminded us that she indeed is the true first lady of South Africa/Azania.

There is, in addition, Grandma Albertina Sisulu, ever resourceful and resilient like the true African mother she is, wife of Mandela's colleague and cellmate Walter Sisulu. She is in the same league as the fallen heroine Ma-Ngoyi (Lillian Masediba), of the famous Women's March to Pretoria in the 1950s. And as other fallen heroines such as Ma-Charlotte Maxeke and Auntie Mary Moodley.

But Mama Winnie is all of them in one—not that she says so, or wanted it to be so, but because the gods have decided it. She has been "widowed," though she and her husband are madly in love and would die to be with one another, like any man and wife. And, like most African mothers, Mama Winnie has had to act many roles: bread-winner, mother, friend and "dad" to her children. In the tradition of so many African women, she is required to hold the knife by the sharp end—or, as Americans would say, bite the bullet—on our behalf.

Are we expected to forgive and forget? We are a "survivalist" people; survival is now our subculture, as one teacher said. We endure pain like Spartans; we do not give up. We would bear pain that would kill even a lion. But that does not mean we can't hit back, can't topple our oppressors, can't kill to survive.

Ask the Young Warriors about that. They are impatient, they are angry. They are raging on behalf of their parents, who still suffer from the hangovers of slavery.

On the one hand, parents might not wholeheartedly approve of what the Young Warriors are doing—especially those things that are done from lack of experience and discipline. On the other hand, parents feel encouraged (and spiritually gratified) that their offspring are not cowards. The Young Warriors are unarmed but unafraid.

And they are winning battles. Were it not for the Young Warriors, Washington would not have done such an acrobatic, 180-degree somersault concerning sanctions against Pretoria. God's little people did it. And God's same little people are going to bring Whitehall to its senses.

Is it true that these Young Warriors are mad? Yes, you have to be crazy to stand up to the might of apartheid. We know it too well, the bullying strategy of Pretoria which has followed. It has threatened and invaded its neighbors and still continues with the policy of regional destabilization that it explicitly disavowed in its Nkomati agreement with Mozambique. If Pretoria bellows, the whole of southern Africa cowers in silence. What else can our neighboring African brothers do against Armscor[2] and the threat of economic strangulation?

They will be free only when we oppressed people of South Africa free ourselves first. *"Nkosi Sikelel'i Afrika* (God Bless Africa),"* Enoch Mankayi Sontonga's anthem, will, after South Africa is liberated, become the official anthem of Africa. Already Tanzania, Zambia and Zimbabwe have adopted our struggle for liberation by making our national anthem their own. Africa will not rest until black South Africa is free. Africa is like a wounded lion, lying in the grass, nursing its wounds, biding time until the opportunity presents itself to strike with all its ferocious might, to avenge its earlier defeat.

Africa badly needs a liberated South Africa—especially in an economic sense, so that an economic bloc comprising Botswana, Angola, Namibia, Zimbabwe, Zambia, Zaire, Kenya, Malawi and Mozambique can be formed along the lines of the Arab oil states.

Southern Africa has been truly blessed with minerals. But in South Africa blacks have been robbed of all their rights to these minerals. We dig and die for gold and diamonds and the white man pays us next to nothing for our labor, later selling these minerals at exorbitant prices, lining his pockets and smiling all the way to the World Bank.

That is why the Young Warriors and the not-so-young Warriors are talking of nationalizing the mines after liberation. If you have gold teeth, know that it was after rockfalls and pipebursts had killed thousands of our brothers. And those exquisite diamonds in your extraordinary necklace choked hundreds of our brothers who dug them from the ground.

You see, apartheid's tentacles spread far and wide. And you are implicated in the oppression of black people in South Africa, protest as you might. You've been drinking wine that is the blood of our brothers and sisters and fathers and mothers in Cape vineyards.

"I didn't know," you say. But that was the same excuse we heard in Nazi Germany. You still have the chance to atone, but it is not for me to tell you how. That is a private matter between you and your conscience. You have always claimed to be my Christian brother. So act. While you rejoice with Christmas carols and tuck your teeth into sumptuous turkey, we'll be eating tear gas and salads called Increased Powers to the South African Defence Forces under the Emergency Regulation. More power to the corrupted. Less rule of law. Less justice. Hell in store for ordinary citizens at roadblocks.

The electorate-which-happens-to-be-white blindly supports all these moves, "to quell the unrest." Yet most do not know where the hell Soweto is—north or south of Johannesburg. All they know is that it is out there somewhere. Far from them. Not a stone's throw. Nor a hand grenade's throw. So they can afford to sleep undisturbed, reassured by the South African Broadcasting Corporation and "intelligence." Have they forgotten how Soweto exploded in 1976 despite the best of "intelligence"? They shouldn't sleep too deeply.

Big business, on the other hand, is worried—for its own sake. Its political partner, Pretoria, is fumbling embarrassingly, wagging fingers, causing the value of the rand to fall and prompting thousands of whites to take the "chicken run" out of the country, fearful for their future. The African gods have spoken: this far and no further. Big business thinks we have forgotten how it waltzed and did the *vas-trap* at the Carlton and Good Hope conferences with Mr. Botha, ganging up on the side of repression. Now, almost two years later, big business appears to be renouncing the agreements reached at those conferences. This because the rand has fallen—and *not* because of any newfound commitment to justice or belief in human rights. Naturally, big business is trying to protect its own interests for expediency's sake; capitalism has never respected human rights.

This does not mean big business cannot be reeducated to make amends for all the wrongs it has committed against black people in South Africa. Neither does it mean that big business is going to be let off the hook easily through bribery and token donations. It is not only political power that has eluded us but, just as important, economic power. On the last point, the West shivers when we talk about killing capitalism and replacing it with something more humane, more considerate. It might well be socialism. Or some part of it. The people will decide that for themselves at their own time and pace. As history tells us, South Africa is a graveyard for predictions, especially about what form of government liberated South Africa is going to have. There will be so many influences to take note of—for example, nonalignment!

Of course there could be a white backlash. But then, the full might of the African giant has yet to be felt. There can't be two bulls in the same *kraal,* says another African proverb. As I said, change is going to come, albeit painfully. We now must decide to what degree the pain will be felt. For whites to become Africans, in the true sense, they have to change their hearts, their supremacist mumbo-jumbo, humble themselves in front of all of Africa (instead of ridiculing it in typical oppressor's arrogance), pledge their allegiance to Africa and not to Europe, and ask to be welcomed into African society not as settlers or passengers but as prodigal sons and daughters. A tall order? Perhaps. Reconciliation is not cheap. It is not just hugging and kissing each other on the cheek as Christians. It is deeper than that, and far more difficult than most people believe.

For instance, the electorate-which-happens-to-be-white expects people who do not have the vote (those of us in Soweto) to celebrate Johannesburg's centenary as if it were our own. As if nothing happened in 1976. As if we would not be commemorating the first decade after the students' demonstration in Soweto. As if all those hundreds of violent deaths were insignificant. As if our hearts did not bleed when stray bullets played havoc with our community and corpses were the order of the day.

The Johannesburg centenary celebrations and the tenth anniversary of the Students' Revolt in Soweto prove, once and for all, that at times the African and European cultures are irreconcilable on certain fundamental issues, as if we were living not just in two worlds, but on two diametrically opposed planets.

When whites are celebrating the centenary of their metropolis, we will be quietly reminiscing about how we died in 1976. About how the white man has everything and we have nothing. About how whites own the very soil Soweto graces. About how we are ruled and regulated from the cradle to the grave. About how, in the land God gave us, all trains, boats and planes are piloted by whites only. About how whites have acres for their homes and we have pieces of ground squeezed to allow only four rooms and an outside toilet. About how white immigrants can come penniless to this country and, within five years, own a chain of stores throughout the land and boast of being citizens to boot. While we who have been here since birth and are children of this soil do not know what it is like to be citizens of our South African fatherland.

After all these things we are still expected to say *"Dankie Nkosi"*—Thank you, Boss—and celebrate! Not on your life! We cannot reconcile with evil, with oppression, with white supremacy. Not now, not ever. So cancel all invitations for Sowetans at your dinner tables, white Johannesburg, for no one is coming. We can't afford the luxury of rejoicing, of celebrating our oppression.

Perhaps white South Africa will listen to us only after there's been another tragedy, another massacre, another indiscriminate bomb blast—an escalation in urban guerrilla warfare à la Beirut or Belfast. In fact, we are already in the first stages of a Beirut or Belfast. An intensification in racism, hopelessness, despair, repression, shootings and countershootings, bombs hurled even by women and children. An increasing use of the army as the heat begins to wear down the police. And the inevitable decision by black clerics that they can no longer justify their exhortations of nonviolence and restraint.

Yes, Beirut and Belfast are staring us right in the face. And if the West is as concerned as it claims, it had better act now. Should the West consider interfering in the domestic affairs of South Africa? No, it should do much more than that—it *must* intervene! It must intervene to prevent this region from becoming engulfed in endless hot pursuits, cross-border conflicts and, eventually, war between white South Africa and the rest of black Africa! White South Africa is accustomed to terrorizing people into submission. We the voteless majority in South Africa know that full well. We know that apartheid has turned the oppressor into a mad beast which knows neither gentleness nor compassion. All it is capable of is *dondering* us to pieces. Brutalizing us. We had hoped that one day this beast would see the light, return to nature, and live in peace with us. Alas, this was not to be. The beast is growing madder by the day, threatening the world community as well.

How should the West intervene? That is your problem, not ours, for you always claim to be on the side of the oppressed, on the side of justice, as the champion of human rights. Now show us your mettle. Live up to your promises, your statements of solidarity with the "downtrodden majority." Did you not say we are one in Christian fellowship, that an injury to one Christian is an injury to all?

Perhaps what I am asking of you is a tall order, impractical and unfair. But should I turn instead to the East? Would you prefer that black South Africa turn its plea to Peking and Moscow in the form of an SOS?

At the moment, hundreds of us are being charged with treason. It is a nightmarish absurdity: noncitizens are being charged with treason against "their country" and executed. And then still others are charged, and others. As if we were able to bring "constitutional" change through the luxury of a ballot box.

That is why, as Young Warriors are being led to the gallows, they tell their mothers to be strong, not to cry, not to mourn, but rather to recite poetry, for they knew there was a price to pay for the liberation of their country. And they knew there will still be a price to be paid by all oppressed black people if they want to be a free people once more.

"Time is running out, South Africa." So goes the famous cliché. Time is running out for peaceful change. And the alternative, said John Vorster, the man who refused to read the writing on his own wall, is too ghastly to contemplate.

Is anyone out there listening? Hearing our pleas?

Looking through my bedroom window, I can see a group of very Young Warriors shouting war chants: *"Nants' e-target* (there's the target!), *madolo phezulu* (knees up!)."

"Hayi, hayi. . . . hayi, hayi!"

NOTES

1. The *sjambok* is a leather whip used as a crowd-control device by South African security forces.
2. Armscor is South Africa's government-owned weapons conglomerate.

WHITE POLITICS

WHITE SOUTH AFRICA CIRCLES THE WAGONS

John de St. Jorre

John de St. Jorre, a former Africa correspondent of the London Observer, *is the author of* A House Divided: South Africa's Uncertain Future. *He was a consultant and senior writer for the Thomas Commission's report,* South Africa: Time Running Out.

O n New Year's Day 1977, South African Prime Minister John Vorster, referring to the riots that shook the black township of Soweto the previous year, warned: "The storm has not yet struck; we are only experiencing the whirlwinds that go before it."

It is not yet clear whether the eye of the storm has settled over the "beloved country," but there is no doubt that South Africa is being buffeted by unprecedented internal and external forces that have created a new atmosphere of awareness and expectation among blacks and a nervous defensiveness among whites. The result is an embattled though still enormously strong and determined white power, and a weaker but equally determined surge of black power. These two realities seem to live in mutual isolation, heightening the contradictions in the apartheid system, depopulating the middle ground and increasing tensions between the races.

De Toqueville's comment that autocratic governments are never at such risk as when they begin a process of reform has been borne out by South Africa's experience. For the Pandora's box of countrywide protest, violence and rebellion that began in September 1984 was unwittingly opened by the government itself through reforms designed to modify the apartheid system.

The foundations of the present crisis were laid during the Soweto upheaval of 1976, which rumbled through the land for a year or more. The Vorster government's response was repression, some minor concessions and more repression. But the events triggered an energetic debate among the more concerned whites (Afrikaners and English alike), a rash of government-appointed commissions examining critical issues like influx control, labor, education and the constitution, and initiatives to "improve the quality of life of urban blacks," such as the electrification of Soweto and the creation of the Urban Foundation.

Those developments took on concrete form after P. W. Botha assumed the leadership in 1978, and the government began to introduce reforms. The process was hesitant, piecemeal, limited, but it was a new departure from the rigid policies of previous Nationalist leaders. In a memorable phrase, Botha told white South Africans they must "adapt or die."

How the electorate was meant to do that has been a matter of intense debate, extraordinary obfuscation and conflicting conclusions ever since. For many, particularly the country's blacks, the issue has become increasingly irrelevant. But since Afrikanerdom continues to rule South Africa, the nature of white power and the direction it is taking continue to demand attention.

P. W. Botha narrowly won the leadership of the National Party in 1978, in the wake of a government scandal that led to the withdrawal of John Vorster. From the relatively liberal Cape Province, Botha had the reputation of a highly experienced politician who had spent virtually all his adult life working for the party, and a successful dozen years as defense minister, during which he built up South Africa's military might and developed important friendships within the military hierarchy. He was also known to be short-fused, belligerent (as defense minister he was sometimes called "Bomber Botha") and intolerant of people who did not share his views.

Considered by many political analysts as either inadequate for the job or, at best, a stopgap leader, Botha surprised his critics by quickly imposing his authority on the Cabinet, consolidating his support in the party and introducing a brisk managerial style to government. He also brought more soldiers into the decision-making process, shook up top levels of the civil service to make it more responsive to government, and reached out to academics, businessmen and journalists for ideas on reform.

Botha began with a flourish, promising to sweep aside the deadwood of previous administrations. Surprisingly, considering his past reputation as a hard-nosed, relatively conservative politician, he appeared to tilt towards the *verligte,* or "enlightened," side of the National Party. Young, enthusiastic planners were given their heads and told to translate the "adapt or die" slogan into practical reforms. A friendly relationship was established with big business—the first time that a Nationalist leader had made such overtures. Even the military men brought into the new, all-powerful State Security Council, which dealt with major policy decisions before they went to the Cabinet, were regarded to be relatively liberal on domestic matters.

The prime minister seemed to be particularly impressed with the arguments of businessmen who stressed the need for a stable and skilled black work force and the merits of creating a black middle class. The legalization of black trade unions in 1979 reflected these concerns and was a

major change, bringing with it unpredictable consequences. The military, after much agonizing, cautiously
opened its doors to blacks. Leasehold rights were granted
to certain blacks in the townships and most categories of
job reservation, which barred blacks from moving into
many skilled or semiskilled trades, were abolished. Black
education was made a budgetary priority and spending
increased dramatically.

Pragmatic considerations lay behind these changes.
Worried by the revolutionary potential of the vast masses
of unemployed, discontented blacks and the need for more
skilled labor (South Africa was booming in the late 1970s),
the government ignored the ideological imperatives of
apartheid that these reforms contradicted. There seems
little doubt that the government was aware of the opposition that its policies would stir among right-wing whites
and of the political role that a class of more skilled and
better-educated blacks might eventually play. But it appeared confident, with its immense coercive powers, of
containing both sets of pressures.

What has happened since then has proved a salutary
lesson in the realities of white and black power in South
Africa. Even the most powerful Afrikaner Nationalist
government is vulnerable to pressure from its ethnic co-
horts on the right; it is also susceptible to mass black
action. In practical terms, those pressures have simultaneously slowed and defined the nature of Botha's reforms,
but neither has so far derailed them.

Early-warning signals of right-wing dissatisfaction came
in the 1981 elections—the first Botha had fought as prime
minister—which on the surface seemed to represent a brilliant personal victory. The National Party was returned to
power with a huge majority (131 out of a total of 165

seats). The Progressive Federal Party (PFP), on the left, gained ground to reach a total of twenty-six seats with 19 percent of the vote. The New Republic Party (NRP), the rump of the once-glorious United Party of J. B. M. Hertzog and Jan Christian Smuts, lost ground and ended up with eight seats. The Herstigte, or "Reconstituted," National Party (HNP), on the right, took 14 percent of the vote but failed to win a seat.

Some analysts, including policymakers in the Reagan administration, interpreted the results as a clear mandate for Botha's reformist policies, believing that those changes would lead, one way or another, to a dismantling of the racially underpinned South African system. The argument was that P. W. Botha, a man convinced that many aspects of apartheid were outmoded and unnecessary and that change was vital for the white man's survival, would now be able to push ahead, relatively unencumbered by the right wing, and introduce significant reforms.

This interpretation, however, was seriously flawed in that it treated the white South African electorate as relatively homogeneous, whereas it is in fact riven by the old Afrikaner-English schism, with the English consigned to a perpetual and powerless minority of less than 40 percent of the total. White South Africans, in spite of social and economical changes and some crossing over, still vote along ethnic lines. Since 1948, successive National Party leaders have managed to rally the bulk of Afrikanerdom behind the party flag both in terms of parliamentary seats and in the percentage of the poll.

The 1981 election demonstrated that the Afrikaner-English divide was as great as ever, and, further, it carried a deeply worrying message about Afrikaner feelings toward Botha's efforts at reform. For, although Botha retained an overwhelming parliamentary majority, he lost almost 40 percent of the *Afrikaner* vote. A third of Afrikanerdom moved to the right and voted for the HNP, which had split off from the National Party in 1969 and set itself up as the repository of Dr. Hendrik F. Verwoerd's "pure" apartheid. A smaller group, estimated at around 5 percent, moved to the left to support Frederick van Zyl Slabbert's PFP.

"It was an ominous signal," said Ton Vosloo, a leading Afrikaner newspaper editor and one of Botha's *verligte* advisers. "The HNP, after years on the edge of politics, became respectable. It was not a happy time for Afrikanerdom."

Unhappier times were to come. The departure of the HNP from the National Party over a decade before had not purged the ruling party of all its right-wing dissenters. Led by Andries Treurnicht, a former pastor in the Dutch Reformed Church and past chairman of Afrikanerdom's influential secret society, the Broederbond, right-wing party members had become increasingly concerned at what they felt was a dangerously liberal tilt by their leader and his *verligte* supporters.

In February 1982, a heated disagreement arose between Treurnicht and Botha over the new proposed constitution that would share some limited political power with the Coloured and Indian minorities but grant nothing to the black majority. The dispute led to the resignation of Treurnicht and seventeen other Nationalist members of Parliament.

The swiftness of the break surprised Treurnicht and his followers, who, many political analysts believe, had intended to remain within the National Party—where they arguably had more influence—or to depart at a more propitious time and take many more Nationalists with them. In the event, Botha, consummate party tactician that he is, outmaneuvered them, quickly closed his party's ranks and declared his determination to introduce the new constitution. Treurnicht and his followers, who regrouped to form the Conservative Party, found themselves facing a still powerful National Party with no hope of a general election to challenge the government for at least another four years.

The Treurnicht breakaway, however, led to a heated debate and serious fissures in many Afrikaner institutions: the Broederbond, the churches, cultural organizations and so on. Nothing like this had happened since 1948, when the Nationalists had first come to power, and nothing could be taken for granted any more. For Botha, the break was a mixed blessing. On the one hand, his party was more unified and more responsive to his notions of reform than it had ever been. On the other, new, powerful voices were out there on the right, openly criticizing government policies.

Meanwhile, Botha sought to achieve a consensus within the white electorate for his constitution by holding a referendum—for whites only—in November 1983. This was a bold step, and it paid off. Two-thirds of white voters endorsed the constitution and, by implication, Botha's other reforms, with many English-speaking voters who normally supported the liberal PFP changing their allegiance and backing the prime minister. This was, for many, Botha's finest hour, demonstrating that while he had lost much Afrikaner support he had made new, compensatory inroads among the English electorate.

Even so, the victory left two major unanswered questions that will have significant bearing on the future direction of government policy. First, can a party as ethnically rooted and ethnically exclusive as the National Party rely on English support—which may be a temporary phenomenon—and afford to lose a major segment of its ethnic base if it is to stay in power? Second, the constitution and the other reforms that have accompanied it triggered the most violent, most sustained and most comprehensive opposition by blacks—supported by many whites, Coloureds and Indians—that South Africa has ever seen. How will that upheaval affect the government's reformist vision?

The fear of a right-wing backlash has been a constant and important factor in white politics for two decades. It is said that the most traumatic moment for John Vorster in his twelve years as prime minister was the breakaway of a tiny group from the National Party to form the HNP in 1969. The right wing has visibly grown since then with the creation of Treurnicht's Conservative Party, the acquisition of the HNP's first seat in parliament and the emergence of a few extraparliamentary groups on the far right. Although they differ in tactics and style, all these right-wing groups have two things in common: an almost exclusively Afrikaner membership and a conviction that the government's policies will lead to the destruction of the political, economic and social hegemony that whites now enjoy in South Africa.

At the moment, the right wing does not seriously threaten the National Party's hold on power. Under the new constitution, the Nationalists do not have to face a general election until 1989. In five by-elections in October 1985, the HNP picked up its first parliamentary seat, and, although the Conservative Party improved its standing, it failed to dislodge any Nationalist incumbents. The government retains a massive seventy-six-seat overall majority. The winner-take-all, Westminster-style constituency electoral system does not favor small parties. If the swing to the right in those five by-elections were to be repeated in a general election, the HNP and CP would collect only thirty-three seats between them, putting them ahead of the Progressive Federal Party but still a long way behind the Nationalists.

Moreover, there is no sign of the two right-wing parties merging, and their message is radical—partition, a white homeland. The HNP, under its tireless, demagogic leader, Jaap Marais, has a populist, blue-collar image and is strident and crude about its support for white supremacy. In the 1985 by-elections, it reversed the Nationalist slogan "Don't Shoot—Think" to "Shoot—Don't Think."

Andries Treurnicht, the Conservative Party leader, is a much more low-keyed figure, and his party, while adamant that old-fashioned "grand" apartheid is the only salvation for South Africa's whites, tries to avoid the brash racist approach of the HNP and seeks to encourage non-Afrikaner membership. The two parties are, however, likely to form some kind of electoral pact in a general election in order not to split the right-wing vote.

The vocal and visible power of the right, especially since it is an Afrikaner right, cannot be underestimated by any Afrikaner government that intends to stay in power. Yet it is paradoxically less threatening now than when Treurnicht and his followers were inside the National Party. With general elections three years away, the HNP and CP can make a lot of noise but exert little influence on the government and its policies. And while it is true that as much as a third of Afrikanerdom now opposes the government from the right, that the Nationalist Party has become sluggish, complacent and lusterless and that the charisma of P. W. Botha's leadership has worn thin, the ruling party nevertheless has a firm grip on all the commanding heights of power, as well as the loyalty of the majority of Afrikaners.

The Nationalists are still a grass-roots party, even after thirty-eight years in power and after a dramatic change in the social and economic status of the Afrikaners. Only 10 percent of the Afrikaners are now farmers. They have become an urban, well-educated, prosperous people, yet they remain ethnically cohesive and the National Party continues to be their political home. The Nationalists, after so long in power, have become inseparable in many people's minds from the government. Directly or indirectly, the state employs 50 percent of all employable Afrikaners (and about one-third of all whites). The print media in South Africa either support the government or criticize it from the left, and the government has exclusive control over radio and television.

The voice of the right wing, outside Parliament, local meetings and what the media chooses to report, is not much heard. The government's coercive powers can be—and have been—used quite ruthlessly against its Afrikaner opponents when they are considered to have stepped too far out of line. The HNP, in the past, and the new extra-parliamentary groups like Carel Boshoff's Afrikaner Volkswag (Afrikaner Sentinel) and Eugene Terre Blanche's *Afrikaner Weerstandsbeweging* (AWB) (Afrikaner Resistance Movement) all claim to have been subjected to surveillance, interference and other heavy-handed government tactics.

A more real danger for the government is the growth of right-wing influence in the civil service, police and military. HNP and CP support in the first two is already thought to be considerable. South Africa's sprawling bureaucracy, despite some streamlining, still contains many powerful officials who hold traditional apartheid beliefs. The police force, although 45 percent black, is also largely conservative, and the government is worried about its members secretly joining the paramilitary AWB under the militant leadership of Terre Blanche. The army is somewhat different in that it has a small permanent cadre with relatively enlightened officers at its head and a broad-based, almost entirely white conscript rank and file. It is thus more representative of the white population as a whole. The effect on the military of being used regularly in the townships against the black population remains to be seen, but it seems clear that its performance has been as tough and brutal as that of the police.

Although it is difficult to quantify conservative influence within the bureaucracy, there is little doubt that it can be used to slow down, if not totally hamstring, the implementation of policies that right-wing bureaucrats dislike. A good example is the government's decision in early 1984 to allow white municipalities to open up their central business districts to black businessmen. Two years later not a single white business district had been desegregated, due to the opposition of government and municipal officials and to bureaucratic red tape.

There are divisions within the National Party. However, the old *verligte/verkrampte* schism is no longer the dominating feature, because the hardliners are now in the Conservative Party, the new home of old-style apartheid. Meanwhile, the mainstream has been largely taken over by the *verligtes.*

The most interesting new development is the emergence of a small group on the left of the parliamentary caucus. These are the "New Nats" or *oerberligtes,* the "over-exposed" or "over-enlightened" ones, as their detractors call them. Well-educated professional men, these Afrikaner Yuppies are far ahead of the government and its policies. Some are even to the left of the Progressives, and they have support from a sprinkling of Afrikaner journalists, academics and businessmen. They believe that the ethnically-based power-sharing of Chris Heunis, the Minister of Constitutional Development and Planning, will not work, and they urge the immediate release of Nelson Mandela and the unbanning of the African National Congress.

While the *verligte* leadership of the party talks of wooing "moderate blacks," the New Nats retort that there aren't any. Afrikaners, they argue, must throw away their ethnic crutches and prepare for survival in a new, black-dominated society, where merit and not skin color will be the critical determinant of individual success. "The New Nats believe that majority rule is not a mere inevitability," said Dries van Heerden, political editor of *Die Vaderland.* "It is a desirability."

But the *oerberligtes* face three serious obstacles. First, they constitute a tiny voice of reason in a confused landscape of prejudice, fear and complacency. Second, white politics, perhaps even more than black politics, remain ethnically hidebound: Afrikaners still do not really trust the English. Finally, even if the New Nats could melt the ethnic glue, there is nowhere—given the disarray of the Progressives—for them to go.

At the other end of the spectrum, the two political parties to the left of the government, the New Republic Party and the Progressive Federal Party, pose far less of a threat to Botha's Nationalists. This is mainly because these parties are predominantly English, although the PFP had made modest inroads into the Afrikaner electorate when it was stylishly led by Frederick van Zyl Slabbert, himself an Afrikaner, before he resigned in February 1986.

The New Republic Party is largely a Natal-based English group and is slowly receding into oblivion. Many of the PFP's English supporters temporarily abandoned the party in the constitutional referendum—Slabbert campaigned energetically for a "No" vote—but appear to have returned to the fold as the normal cycle of parliamentary politics and by-elections reestablished itself.

The PFP has always had a difficult task in persuading the government—and the bulk of the electorate—that its democratic, federalist policies will not turn South Africa over to black majority rule. On the other hand, the PFP's credibility with black opponents of the government is undermined by its participation in the new constitutional system, which is racially based and excludes blacks. An attempt in September 1985 to launch a "Convention Alliance" with the Zulu leader Chief Mangosuthu Gatsha Buthelezi and some Coloured and Indian groups, which called for a national convention of all races and parties to devise a new political structure, ended in failure.

The sudden resignation of Slabbert as both opposition leader and member of Parliament, followed by the resignation of Alex Boraine, a leading PFP liberal and a possible successor to Slabbert, left the party in disarray in early 1986. Provoked and frustrated by the government's inability to implement serious reforms, Slabbert had characterized P. W. Botha's legislative program for 1986 as another "false start" and described the tricameral Parliament as "a grotesque ritual of irrelevance." It seems likely that the Conservative Party will become the official opposition at the next election, shifting the emphasis of the parliamentary debate from the reformist left to the reactionary right. However, some form of white parliamentary liberal presence is likely to survive, perhaps as a group of individuals rather than as a cohesive party, as the voice of white South Africa's liberal conscience playing its traditional role of trying to curb government excesses and cajole, nudge or shame the government into significant reforms.

Botha and his Nationalists command the support of the majority of the white electorate. This majority is made up of about two-thirds of Afrikanerdom plus a considerable percentage of the English and other non-Afrikaners, such as disillusioned white Rhodesians and Portuguese who have settled in South Africa and taken up citizenship.

But can the National Party, under Botha or his successor, continue to retain this degree of support? The key, as always, lies in ethnic politics. As long as Botha retains the allegiance of the majority of the Afrikaner voters, regardless of what happens to the rest, he and the Nationalists will stay in power.

Botha has been careful to carry the majority of the white electorate with him as he introduces changes. Among these changes have been the new constitution, the repeal of the Mixed Marriages and Immorality Acts, leasehold rights for blacks in the townships, the reduction of population removals, the lifting of the prohibition banning political groupings across the color line, the opening up of white downtown areas to black businessmen, the repeal of the pass laws and the restoration of South African citizenship to many blacks who had lost it.

"The government has been successful in persuading the bulk of whites that change is necessary and the Nationalists are the only people that can do it," said Robert Schrire of Cape Town University. "It has also convinced whites that change will not affect their status, security or living standards."

While most whites appear to believe that some reforms are necessary or inevitable, there seems to be a solid consensus on the limits of the reform process. Surveys conducted in 1985 show that the majority of South Africa's whites strongly oppose the desegregation of their schools, hospitals and residential areas and the granting of full political rights to blacks in a unitary state. A 1985 survey done by the Human Services Research Council in Pretoria, for example, revealed that 80 percent of Afrikaners favored continued segregation of schools, hospitals and neighborhoods. A Markinor Gallup poll of urban whites in October of the same year showed that two-thirds of those polled believed that black rule was not inevitable. In short, while whites believe they have come a long way from the days of rigid, doctrinaire apartheid, they remain opposed to accepting blacks' basic social, economic and political demands.

There is an endless debate in South Africa about whether the government is behind, or in front of, the electorate's appetite for change. There is also a belief—held more widely abroad, perhaps, than at home—that, given its head, the Botha government would take a leap of faith and produce some dramatic reforms. And there is a judgment, held firmly by the practitioners of the U.S. policy of "constructive engagement," that, even if Botha cannot bridge the gap between white concessions and black demands, either the dynamic that he has set in motion or his successor will do it for him.

Since Botha came to power, he has often been depicted in the West as a true reformer, a statesman of vision who is eager to create a new and more equitable system in South Africa that would replace apartheid and bring peace and justice to that land. His cautious, piecemeal approach was initially ascribed to the restrictive power of the right wing inside and outside his party. However, as black opposition intensified and violence escalated and as his government appeared to flounder, he was criticized for a failure of leadership and nerve.

This analysis does him less than justice, condemning him for failing to bring changes he never promised and for being the leader he never was. P. W. Botha is an experienced party politician of limited imagination and charisma, cast in the traditions of his party and *volk,* who is prepared to take risks to modernize the system but who, at the age of seventy, has no intention of becoming an Afrikaner Samson, bringing the temple of white domination and white exclusivity crashing down around his ears.

His vision of the future is, like that of most Afrikaner leaders, a limited one. It is also, in the judgment of South African blacks and Western observers, woefully inadequate to end the crisis and solve the country's problems. But his government, the National Party and the majority of the white electorate support that vision, if only because, having rejected the pure brand of apartheid of the past, they see no other alternative that will secure their racial identity, social position, economic privileges and, most important of all, their physical control.

"White South Africans share a whole complex of fears and prejudices about race and color, rooted in the colonial era, which retains remarkable force," Gerald Shaw, deputy editor of *The Cape Times,* observed. "The mainstream of white South African opinion is solidly cast in a mould of conservatism."

Much of the debate in South Africa is confused by the semantics of apartheid and by the lingering controversies the term evokes. This is not to say that the racially based structure of the South African state has been or is in the process of being, removed, although there has been some erosion of racial barriers in public, in the workplace, even in politics. It hasn't, and it isn't, and South Africa remains unique for that reason.

But there has been a major collapse of ideology in both the theory and the practice of apartheid. The new constitution, the repeal of the Mixed Marriages and Immorality Acts, the ending of the pass laws, and the tacit acceptance of the unworkability of the homeland strategy as a final political solution for South Africa's blacks are large nails in the coffin of ideological apartheid.

Instead, it helps to concentrate on the much simpler notion of white power and white control, ignoring as best one can the philosophical, ideological and religious baggage of apartheid which, insofar as it is still around, has been carted off by the political parties of the far right. Narrowing it further, the true focus is Afrikaner power and control, and here it is plain that very little has changed.

The majority of Afrikaners, who make up roughly 60 percent of the white population of 4.8 million, still support the National Party under P. W. Botha's leadership. The military, the police and the vast civil service, all dominated by Afrikaners, remain loyal to their government. The opposition parties, largely English on the left and almost wholly Afrikaner on the right, continue to be weak and ineffective. There is no diminution of will or capacity on the part of the Nationalist government to govern, despite some anxiety and soul-searching among its supporters.

Put simply, the government intends to stay in power, crush dissent, control the pace of change, and establish a "consociational" political system, which will build on the existing pattern of homelands and black urban areas and co-opt as many nonwhite leaders and groups as possible.

The new constitution that was installed in September

1984, offering Coloureds and Indians limited participation in the central political system on separate voters' rolls and in separate parliamentary chambers, will stay. Blacks will not be offered a fourth chamber or any direct representation in Parliament. The homeland strategy will continue. It is significant that the government is pressing ahead with the consolidation and "independence" of KwaNdebele. But it is now generally accepted by government planners that another mechanism for black political participation, especially for urban blacks who have no connection with or interest in the homelands, is needed. The government has also acknowledged that South African citizenship, though not political rights within the central system, should be restored to blacks who lost it when homelands deemed to be their own became independent.

The government's constitutional proposals retain its commitment to the concept of ethnic groupings and to the division between "own" and "general" affairs, a principal enshrined in the 1984 constitution. Thus new provincial authorities with executive powers, "representing all population groups," are to be established, replacing the old, all-white elected legislatures. The new multi-racial bodies will, however, be government-appointed rather than elected. Regional Service Councils will be installed, bringing blacks, browns and whites together at the municipal level to run common ("general") services such as water, power, roads and sewage, while each racial group will look after education and health ("own affairs").

Some government supporters believe that Chief Gatsha Buthelezi, with the carrot of a federal arrangement for the provinces of Natal and KwaZulu (the so-called KwaNatal option), could be brought into this process at a later stage. But the African National Congress and other black nationalist organizations are ruled out as possible partners in any new multiracial prototype.

P. W. Botha revealed a little more of his reformist hand in a speech at the opening of Parliament on January 31, 1986, and in a subsequent publicity campaign. South African citizenship, he announced, would be restored to blacks who had lost it when their designated homelands opted for independence, and passes for blacks would be scrapped by the middle of 1986, to be replaced by a single identity document for all South Africans. The political aspirations of all South Africans, the President said, would be accommodated in a democratic system of government in "a unified South Africa," and a new "National Statutory Council," in which white and black leaders would meet to "consider and advise on matters of common concern" would be set up. "We have outgrown the colonial system of paternalism as well as the outdated concept of apartheid," Botha said.

While the speech did not reveal anything fundamentally new, it was conciliatory in tone and clarified some earlier promises. But it was full of the code words—"group" or "community" rather than "individual" rights, references to South Africa as a "nation of minorities" and so on— that experienced observers of the reform process have come to recognize as meaning the continuation of white control. The speech's impact, moreover, was marred by President Botha publicly chastisement of his foreign minister, Roelof F. ("Pik") Botha, for saying that government policy could result in the country having a black president and by the sudden resignation of PFP leader Slabbert, who declared that he had lost faith in the government's ability to introduce significant change. These events also turned Chief Buthelezi against the new National Statutory Council after he had initially responded favorably to the idea.

Once again, the South African government appeared to be offering too little too late and to have an uncanny knack of shooting itself in the foot.

Looked at through the prism of the other reality, that of black South Africans and others who believe that fundamental change must come soon if a spiraling descent into civil war is to be halted, the government's plans appear totally unreal, even mad. But what seems significant is that while the pace of Botha's reforms has been slowed by the upheavals that followed the introduction of the new constitution, the general direction has not been affected. Nationalist policies, inchoate, unclear and contradictory though they often appear to be, hang together when their purpose of protecting white political control and white separateness in the key areas of education, housing and health is considered.

Optimists looking for a light at the end of the tunnel turn to the succession which they hope will come before, rather than after, the 1989 general elections. There appeared to be two frontrunners, F. W. de Klerk, Minister of Home Affairs and leader of the powerful Transvaal wing of the National Party, and Gerrit Viljoen, Minister of Education and Development Aid (black affairs). For those who believe fundamental change by a Nationalist government is possible, Viljoen is the favorite son. The government's leading intellectual, a former leader of the Broederbond and head of the Rand-Afrikaans University, Viljoen is seen as an intelligent and sensitive *verligte* reformer. In contrast, de Klerk is a traditionalist, rooted in the center of the party and with little understanding of the broader and strategic dimensions of the problem.

But even if Viljoen, or someone else who shares his *verligte* and pragmatic beliefs, takes over from P. W. Botha, there is no evidence to indicate that the government's basic direction would change. Viljoen has made it clear that the Nationalists have no intention of incorporating blacks either into the central political system or into a racially integrated social and economic structure that would remove the barriers held in place by the Group Areas Act and other segregationist legislation.[1] The post-Botha era, at best, promises a change more of style than of substance.

In 1984 and 1985, the Government withstood a severe buffeting. The violence that began in September 1984, when the new constitution was introduced, appeared unstoppable. For the first time in two and a half decades, the government had to bring the army into black townships. In July 1985, Botha declared a state of emergency in a number of areas, less for the new but only marginally more comprehensive coercive powers a state of emergency bestows than to satisfy right-wing criticism inside and outside the National Party. But the violence continued, and a much-touted speech by Botha in August that was supposed to announce major reforms turned into a defiant and bellicose blast against South Africa's "internal and external enemies."

The effect of that address was dramatic. Foreign bankers refused to renew their loans. The rand fell dramatically. The love affair between Pretoria and South African big business turned sour, and a group of leading businessmen trekked to Lusaka to talk to the ANC. The economic recession, already the worst since the depression of the 1930s, deepened. White unemployment began to cause concern and some whites began to vote with their feet by emigrating. Even friendly America turned aside and imposed minor sanctions.

President Botha would welcome a formula to release

Nelson Mandela, the imprisoned African National Congress leader, but he has so far failed to separate Mandela's release from the conditions that Mandela himself has set for his own liberty. Botha is not yet prepared to accept those conditions, which include the unbanning of the ANC, allowing normal political activity and organization, and implicitly starting negotiations for a new constitution and a transfer of power. The fact that these conditions— the "Mandela package"—are also being pressed on him by domestic political opponents, by the United Nations, the Commonwealth, and the majority of South Africa's western trading partners, including the United States, makes it harder than ever for him to accept.

The Cabinet appears to be divided on the Mandela issue. Foreign Minister Pik Botha and other soft-liners, who are concerned about South Africa's international image, have been pressing for Mandela's release. Louis Le Grange, the Minister of Law and Order, and the security establishment want to keep him in jail. Botha himself is believed to be a hard-liner but amenable to persuasion if important elements in the National Party and the Afrikaner power establishment are prepared to endorse and actively support the decision.

Mandela's release poses three major problems for the government. First, will his freedom and the opening-up of black politics result in a calmer or in a more violent situation, giving the government more or less control over events? Second, is the government ready to come to terms with the Mandela package and, by implication, move toward a transition to black rule? And third, how detrimental will it be for the government if Mandela is not released and dies in prison?

The answer appears to be, first, that the situation will become more volatile and less controllable. There will be a real risk of having to put Mandela back in jail. Second, P. W. Botha and the Afrikaner establishment are nowhere ready to surrender part or all of their power to the black majority. And third, Mandela's continued incarceration—and his eventual death in prison—will cause the government serious problems, particularly in the international community. But, given the alternatives, keeping him in jail appears to be safer for Pretoria than releasing him and opening up an unquantifiable Pandora's Box of risks.

Meanwhile, the government has adopted two tactical approaches to the problem. It is trying to split the ANC by inviting home exiled "nationalists" as opposed to "communists" who renounce violence. And further, it is sending occasional encouraging diplomatic signals about Mandela's release in order to keep its options open.

The government seems to calculate that by pursuing its mixture of moderate repression and moderate reform it can weather the storm. And then, if the violence wanes, it will have won a useful respite. It calculates, probably rightly, that with peace restored and more reforms in the pipeline, South African businessmen will turn their backs on political matters and redirect their energies to making money. Likewise, the foreign bankers. And then there is always the hope of a "goldfall," a significant rise in the gold price which would bring the kind of economic windfall that has often saved South African governments in the past.

The opposite side of the coin—worsening violence and growing isolation—would almost certainly result in the government using more of its coercive power and consolidating its Afrikaner base by moving rightwards. The critical factor will be the level of violence against whites and changes in white standards of living. If more whites are killed, as seems likely after the ANC's threat to broaden the struggle into a "people's war," and the economic costs become more punitive for the white population, the Nationalist government is likely to hunker down in defense of a siege state.

Neither of these scenarios is attractive. The first would see a slow modification of the status quo that shies away from the central issue of the transfer of power to the black majority, deepening the gulf between white and black, peace and war. The second is an increasingly brutal and costly sharpening of racial confrontation, possibly leading to negotiation if rational minds prevail but more likely descending into a widening, insoluble conflict: the "Lebanization" of South Africa.

Returning to the upheavals of 1976, Afrikaner historian F. A. van Jaarsveld criticized his countrymen for not addressing the central problems and for letting the initiative slip out of their hands. "The Afrikaner stands alone before an approaching and inevitable war," he wrote, "and he stands alone."

NOTES

1. Viljoen gave a revealing account of government policy and his own views in an interview in *Leadership SA,* vol. 4 (First Quarter 1985).

A VISIT TO STELLENBOSCH

J. M. Coetzee

J. M. Coetzee, the South African novelist, is author of
Waiting for the Barbarians *and* Life and Times of Michael K.

S ome forty miles from Cape Town, on the fringe of the
wine-making region of the Cape Province, lies Stellenbosch, the second oldest town in South Africa. Though
it is the seat of a major university, Stellenbosch is not a
notably liberal place. Its students are well behaved, and its
white voters have always stood firmly behind the National
Party.

A few months ago, the highway between Cape Town
and Stellenbosch was effectively closed. Bands of black
and Coloured youths hung about on the verges or waited
on overpasses to stone cars; burning barricades sometimes
blocked the road. On bad days even the airport, which lies
along this route, could be reached only under police es-
cort.

Today, as I drive out to Stellenbosch, the highway is
reputed to be safe. I pass an armored troop carrier parked
under a tree. A soldier, crouched on the embankment,
stares at something through binoculars. From the vicinity
of the Crossroads squatter camp a pillar of yellow smoke
rises into the air. The sun blazes down. All is quiet on this
southern front, by South African standards.

I am on my way to meet some of the citizens of Stellenbosch, strangers as yet to me, to hear how they feel about
what is going on in our country. As I discover, the people

I interview do not conform to the reigning stereotype of the Afrikaner. They do not speak contemptuously of blacks. They are not notably intolerant in their attitudes, heartless in their conduct or indolent in their daily life. They seem not to bear the worst marks of apartheid, a doctrine and a set of social practices that scars the moral being of whites as it degrades and demeans blacks. Whether they can be said to be representative of their three million compatriots I do not know. They all identify themselves as Afrikaners, but their allegiances seem to lie as much with the broad South African middle class as with the Afrikaner tribe. In this respect they are typical of the generation born after 1948, a generation that, having grown up under Afrikaner hegemony, can afford to be more self-assured, less belligerently nationalistic than their fathers.

Indeed, I am struck above all by the calm of those I interview. They do not talk like people perched on the lip of a volcano. All of them believe the world around them is changing (and should be changing faster), but nowhere do they seem to envisage an eruption of change that might sweep them and their children away. Yet they live in a country seething with black anger and at war on its borders. Have the ring of steel around the black townships and the clampdown on news coverage fostered in them an unreal sense of security, a culpable ignorance, a foolish calm? Or do they in truth have darker fears, more dire visions of the future, than they are ready to divulge? Are they telling the truth, the whole truth, or have they chosen to engage in acts of self-presentation for an audience of strangers?

I put the question, yet it seems to me falsely put. How often in our lives does the truth of ourselves, the whole and unmixed truth, emerge? Are we not routinely engaged in acts of self-presentation, acts which it would be excessively puritanical to condemn as insincere? Surely, in getting to know the truth of another person, we neither accept nor reject his self-presentations but read them, as best we can, in whatever context we can summon up. A few hours of conversation will not give us privileged access to "the Afrikaner"; it would be naive to expect that. What we have here are excerpts from the texts of four lives, uttered (I believe) with due deliberation, for the record, at particular moments in four life histories—fragments of the text of a national discourse, to be read and weighed alongside whatever other fragments we can come into possession of.

In one of the pleasanter white suburbs, I meet Kaffie Pretorius, an attractive, matronly woman in her thirties. Brought up in Lambert's Bay on South Africa's west coast, where her father kept a store, she married an academic, settled in Stellenbosch, paints in her spare time. But she still hankers for the desolate west coast landscape: when she goes there on vacation, she takes her children on long rambles in the *veld* to teach them the plant lore she learned as a child.

We speak in Afrikaans, our common tongue, the language of most of rural South Africa. Like everyone else I speak to, Kaffie Pretorius is depressed about the failing economy, about accelerating inflation and the collapse of the South African currency, which has led in only a few months to a doubling in the prices of imported goods, including gasoline. Yet, to my surprise, she observes that these economic woes may not be such a bad thing: "For the first time, whites are truly affected—for the first time they must think seriously about the future." And then, after a pause, "How did we think we could hold on to all of this?" She waves a hand to embrace her spacious home, the prosperous neighborhood, and beyond it the town of Stellenbosch, surrounded by thousands of acres of farmland. "How did we ever think we could hold on to it?"

I have no reply. I am touched by her words, by their suddenness, by the feeling behind them. Perhaps one can be so naked only with strangers. Yet afterward, I wonder whether I would not have been equally touched, though in a different way, had she lamented, "How can they take all this away from us?" And is it a good idea to indulge, in oneself or anyone else, these fits of voluptuous self-recrimination?

"Things go in phases," she resumes. "We are the generation that will have to make the adjustment. Our children will find it easier. Already, children find it easier to relate to Coloured friends than we ever did."

In what spheres of life, I ask, are whites going to find it hardest to adjust? "First, education. When schools are integrated, standards drop. It's unfortunate, but it's a fact. Look at Zimbabwe. Second, neighbors. "Would she personally mind black or Coloured neighbors? "Not at all," she replies. "If a black family could afford to move in next door, I would welcome them."

I am struck, as we talk, by how vague and shifting her fears are, and by how typical she is of most whites in this respect. At one moment, she envisages a future social order much like the present one, though without the racial laws. At other moments, she seems to have a grimmer picture before her eyes: a hand-to-mouth existence as an unwelcome guest in the land of her birth. It is one of the bitterest consequences of the decades-long suppression of black dissent that ordinary whites now not only have no one with whom to imagine negotiating their future but have not the vaguest idea of what blacks might be prepared to settle for.

"Our women are the worst," Kaffie Pretorius remarks. "It is because domestic help is so easy to get. Utter idleness. They get into their cars in the morning and drive around aimlessly all day. If they are the most conservative, it is because they have the most to lose."

Does she herself have a servant, and how have interpersonal relations been during the present unrest? "Martha is going to have a baby soon, which has led us to talk to each other more openly. It strikes me how hard we find it to think our way into the life our servants lead. I wonder how I would feel, in this awful summer heat, living in a corrugated steel house in Ida's Valley."

After lunch, some teenage friends of the family stop by. They have just written their school-leaving examinations. For the boys, the choice is whether to enroll in college and postpone military service or to go into the army. I ask whether they have any doubts about serving in Namibia or patrolling South Africa's black townships. No, they reply: one must be prepared to make sacrifices for one's country. All the same, they are cynical about South Africa's occupation of Namibia and its professed aims there (to protect the right of the territory to self-determination). As for the strife at home, they agree that blacks should be given more freedom. But then, says one of them, Dawid, whites should have freedom too—freedom to found a state in which they will be their own masters. I ask where this state should be, thinking he will propose some tiny Spartan colony on the Orange River. "The Transvaal, the Orange Free State, and northern Natal," he replies, naming a vast area containing perhaps three-quarters of South Africa's economic resources—"our forefathers shed enough blood for those parts of the country to justify our claim to them."

He speaks the language, arrogantly possessive, of the enduring right-wing dream of a national homeland where the Afrikaner will be left to run his affairs without interference, and where blacks will face a clear and simple choice: to stay on as rightless, wage-earning sojourners, or to pack their bags and seek their salvation elsewhere.

Dawid's friends shake their heads and smile. Clearly they don't take him seriously. As for Dawid, his face is inscrutable. Does he believe in what he says, or is he trying to shock me? I know the streak of sly humor behind the Afrikaner's mask of dourness. Is Dawid a joker? "What are your ambitions?" I ask him. "To qualify as a clinical psychologist and then go into politics," he replies.

"I travel widely, I talk to many people," says Michiel le Roux. "I would say that, down to the smallest town in South Africa, there is a perception that things have changed, totally and drastically; 1985 has left a mark on everyone. There is an awareness that the country is in a crisis situation, and this cuts across boundaries of age, class, language.

"No one thinks we need only take a few deep breaths for things to go back to normal, as they did in 1977. For this reason it has become possible for a strong leader to take South Africa in a direction that would have been unthinkable in 1984. Anything is thinkable in 1986, provided that the leadership is strong enough."

Le Roux, a graduate in law, is, at the age of 36, an executive in a Stellenbosch-based liquor company. We meet in his spacious office overlooking a courtyard in which stands an old wooden winepress, tall as a house, preserved for posterity.

Does the strong leadership he refers to exist? "No, clearly it doesn't. President Botha gave strong leadership —stronger than one expected—up to a certain point. Then he faltered. The issue over which he faltered was residential segregation. The feeling that we are directionless is widespread. People have no feeling of being on the road anywhere, or of knowing where we are on the road to."

If the last year has been a year of crisis, how has the crisis manifested itself in this quiet, civilized town with its oak-lined streets and painstakingly restored eighteenth-century houses? Race relations are good, or seem to be, Michiel replies. He is conscious of no hostility when he visits Coloured areas; calls for a boycott of white businesses have met with little success. Yet, he concedes, it is quite possible he is deluded. A Coloured school principal warned him of a "tremendous level of aggression" just beneath the surface. What more can he say? One can report only what one sees.

Where we go from here neither of us is sure. I remember the soldiers I passed on the highway, the smoke over the shantytowns. Which is the true face of South Africa— Crossroads, burning, or Stellenbosch, on the surface so placid? Months ago, I remember, on a quiet Sunday afternoon, I cycled through this town. "*Amandla!* (Power!)," shouted a voice behind me. I glanced around. A man, not black, but Coloured, waved a fist at me from the sidewalk. "*Amandla!*" he shouted again, in case I had misunderstood him. Was his the true, hidden face of Stellenbosch?

We talk about American stereotypes of the Afrikaner. Michiel shrugs them off. "Stereotypes are always a generation out of date—that is their nature." Would he regard himself as a representative modern Afrikaner? "It is curious how a society changes," he replies. "It is like a child growing: day by day you see no difference, then all of a sudden the child is grown up. For Afrikaners of my generation, born after 1948, the old issues have never really had relevance. It is a question of self-confidence. The Afrikaner's language is no longer threatened. He rules the land. The things that matter to him today are the same things that matter to an American, an Englishman, a German: his children, his job, his salary, his car, his vacation. He has been absorbed into a cultural pattern that is basically American. If you ask me to put my finger on anything that is *different,* from a political point of view, about the Afrikaner, I would say it is simply that he tends to be twenty or thirty years behind the times. Take racial discrimination. Before World War II, racial discrimination was a fact of life all over the West. The West came to realize it was wrong. Now it is gradually becoming accepted here that you don't judge a person on the basis of skin color."

If Afrikaners have been swallowed into an American lifestyle, is the same future in store for blacks?

"The black man is oppressed in his own country. That is why, at the moment, it is important for him to assert his own culture—black art, black writing, black theater. But the American cultural current is very strong. Ultimately, black theater doesn't stand a chance against 'Dallas.' It is 'Dallas' that blacks will prefer to watch.

"It is striking what a hold Western values have taken among blacks, values like freedom of choice, freedom of speech, freedom of assembly. Who knows, perhaps blacks will guard these values all the more jealously because they have been denied them so long. On the other hand, if black liberation comes only after a long military struggle, we may have a military cast of mind imposed over everything —military discipline, military organization, as in so many other African countries. It is a matter of *how* the transition takes place."

My next stop is at the farm of Jan Boland Coetzee. Whether Jan Boland has heard of me I doubt: he is not much of a novel-reading man. But I have seen him scores of times from the sidelines, in his rugby-playing heyday, and can make a fair guess at his approach to life: hard work, no nonsense. Within minutes we have compared genealogies, as is the custom in our country, and established that, like so many Afrikaners, we are probably distant relations—fourth or fifth or tenth cousins.

For our interview he conducts me into the cavernous cellars of his winery, which are lined with huge oak casks imported from France (the craft of cooping has died out in South Africa, he tells me). In a subterranean hush, we sit down to talk.

How is apartheid faring in the countryside, I ask. "Apartheid has never been a word in my book," he replies, establishing his footing at once; and he proceeds to reminisce about the farm on which he grew up, where his grandfather drove to town to do the shopping for everyone, black and white alike. "It was only later, when I left the farm, that I first experienced apartheid." For a while he muses. "Apartheid has created a gulf between people. We no longer know each other. Also, we whites have simply appropriated things for ourselves, leaving the blacks and Coloureds to do the producing. It is not just. It is not a healthy state of affairs."

He is not, strictly speaking, answering my question, and knows it. I understand the difficulty he is having. Like me, he was born in the twilight of a centuries-old feudal order in which the rights and duties of masters and servants seemed to be a matter of unspoken convention, and in which a mixture of personal intimacy and social distance —a mixture characteristic of societies with a slaveholding past—pervaded all dealings. To whites brought up in this old order, the codification of social relations into the system of racial laws known as apartheid always seemed gross and unnecessary, the brainchild of academic ideologues and upstart politicians. So for Jan Boland Coetzee to shake his head over apartheid, yet look back nostalgically to an age when everyone knew his place, by no means proves him a hypocrite, though I suspect he forgets the iron hand needed to keep the old order running.

Coetzee is known not only as a winemaker but for his part in the movement among progressive farmers to improve labor relations in the countryside. The age of the average farm laborer in South Africa, he tells me, is fifty-two years. Two generations of workers have quit white farms to seek their fortunes in the cities. In another generation, there will be no one left to till the soil. Therefore he has striven to create an exemplary environment on his own farm that will draw younger Coloured men back to the land: decent wages, productivity incentives, comfortable housing, health care, recreational opportunities. "During the present unrest we have found many younger Coloured people wanting to come back to the farm simply in order to be part of an ordered little community with civilized standards and a regular routine. For years we farmers were preoccupied with land and capital. Now we have begun to pay attention to people again, and the result is a change in attitudes that cannot be described—it truly has to be experienced."

There is a certain Utopianism in the vision he projects of a rural order based on small, rationally organized laboring communities. Utopian less because his brand of upliftment does not work—it clearly does, here and now, within its self-imposed limits—than because it draws much of its attractiveness from somewhat sentimentalized memories of a feudal past. Farmers like Coetzee reject such vast centralized blueprints for the future as Hendrik Verwoerd's "grand apartheid" in favor of small-scale, independent, pragmatic local solutions. As long as the politicians (and perhaps the police too) will leave us alone, Coetzee seems to be saying, we countryfolk can find ways to live harmoniously together. In much of the talk rife among more progressive whites today, the same spirit is to be detected: loss of faith in large-scale national policies, impatience with red tape, readiness for ad hoc approaches to local problems. The irony is that this is precisely the moment in history when black South Africans are grouping together in larger and larger political blocs, and black leaders prepared to limit discussion to merely local issues are proving harder and harder to find.

Only the darkest cynic would claim that the effort Jan Boland Coetzee and his wife have put into the social upliftment of their work force has not been sincerely intended. While their workers are well housed, the Coetzees themselves live in a cramped bungalow—renovation of the old farmstead is barely under way. Nevertheless, looking toward the future, one may ask whether marriage will ever be possible between the kind of enlightened paternalism they stand for and the egalitarian black nationalism sweeping across the land. When I ask Jan Boland what he thinks the effect will be on this part of the country, once restrictions on black mobility ("influx control") have been lifted, he is dismissive: "There is no tradition of blacks living in the Western Cape," he says. True; but only because the full force of the law has been brought to bear to keep blacks out. Can a farm remain an island of tranquility in a country in turmoil? Can the Western Cape, this tiny tip of the continent, declare itself independent of Africa?

Can Jan Boland imagine circumstances that would make him give up his farm and quit South Africa? Vehemently, he shakes his head. "Never. I stay. I have enough faith in my countrymen, black, white and Coloured, to believe we can work out a solution. I can't believe that South Africans are such bad people as the Americans and the rest say." He tells a story of how, while touring France with the national rugby team, the Springboks, he found himself in a bus with some American tourists. "They asked us what language we were speaking, and we told them it was Afrikaans. They had never heard of such a language, they didn't even know there were such people as Afrikaners. Well, now they know! What I mean to say is: rather be proud of your language than your skin color. As for the norms of the so-called civilized world, we will live those norms, not just talk about them."

"You must understand that I am a believing Christian," says Lydia Roos. "I can't sit here and despair, I can't say there is no future for us, I can't say it is too late. Because things have begun to change. But we must move faster. Whether the government understands this, I don't know."

Lydia Roos is a domestic science teacher in a high school. We meet in her home in an unpretentious white suburb of Cape Town. The schools have just closed for the summer vacation. It has been a hard year, a year of bad news and official lies, the lies sometimes harder to bear than the bad news. We all ache for relief. But the end is not in sight. "December 16 MARTYRS DAY" reads an ominous sign daubed on a wall in the town. Under the writing is a picture of a neat little house, like the one in which we sit, with flames licking around it.

"We are going to have to make sacrifices," she says. "Prices are rising all the time. Yet the other day I thought: if high prices mean that farm workers will at last get a good wage, maybe it's a good thing."

A drop in living standards: will that be the extent of

white sacrifice? What of social apartheid? Is she prepared to see the neighborhood opened up?

There is no hesitation in her reply: "Absolutely. Nor do I think other people in the block would object. Coloureds, blacks: if they can afford it, let them come and live here."

Her readiness to jettison the Group Areas Act, which enforces segregation of housing, marks Lydia as, in her word, *verlig,* enlightened. Her vision of the future, she says, is of a South Africa in which there will be many tribes, white and black, the Afrikaners one of them, none in a position of dominance, each maintaining its own cultural identity "We will keep our *boerekos,* our Afrikaner dishes, just as the Indians have kept their curry."

I am dubious. Is the struggle in South Africa not about more than the preservation of national cuisines? What of the realities of power?

"I think we will end up with a federal system," she says, "provinces with local self-government and a national government over them. The Western Cape should be one province, with Cape Town as its capital. I don't know about the Eastern Cape—that is a matter for the blacks."

Will whites elsewhere in the country, living in the midst of vast black majorities, not see her prescription as a form of smug isolationism that only the Western Cape, with its small black African population, can afford?

She smiles. "Perhaps," she concedes. "I see my brother once a year. He lives in Pretoria. After the first day or two we don't talk politics anymore. We disagree too much. But families don't break up over questions of politics. We have ways of living with our differences."

I think of the poet Breyten Breytenbach and his brother, an officer in the security forces, who do not speak to each other, of the many friendships I have seen break up under the stresses of this last year. Is it uncharitable to think that Lydia and her brother do not yet disagree enough?

Have her *verlig* leanings brought her into conflict with other Afrikaners? No, she replies. Personally she is not combative. When the gulf yawns too wide she prefers to keep quiet. But she finds she has lost respect for colleagues at school who are absolutely unsympathetic to black aspirations. "Within myself I doubt their integrity." *Opregtheid*, uprightness, integrity, is a key word for her. It measures the distance between professed Christian faith and day-to-day practice. Her parents have worked all their lives in the "mission" church, the branch of the Dutch Reformed Church that ministers to Coloured people. She is a regular churchgoer, and on Thursday evenings runs needlework classes for black domestic servants. "We must each do our bit," she says.

At school, among the teenagers she teaches, she encounters little spirit of conciliation: "They talk only of shooting the troublemakers," she says. "It hurts me, that kind of talk. They pick it up from each other, or they hear it at home. The school I teach at draws on a less prosperous neighborhood. In the better parts of town you will probably find a more thinking attitude. But signs of the unrest are all around us: buses with broken windows, sirens all the time, helicopters overhead, blacks singing freedom songs in the streets. No one can escape it. You can't expect children not to be affected.

"I taught in a Coloured school for a while, in Elsie's River. I went back for a visit. When I taught there I had good relations with the children, open relations. Now things have changed. The old openness has gone. Hostility? I wouldn't call it personal hostility, though I couldn't help hearing remarks passed behind my back. But hostility toward the system—yes, definitely.

"I remember, during my time there, there was never any celebration of our national day, no singing of the national anthem. I suppose one can understand that. The anthem has certain Afrikaner connotations—the line about the creaking ox wagon and so forth. But I love the anthem. To some extent it is our fault that they won't sing it. But still . . .''

December, 1985

WHITE VOICES

Andries P. Treurnicht, Conservative Party

Andries P. Treurnicht is leader of the Conservative Party of South Africa. The following is an excerpt from a speech he delivered in Pretoria at the Conservative Party Congress of the Transvaal on August 19, 1985.

People who think that Mr. Botha's "crossing of the Rubicon" and his abdication of white government mean the end of the Afrikaner and broader white nationalism are making a big mistake. We will not allow the Oppenheimers[1] and American pressure groups to create a potpourri of people or to establish a nonracial economic empire upon the ruins of a white Christian culture and civilization. A people is only conquered when it has destroyed its own spirit. We are not prepared to consider national suicide. We do not as a people cherish a death wish. If nonwhite students at Wits University can shout, "We shall not be silenced!" we can say here tonight, with the simplicity of our faith and our will, "We do not wish to silence anyone's call for rights or freedom, but no one will silence the awakening white nation. The battle for the return of our political self-determination has only just begun." I remind you of the words of N. P. van Wyk Louw in "Die DieperReg" where the Advocate said, "If you enslave a proud people then resistance becomes its right."

I want to give a rational explanation to those people who ask if our policy is morally justified—whether it is in accordance with Christian principles. Any person, whether Nat or Prog² or Bishop Tutu or Dr. Boesak or our own supporters has the right to test the feasibility of our policy—just as we naturally have the right to test the feasibility of integration, of power sharing, of government by consensus, of multiracial coalition government, of self-determination of different peoples within the same territory, of a racial federation or a territorial federation. The question to the Conservative Party is: How does your policy of separate development—partition—accord with the demands of Christian principles?

I want to answer on behalf of the Conservative Party. We acknowledge and profess the unity of all true believers in the Holy Trinity, that is to say, believers regardless of where they come from. We respect the faith of our fellow man, be he of another nation or race. We deplore hatred or envy or contempt towards any fellow man. We say: Respect the brotherhood of man. Show a Christian disposition and willingness to help. Acknowledge that your fellow man also has rights. We also declare that God is responsible for the origin of peoples and nations in all their diversity, variety, heritage, national identity, nationhood and claim to a territory.

God's ordination includes certain boundaries, however. Boundaries between certain communities are not in conflict with God's reconciliation. Real reconciliation definitely does not mean a return to the Babylonian attempt at unity. Ethnic differences are not a curse which must be expiated, but these differences are counter to the Antichrist plan—world domination and false concepts of oneness. Reconciliation and Christian love do not replace justice or the right to personal community rights or the right to nationhood. Morality demands that justice is enjoyed by different nations, constitutionally and culturally.

If Tutu and Boesak and Buthelezi demand justice for their own people, we acknowledge the right to do so as well. But morality also demands that they not be denied their freedom, their political power and decision-making within their own territory in a new dispensation, as is occuring in the new dispensation. Morality demands that whites also retain the power to protect their legitimate freedom. Christian reconciliation does not demand a unitary state for different peoples, or common residential areas, or multiracial schools or universities, voters rolls, mixed marriages or uncontrolled immorality or even one common religion for the faithful of different religions.

Some frocked clergymen, in their campaign against so-called white racism and apartheid as so-called heresies, are actually the perpetrators of black racism and hatred instead of reconciliation. That kind of reconciliation demands white capitulation. It implies black domination. It must of necessity encourage white resistance. We say: You must distinguish between Christian reconciliation and liberalism with its superficial egalitarianism, its glorification of integration. I ask: How do certain ministers reconcile the cross of Christ worn around their neck with the communist flag under which they stand and preach? Must white Christians reconcile themselves to that or may they pray to be protected from such a Christianity?

If supplicants in the streets associate themselves with black power, have white Christians not the right to pray for protection against black domination? We say: You supplicants are not being devout if you bow before threats of black revolution or if you try to talk the white man in to succumbing to a guilt feeling regarding the past and into a consensus government, as though it is the Christian recipe for constitutional reconciliation.

It was Michael Hurry who said, "If a people can be

undermined psychologically for a period, its enemies are sure of victory. A despondent, confused and guilt-laden people does not offer much resistance. A people which has been deprived of spiritual muscle, without patriotism and national pride, will be like grain before the communist scythe."

State President P. W. Botha, National Party

P. W. Botha is leader of the National Party and State President of the Republic of South Africa. The following is an excerpt from his speech to the annual congress of the National Party in Durban on August 15, 1985.

We know that it is a hard fact of South African life that it will not be possible to accommodate the political aspirations of our various population groups and communities in a familiar or ready-made political system.

We have often found that our efforts to find solutions have been impeded and frustrated because different interpretations have been put on the terminology that we use to describe our particular form of democratic solution.

Some years ago, with the best intentions on my part, I advocated a confederation of South African states which would cooperate with one another. The idea was belittled and prejudice was created against it.

Now let me state explicitly that I believe in participation by all the South African communities on matters of common concern. I believe there should be structures to reach this goal of coresponsibility and participation.

I firmly believe that the granting and acceptance of independence by various black peoples within the context of their own statehood represent a material part of the solution. However, I would like to restate my government's position in this regard, namely, that independence cannot be forced upon any community. Should any of the black national states therefore prefer not to accept independence, such states or communities will remain part of the South African nation. They are South African citizens and should be accommodated within political institutions within the boundaries of the Republic of South Africa. This does not mean that regional considerations should not be taken into account and that provision should not be made for participation in institutions on a regional and/or group basis.

I know for a fact that most leaders in their own right in South Africa, as well as all reasonable South Africans, will not accept the principle of one-man-one-vote in a unitary system. That would lead to domination by one over the others and chaos. Consequently, I reject it as a solution.

Secondly, a so-called fourth chamber of Parliament is not a practical solution and I do not think responsible people will argue in favor of it. We must rather seek our solutions in the devolution of power.

I admit that the acceptance by my government of the permanence of black communities in urban areas outside the national states means that a solution will have to be found for their legitimate rights. The future of these communities and their constitutional arrangements will have to be negotiated with leaders from the national states as well as from among their own ranks.

But let me be quite frank with you. You must know where you stand with me. It is the right of the party congresses to state whether they agree with their leader or not.

I am not prepared to lead White South Africans and other minority groups on a road to abdication and suicide. Destroy White South Africa and our influence, and this country will drift into faction, strife, chaos and poverty.

Together with my policy statements in Parliament earlier this year, I regard this speech as my manifesto.

In my policy statements in January and June of this year, I indicated that there would be further developments with regard to the rights and interests of the various population groups in Southern Africa. Since then we have had to contend with escalating violence within South Africa, as well as pressure from abroad in the form of measures designed to coerce the government into giving in to various demands.

Our enemies, both within and without, seek to divide our peoples. They seek to create unbridgeable differences between us so as to prevent us from negotiating peaceful solutions to our problems. Peaceful negotiation is their enemy, because it will lead to joint responsibility for the progress and prosperity of South Africa. Those who espouse violence do not want to participate. They wish to seize and monopolize all power. Let there be no doubt what they would do with such power. One has only to look at their methods and means. Violent and brutal means can only lead to totalitarian and tyrannical ends.

Their actions speak louder than their words. Their words offer ready panaceas such as one-man-one-vote, freedom and justice for all. Their actions leave no doubt that the freedoms we already have, together with the ongoing extension of democracy in South Africa, are the true targets of their violence. . . .

The violence of our enemies is a warning to us. We who

are committed to peaceful negotiation also have a warning to them. Our warning is that our readiness to negotiate should not be mistaken for weakness. Reform through the process of negotiation is not weakness. Talking, consulting, bargaining with all our peoples' leaders is not weakness. Acceptance of one another and joint responsibility for the welfare and stability of our country is not weakness. It is, in fact, our strength.

Our strength is the courage to face and accommodate the problems bequeathed to us by history. The reality of our diversity is a hard reality. We face it because it is there. How do we accommodate it? How do we build a better future out of the variety of cultures, values, languages that is demonstrably real in our heterogeneous society?

We are resolved—we are committed—to do so in two fundamental ways.

Firstly, by letting the people speak through their leaders and by negotiation among all these leaders. In these negotiations we will all endeavor to improve our common well-being. We will not prescribe and we will not demand. To do so would be to take only. We will give so that others can also give—for a better future for everyone.

Secondly, the overriding common denomimator is our common concern for each other's freedom and well-being. Our peace and prosperity are indivisible. Therefore, the only way forward is through cooperation and coresponsibility. . . .

The implementation of the principles I have stated today can have far-reaching effects for us all. I believe that we are today crossing the Rubicon. There can be no turning back. We now have a manifesto for the future of our country, and we must embark on a program of positive action in the months and years ahead. The challenges we face demand that all concerned should negotiate in a spirit of give-and-take. With mutual goodwill we shall reach our destination peacefully.

Frederick van Zyl Slabbert, Progressive Federal Party

Frederick van Zyl Slabbert, a member of the Progressive Federal Party, was a member of Parliament and leader of the opposition until his resignation from public office on February 7, 1986. The following is an excerpt from his annual motion of no confidence, made in Parliament in Cape Town on February 3, 1986.

O ne cannot enter into negotiations, and neither can one create a climate conducive to negotiation, as long as apartheid has not been dismantled. It cannot be done. That means that dismantling apartheid is a priority, and nobody but this government can do that. They put apartheid on the statute books—they have to remove it. We cannot dismantle apartheid, neither can the United Democratic Front, the African National Congress or the Black Sash—only this government can dismantle apartheid.

What does it mean to dismantle apartheid? It is fascinating that, when one goes overseas, one hears people saying that one must tell the State President to get rid of apartheid. When one asks them what they mean, six out of ten times those people do not really know what they mean. They simply want to remove the concept from the agenda.

Apartheid depends on laws. The essence of apartheid is the denial of freedom of choice on the basis of race or ethnicity—that is the essence of apartheid, which is re-flected in laws such as the Population Registration Act, the Group Areas Act and the Reservation of Separate Amenities Act. Last year we got rid of Section 16 of the Immorality Act and of the Prohibition of Mixed Mar-riages Act. However, the very fact that we restored free-dom of choice as far as those acts were concerned high-lighted the absence of freedom of choice in all other areas. That is the essence of apartheid. We have to get rid of laws and statutes that compel people to form part of groups on a racial and ethnic basis against their will. It is as simple as that. That is the first step.

Secondly, the government must declare that under those circumstances of freedom of choice they will have removed what the ANC and others cite as the cause for their commitment to violence and the armed struggle. Therefore they would then be able to operate legally and peacefully in South Africa together with other organiza-tions and movements. The government must also declare that all political prisoners will be released to do the same.

Who is also pleading for this? I can promise the govern-ment that it is not the communist wing of the ANC. They do not want to be legalized. However, Chief Gatsha Bu-thelezi says that the government must unban those people so that he can compete with them in the domestic political market. We need to do that ourselves. We need to know the who's who of politics in this country. That is why this second step is so essential. This morning in *The Cape Times*, Percy Qoboza, who by no means is a radical, says, "Talking and negotiating with the ANC and PAC has become something the government cannot duck any longer. They may take all the refugees they want out of Lesotho, Botswana or even Swaziland but they will not defuse those bombs. The problem is not in those countries but right here inside our borders."

To legalize those organizations is not to legalize violence. I want to make that point quite clear. To legalize them is actually to let them move away from violence. If they do become involved in violence, all the machinery of the state is available in any case to stop the violence.

Thirdly, after this has been done, the government must announce a package of reform plans to do away as best as possible with the de facto inequalities in housing, education and welfare. They must do that instead of doing so now in a piecemeal fashion and getting no credit for it. What is happening now is that the government is introducing these piecemeal reforms in the absence of dismantling apartheid and allowing freedom of choice. The government is always walking backwards in this situation under pressure. It is the law of diminishing options which is the dilemma of reform. Only once one has done that can one go on towards equalizing the situation.

Fourthly, the government must allow for a period of time for political organizations to consolidate their support and stabilize the communities. We cannot stabilize the communities with security forces. It cannot be done. Those communities will have to stabilize themselves and the government will have to create the conditions under which they can do so.

Fifthly, the government must make it clear that under these circumstances lawlessness and subversive action will be dealt with firmly and without hesitation. That can obviously be done under those circumstances because the Government has created the circumstance in which they can operate.

Sixthly, the government must appoint a multiracial monitoring board of appeal to which people can bring their grievances and suggestions on problems they are experiencing as a result of the changes. Yes, there are going to be painful adjustments. It is going to be difficult to go through a process of reform, but the government can anticipate that by appointing the kind of body that the State President has referred to. Then it can fulfill a function and people can come forward and participate in it.

Seventhly, the government must then appoint a negotiating forum to which they can invite the recognized political and community leaders to discuss how best a new constitution for South Africa can be brought about. Then only can negotiation really get off the ground.

There are, of course, risks and uncertainties involved in these suggestions. However, one thing is sure and that is that if the government continues acting the way they are acting now, there will be no uncertainties—conflict, siege and escalating violence are inevitable.

NOTES

1. Harry Oppenheimer is former chairman of the Anglo American Group, Ltd., South Africa's largest industrial and mining conglomerate.
2. Members of the Nationalist Party or the Progressive Federal Party.

BLACK POLITICS

BLACK POLITICS: THE ROAD TO REVOLUTION

Thomas G. Karis

Thomas G. Karis is Professor Emeritus of Political Science and Senior Research Fellow at the Ralphe Bunche Institute on the United Nations at the Graduate School of the City University of New York. He is coeditor, with Gwendolen M. Carter, of the four-volume work, From Protest to Challenge: A Documentary History of African Politics in South Africa, 1882–1964.

R evolution is in the making in South Africa, but the end is not yet in sight. Interrelated crises confront the regime with political challenges it appears unable to meet: a crisis of legitimacy in relations with blacks, the threat of ungovernability in African areas, a politically generated economic crisis and deep anxieties among whites. The outlawed African National Congress has grown in prestige and popular support, and black trade unions, stronger and better organized than ever in the past, are becoming overtly political in demanding fundamental change.

The roots of black resistance to white rule reach deep into South African history. But the genesis of the current revolutionary process can be traced to the coming to power of the National Party in 1948 and the sharp upsurge in black activism its harsh racist policies provoked. The process moved from nonviolent protest to armed resistance in 1961, a year after the oldest and largest black opposition movement, the African National Congress, and its offshoot, the Pan Africanist Congress, were outlawed in the wake of killings by the police at Sharpeville. The ANC's military wing then embarked on a program of "armed struggle" against the regime.

In the quarter century since then, black opposition has manifested itself in a variety of ways, ranging from the sharply defiant Black Consciousness Movement to the tribal machine politics of Chief Mangosuthu Gatsha Buthelezi. It reached a major watershed in the Soweto student uprising, which began on June 16, 1976, and reverberated in many parts of South Africa until the end of 1977. Soweto marked a qualitative change in youthful defiance and produced the first substantial exodus for guerrilla training.

Since September 1984, the process of revolutionary challenge has dramatically accelerated, although it is still far from threatening to bring down the regime. The trigger for the current stage was the constitutionalization of white supremacy, which the National Party government had been institutionalizing by statute since 1948. On September 3, 1984, a new constitution was promulgated in an attempt to divide black opposition by providing new, racially separate chambers of Parliament for Indians and mixed-race "Coloureds." The tricameral Parliament is controlled by whites and excludes Africans. Not coincidentally, September 1984 also marked the beginning of a new period of intensified protest in African townships, accompanied by more extensive and persistent violence than at any earlier period and by much greater police counterviolence.

For South African blacks, this upsurge in violent opposition has sharpened the long-standing debate on several central tactical issues, including the question of participation in government-sponsored institutions, the acceptability of white allies in the fight against the regime, the role of violence in the antiapartheid struggle, and the relative importance of race and class in analyses of South Africa's situation. All of these questions are being debated against the background of renewed activism within the black community and growing black support for the ANC.

Aided by the increasing visibility of its sabotage and guerrilla actions, the ANC has experienced an extraordinarily open, countrywide resurgence. African support for it is nationwide, cutting across tribal and ethnic groups, classes, regions, age and education. Its best-known leader, Nelson Mandela, who has served over twenty years of a life sentence for planning sabotage, easily ranks as the most admired African leader in the country. It seems increasingly unlikely that the ANC can be excluded from any serious attempt to find a lasting solution to South Africa's deepening crisis.

For all its drama and importance, the most recent period of conflict in South Africa represents only a brief stage in the long history of black resistance to white rule. Violent resistance by indigenous people at the Cape began more than 300 years ago, and resistance by Bantu-speaking Africans began over 200 years ago. Christian mission schools in the nineteenth century and, after 1853, the Cape Colony's nonracial qualified franchise, contributed to the rise of African political liberalism and hopes for movement toward racial equality.

An important advance in the development of black politics in South Africa came in 1912, when professional and middle-class Africans took the lead in forming the African National Congress. The new group aimed to become a national voice overriding tribal differences and pressing for inclusion of Africans within a common nonracial society.

For almost four decades, the ANC and its moderate leaders responded to South Africa's segregationist and exploitative policies by organizing deputations, petitions and public meetings. A year after the National Party came to power in the watershed election of 1948, the ANC responded by adopting a program of illegal but nonviolent tactics of civil disobedience, as well as boycotts, strikes and noncooperation. These tactics were not in themselves revolutionary, but, given the gap between the policies of the new government, which proceeded to entrench itself in power, and the contrary direction of the ANC, the program adopted in 1949 marked the beginning of a revolutionary process.

In the face of mounting repression, ANC leaders also reassessed in the early 1950s the need for non-African allies. They welcomed the formation of a multiracial Congress Alliance headed by the ANC and including congresses representing Indians, Coloureds and whites. In forming the alliance, ANC leaders wrestled with the issue of their relationship to the small Communist Party of South Africa, which had been outlawed in 1950. Formed by whites in 1921, the Communist Party was the oldest Marxist-Leninist party on the continent. It opened its ranks to Africans in the mid-1920s, and some of its leading African members also joined the ANC.

In 1955, the Congress Alliance issued its Freedom Charter, a document that remains a central definition of the aims of the ANC. Its most important feature was its opening declaration, "South Africa belongs to all who live in it, black and white." This formulation was at the center of bitter disputes and led to a major split within South Africa's black political ranks that is still visible today.

The disagreement centered around a small "Africanist" faction within the ANC that was opposed to the growing role of non-Africans in the ANC's struggle. That group broke away from the ANC in 1959, forming the Pan Africanist Congress under the leadership of Robert Sobukwe. While sharing the ANC's nonracial aims, the PAC rejected the Freedom Charter and insisted with mystical overtones that Africans were the indigenous owners of the soil. They charged radical whites with manipulating events and with pressing for premature action that harmed rank-and-file Africans.

The 1950s were a time of sporadic and turbulent protest by Africans, much of it spontaneous. During this period the ANC operated on the fringes of legality and faced innumerable problems of organization. Formal membership was never a valid measure of its political influence, and its rallies attracted thousands.

The decade ended in a watershed for African politics when, on March 21, 1960, a line of jittery police at Sharpeville, south of Johannesburg, opened fire on a peaceful crowd of demonstrators at a PAC-sponsored protest against laws requiring Africans to carry passes. Sixty-nine Africans were shot dead, the great majority hit in the back as they ran; 186 others were wounded, including forty women and eight children. In the wake of the shootings, both the ANC and PAC were outlawed and went underground. Many of their leaders were arrested and thousands were detained under emergency regulations.

Neither the ANC nor the PAC was prepared for clandestine activity. Yet they saw in the government's reaction to Sharpeville final proof that peaceful opposition to white rule was no longer possible. In December 1961, the ANC's newly formed military wing, Umkonto we Sizwe ("Spear of the Nation"), announced its existence. On December

16, the day when South African whites celebrate the defeat of the Zulus in 1828, Umkonto exploded homemade bombs at symbolic targets at times when no one would be injured.

During the next decade, South Africa became a powerful police state, making widespread use of detention and torture but also winning some black collaboration. The police smashed underground cells and demoralized the radical opposition. Umkonto's headquarters were unearthed in mid-1963, and Nelson Mandela and other ANC leaders were sentenced to life imprisonment. Mandela's former law partner, Oliver Tambo, who had been sent abroad, had to add long-range military preparation to his diplomatic and propaganda efforts on behalf of the ANC.

By the end of the 1960s, the ANC seemed to be little more than a shadowy presence in South Africa. But during the political lull in the late 1960s, a new generation of outspoken African, Indian and Coloured students began to exert a pervasive influence within South Africa in what became known as the Black Consciousness Movement. In its terminology, "black" was defined not as a color but as a term for all those suffering from white racial oppression, thus encompassing Africans, Indians and Coloureds. Making use of symbols of defiance such as the clenched-fist salute of black power, Black Consciousness sought to deal with the psychological problem of overcoming black attitudes of inferiority and subservience. "Black man, you are on your own" was a key slogan.

In its rejection of white allies, the new movement came within the minor Africanist-PAC stream of thinking, yet its definition of "black" gave it a wider appeal. It presented a challenge not only to the ANC's role as the primary focus of black activism but also to its commitment to multiracial cooperation and its relationship to the

South African Communist Party. At a conference in Tanzania in 1969, ANC leaders emphasized the primacy of African "national consciousness" but also invited revolution-minded whites, Indians and Coloureds to join the ANC.

Marxists accused Black Consciousness of failing to understand the nature of capitalism and the class struggle, but Black Consciousness leaders saw racial polarization and confrontation with the white enemy as necessary stages in the liberation struggle. Liberal whites understandably feared that Black Consciousness was antiwhite. But Black Consciousness advocates saw themselves as pro-black rather than antiwhite, and they included whites within their vision of a future South Africa.

Another major focus of black political activism that emerged in this period centered around a hereditary Zulu leader, Chief Mangosuthu Gatsha Buthelezi. In the early 1970s, many Africans saw Buthelezi as a political leader who could help to encourage a united African nationalism. As a member of the ANC Youth League, Buthelezi had won an early reputation as an African nationalist. A descendant of Zulu royalty, he followed the pragmatic advice of Albert Lutuli and other ANC leaders, who urged him in 1970 to participate in the setting up of the KwaZulu homeland in Natal. They wanted the strategically located KwaZulu to have a sympathetic leader who would refuse independence, as Buthelezi was to do.

For a time in the early 1970s, it appeared that Buthelezi might also have a role in the Black Consciousness movement. Alongside Steve Biko, the movement's leading personality, he spoke at a conference on the formation of a Black People's Convention. When it was formally launched in 1972 and appeared headed for confrontation with the white authorities, however, Buthelezi joined older and more cautious black leaders and moved aside.

In 1974–75, Buthelezi revived Inkatha, a dormant Zulu cultural organization, seeking to make it the basis for a political mass movement open to all Africans, although the membership today is still almost entirely Zulu. Organizationally, Inkatha overlaps to a large degree with the KwaZulu government, its organs and its schools. In the early stage, Inkatha grew rapidly among rural and poorly educated people through the mobilizing role of Zulu chiefs and reached out to include Zulu migratory workers living in hostels on the Witwatersrand. Inkatha's emphasis on stability and order also appealed to the older generation and to some middle-class Africans.

Inkatha benefited from the typical pressures of a political machine that can influence privileges and status and distribute patronage. Teachers, civil servants and, for example, traders seeking licenses and men seeking work felt compelled to join. Between 1982 and 1985 the number of card-carrying members it claimed more than tripled, to more than one million.

African workers also displayed a new sense of power in the 1970s. In early 1973 nearly 100,000 workers in some 150 firms in the Durban area, acting with almost no visible leadership, took part in a wave of largely spontaneous illegal strikes. During World War II, African unions had attracted 150,000 members, but after 1948 the National Party government banned many organizers and harassed the unions. By 1969 only thirteen African unions existed, with about 16,000 members. The strikes of early 1973, therefore, were a major phenomenon and were politically significant in demonstrating the potential power of black workers.

A new era in black protest was signaled on June 16, 1976, in the black township of Soweto on the outskirts of Johannesburg. The collapse of the Portuguese government and, in 1975, the coming to power of revolutionary governments in Mozambique and Angola heightened black expectations inside the Republic. And, when Soweto students demonstrated against mandatory instruction in the Afrikaans language, they were met by police guns.

The students' protest quickly turned into a widespread uprising. According to official statistics, 575 people died in the shooting and rioting that followed, 134 of them under the age of eighteen. Other estimates were much higher. Protests, arson and violence (mainly by the police) spread to many parts of the country. What made "Soweto" a watershed was the qualitatively new level of defiance and fearlessness demonstrated by black youth. It also resulted in the first substantial exodus of blacks for guerrilla training.

On October 19, 1977, the government cracked down, banning all the major Black Consciousness organizations. Shortly before the crackdown, the movement's best-known leader, Steve Biko, died in police custody after beatings and alleged torture, prompting an international outcry. Other major Black Consciousness figures were jailed, and the movement was decapitated. A new Black Consciousness group, the Azanian People's Organization, was established six months later.[1] But, in the face of the government's repressive capacities, it became clear that the kind of spontaneous, loosely organized protest represented by Soweto could not be effective. The focus of black activism shifted toward organizing at the community level, and also toward opposition groups in exile.

After going underground in 1960, the two major exile groups, the PAC and ANC, had taken different paths. The PAC, based in Dar es Salaam, Tanzania, had been largely crippled by internal struggles, which worsened after the death of Robert Sobukwe in 1978. The ANC, however, had grown into a well-organized liberation movement with extensive international connections. It was thus able to benefit from the flood of new recruits that left South Africa in the wake of the Soweto uprising.

The ANC's armed efforts had often been amateurish and abortive, but they were also marked by restraint. Its leaders acknowledged that its sabotage and small-scale guerrilla attacks were primarily exercises in "armed propaganda." ANC guerrillas attacked such targets as police stations and the offices of government departments and officially sponsored black councils. They also struck at symbolic targets of strategic significance such as railway lines, oil depots and electricity substations. The ANC also took responsibility for a small number of attacks on African policemen and the assassination of a few informers and state witnesses, actions obviously designed to deter such collaboration. But it rejected indiscriminate killing, kidnapping and other measures used by extremist groups elsewhere.

In the years following Soweto, the ANC's sabotage and guerrilla attacks became more frequent and sophisticated. The ANC expanded its structures within South Africa and its network for training in Africa and Soviet-bloc countries, the latter supplying nearly all of its military support. It also established routes for the infiltration of guerrillas into South Africa.

At least until May 1983, the number of lives lost in ANC actions was very small. In January 1983 a Defense Force official provided this writer with a memorandum summarizing casualties over the previous five years in the Republic, Transkei, Ciskei and Venda. In incidents attributed to the ANC but not in every case confirmed, twenty-two people died, four of them white. Some observers have claimed that many incidents of sabotage and clashes with government forces have been unreported.

In response to the ANC's attacks, the government conducted a systematic campaign against the group, including the open use of South African forces to attack alleged ANC centers in neighboring countries. The government was also suspected of responsibility for the assassinations of prominent ANC officials both inside and outside South Africa.

For Gatsha Buthelezi and Inkatha, the Soweto unrest and the police crackdown that followed provided a tempting opportunity to move into a leadership vacuum. In the mid-1970s, Buthelezi had become increasingly estranged from the Black Consciousness Movement. Debate within the movement's student organization about the merits of "infiltration politics" was resolved, under Steve Biko's leadership, against Buthelezi. The hostility of young radicals who labeled him a "sellout" for his homeland role came to a head in 1978 at the funeral of PAC leader Sobukwe. In the presence of a mass gathering that included prominent whites, young militants spat, jeered and hurled stones at Buthelezi, forcing him to leave. He departed, said one observer, "in a shaking, crying rage of humiliation." The impact of this episode on Buthelezi, a proud and sensitive man, is difficult to overstate.

In contrast, the ANC leadership maintained informal relations with Buthelezi throughout the 1970s. Unlike the Black Consciousness leaders, they distinguished between Buthelezi and those homeland leaders who had accepted independence. They also considered Inkatha to be a potentially important mass movement, with rural-urban links, that might eventually mesh with the ANC. Meanwhile, Buthelezi was meeting with leaders of the white Progressive Federal Party, English-speaking and Afrikaner businessmen, and prominent members of the National Party. Increasingly, he began to extol the benefits of the free-enterprise system, seeking a partnership of Inkatha, business and the ruling National Party and calculating that, as pressures mounted for radical change, whites would be compelled to turn to him as the most acceptable black leader.

By mid-1980, however, Buthelezi's hopes for a "united front" with the ANC appeared at an end when Oliver Tambo declared that he had "emerged on the side of the enemy against the people." The cycle of black protest, white repression, and black radicalization was again leaving Buthelezi behind. Facing its perennial problem of keeping ahead of its followers, the ANC leadership found itself obliged to react to the growing hostility toward Buthelezi inside South Africa. The immediate catalyst for the split was Buthelezi's condemnation of school boycotts and other campaigns supported by the ANC. Warning that troublemakers might have "their skulls cracked," he announced his intention "to create well-disciplined and regimented *impis* (bands of warriors) in every Inkatha region" to keep order.

A final important outgrowth of the Soweto period was a change in official South African attitudes toward the black labor movement. Both government and business hoped that the emerging unions could become forces for stability in industrial relations if they were legalized and made subject to the rules governing registered unions. The government legalized African unions in 1979, and in that year the Federation of South African Trade Unions was formed.

The new federation was wary of challenging the state by premature and politically provocative action. It saw "the bosses," not the state, as its primary enemy. Through skillful use of new legal options, the emerging unions rapidly strengthened themselves on the shop floor.

The most recent stage in black challenge to white rule began in July 1982, when the Nationalist government announced its proposal for a new constitutional system, providing for a tricameral Parliament that would preserve white control but permit participation by elected representatives of Coloureds and Indians.

The new constitution was only the latest—but the most dramatic and detested—in a long series of attempts by South African authorities to formalize the mechanisms of white supremacy and to divide and co-opt potential black opposition. Fundamentally rejecting liberal conceptions of a common nonracial society, the National Party government has sought to defeat African nationalism by treating Africans as members of separate nations. Over three decades, its "homeland" or "Bantustan" policy has succeeded in winning sufficient collaboration to create four nominally independent "national states"—Transkei, Ciskei, Bophuthatswana and Venda. These states are recognized only by South Africa, but they have bureaucratic elites with vested interests in the status quo, and they play an important role in South Africa's counterinsurgency efforts against the ANC.

In its rhetoric, the government has come to abandon reliance on so-called grand apartheid. And it has taken some steps that recognize urban Africans as permanent residents with an indirect say in national policy-making; on September 30, 1985, President P. W. Botha expressed his commitment to "a united South Africa, one citizenship and a universal franchise." Yet a fifth national state is soon to be created, and there is no sign that citizenship for

Africans will carry with it a right to vote for representation in the central Parliament.

Pretoria's preoccupation with complex political schemes reflects the fundamentally political nature of South Africa's crisis. Yet the government has repeatedly failed to engage the cooperation of popular or credible African leaders or to create effective mechanisms for negotiating with them. This was so in 1979 when a Cabinet member attempted to set up a series of regional advisory committees on the future of urban Africans. A Special Cabinet Committee created in 1982 for the same purpose was equally ineffective. In January 1985, President Botha announced the creation of "an informal, nonstatutory forum," apparently designed to include leaders opposed to participation in officially sponsored institutions. But this, too, has remained empty. It excluded not only those who did not renounce violence but also those who had "unconstitutional aims." On January 31, 1986, Botha announced his intention "to negotiate the establishment of a national statutory council" that would "advise on matters of common concern," but the prospects of this body also seem dim.

The strategy behind the new constitution backfired badly. Far from defusing opposition to the regime, the constitutional proposals served to focus attention on basic issues of political power, provoking a widespread boycott of elections to the new Coloured and Indian parliamentary chambers and sparking a wave of protest and violence that has bordered on countrywide insurrection.

The debate on the constitution had a polarizing effect. White voters approved the plan by a two-thirds majority, with an estimated 76 percent of eligible voters participating. The Progressive Federal Party called for a "No" vote, but many of its usual followers disagreed, believing that the government had a hidden agenda and was taking a step in the right direction.

On the other hand, virtually all African leaders expressed intense opposition to the plan. The effectiveness of a boycott campaign in the separate Coloured and Indian elections indicated how far the government's legitimacy had fallen with those groups. Fewer than one in five eligible Coloured voters and only one in seven of eligible Indian voters voted. In the politically conscious Cape Peninsula, only 5 percent of eligible Coloured voters went to the polls.

In 1983, opponents of the proposed constitution formed two new coalitions which continue to play a central role in opposition to the regime. The two groups represent differing orientations in black political thinking but have some overlapping sponsorship and participation.

The larger and more important coalition is the United Democratic Front, which serves as an umbrella organization with a decentralized federal structure. It now claims some two million adherents belonging to some 680 affiliated organizations. These include political, community, labor, religious, youth and other groups representing all races. In its multiracialism, the UDF resembles the Congress Alliance of the 1950s, but it differs organizationally in that the Alliance was composed only of national organizations.

The UDF has obvious sympathies with the African National Congress, and its three presidents—Oscar Mpetha, Archie Gumede and Albertina Sisulu, the wife of Walter Sisulu, the ANC's imprisoned secretary-general—are veteran ANC activists. The list of UDF patrons includes Mandela, Sisulu, Govan Mbeki and other prominent leaders or associates of the ANC.

Still, in an effort to encompass the widest possible opposition to the new constitution, the UDF has avoided making adherence to the ANC's Freedom Charter a condition of membership. Describing its goals as a "united, democratic South Africa based on the will of the people" and an end to "economic and other forms of exploitation," the UDF has not gone far beyond general principles to define a constitutional or economic policy.

Prominent among the UDF's affiliates are the Congress of South African Students, for high school students, which was outlawed in August 1985; the Azanian Students Organization, for college students; the Soweto Civic Association, headed by Dr. Nthato Motlana, the Natal Indian Congress, which Mohandas Gandhi helped establish in 1894; and the Transvaal Indian Congress. Also among its affiliates are white liberal organizations such as the National Union of South African Students and the Natal region of the Black Sash.

Early in 1985 the government moved to crush the UDF, arresting leaders on charges of high treason, and in the eyes of many observers the possibility of nonviolent protest appeared to be at stake. For legal reasons, the major trial collapsed in December 1985, but Botha apparently continues to regard UDF leaders as traitors.

Ideologically in contrast to the UDF is the National Forum, which is a convocation rather than an organization. Like UDF leaders, its leaders have also been subject to official repression, although to a lesser extent. At its first meeting, the National Forum attracted representatives of nearly 200 black organizations. Notable among them were the Azanian People's Organization, led since 1985 by former Black Consciousness activist Saths Cooper, and the Cape Action League, headed by Dr. Neville Alexander, a Marxist intellectual. Cooper and Alexander, both of whom have served prison sentences on Robben Island, are the main intellectual influences within the National Forum.

The most important recent development affecting the future of black resistance was the formation of the Congress of South African Trade Unions on November 30, 1985. After four years of difficult negotiations, COSATU emerged as the largest union federation in South African history. Remarkably, it did so during a state of emergency and a time of severe recession and unemployment. It brought together the Federation of South African Trade Unions, the National Union of Mineworkers and other independent unions, including some that were affiliated to the United Democratic Front.

COSATU went far in merging two traditions—the promotion of working-class interests and the struggle against white political domination. The unity talks that led to COSATU's formation had grappled with long-standing debates over the relative importance of class and race, and also with disputes over the need for building shop-floor strength as opposed to the need for joint action with popular political movements. The outcome of the talks was a federation with well over 500,000 signed-up members, most of them Africans. It is nonracial in policy, committed to merging thirty-four affiliates into twelve national industrial unions based on shop-floor strength, and politically sympathetic to the ANC.

Still outside COSATU are the Council of Unions of South Africa and the Azanian Confederation of Trade Unions, both inspired by Black Consciousness. The former claims some 180,000 members and important industrial unions among its affiliates: the latter, some 70,000 members belonging to general unions.

The rise of the mainly African unions has been phenomenal. It must be remembered that as yet not much more than about 10 percent of all the economically active African population within South Africa's traditional boundaries is unionized. But that fact greatly underestimates the strategic power already attained by the new unions in several key industries and companies and the influence of important new union leaders such as Cyril Ramaphosa, the 33-year-old head of the National Mineworkers' Union.

The politicization of the emerging black unions is a development that the government hoped would not happen when it decided in 1979 to legalize them. Government and business leaders should have recognized, however, that the organization of the new unions was itself a political act. Black union leaders have no intention of confining themselves to narrow issues of labor-management relations, and the unions have become increasingly involved in pressing for action on community-related issues. But experienced organizers remain concerned that the planning of campaigns should be realistic and have rank-and-file support.

The black union movement has already sunk deep roots. The number of shop stewards rose from 6,000 in 1983 to about 12,500 in 1985, and the government would face a countrywide strike if it attempted any major repression of the new union leadership. The leadership of COSATU is anxious to avoid premature or unrealistic timetables for political action. When the new president of COSATU, Elijah Barayi, called at a mass rally for the burning of passes if they were not scrapped within six months, the COSATU executive in effect retracted the threat. But now in the political battle, COSATU cannot avoid responding to actions by the government. It also faces an antagonist in Chief Buthelezi, who has attacked COSATU as a "new front" for the ANC.

The period after September 1984 began with bloody clashes—"unrest" is the common euphemism—and confrontation with the police in African townships in the Vaal

Triangle, an urban complex south of Johannesburg. Protest centered on the issues of political power raised by the new constitution, combined with local grievances—in particular, raises in rent—at a time of economic recession and unemployment. A cycle of violence soon developed: protest demonstrations, police killings, funerals in a charged political atmosphere, often with ANC trappings, new clashes and deaths at the funerals, and so on. Schools have been boycotted, government property and that of local black officials damaged or burned, indoor meetings banned (outdoor meetings have been banned for some years) and leaders detained.

What is particularly new is the substantial amount of black violence against blacks who are seen as collaborators. In seven months, according to government officials, fifteen black councillors were murdered in the Vaal Triangle, and over seventy-five, including thirty chairmen, resigned. They had taken on new significance as symbols of African exclusion in the new constitution. Today the countrywide third tier of African local government is, in effect, destroyed, and plans for the indirect representation of African local authorities at a second tier of multiracial "regional service councils," to be established in 1986, have been undermined.

Another new element that has escalated tensions has been the use of army troops on a large scale in African townships. In earlier years the army had been used mainly on a standby basis. But in October 1984 troops cordoned off the 160,000 residents of Sebokeng, south of Johannesburg, and, beginning at 2 A.M., the police conducted a complete search of every house, arresting 2,300 persons on minor charges.

The violence that has occurred since then has become almost routine. A particularly notorious example occurred on March 21, 1985, on the twenty-fifth anniversary of the Sharpeville shootings. As several thousand Africans walked peacefully in a funeral procession from one township to another, passing through white residential areas of Uitenhage in the eastern Cape, the police killed twenty, shooting ten from behind, and wounded twenty-seven, most of them as they fled. An investigating judge later found that the police had lied in claiming that the crowd had attacked them.

It is difficult to describe adequately the anger and hatred fanned by this kind of police action. The very presence of the police and army in black townships has been provocative. Although blaming the turmoil on agitators, the police have often been indiscriminate, as well as appearing to act with relish, in their use of whips and guns. Stone-throwing and firebombings by black youths have been met by tear gas, mass arrests, beatings, rubber bullets and, more and more, live ammunition.

Ironically, the action used to quell disturbances led to results that made it necessary for the government to proclaim a state of emergency on July 21, 1985, in some of the most populated parts of South Africa. The state of emergency was the first since 1960.

In late August the government banned the Congress of South African Students, the most popular national organization of African secondary school students. Over 500 of its members had been detained during the first month of the emergency. Violent "unrest" spread that month to the Cape Town Coloured communities, whose usual placidity had been shattered after the Soweto uprising. In late October, the state of emergency was extended to the Cape Town area.

During the sixteen months ending in December 1985, more than a thousand people, almost all of them black, died in the townships, some two-thirds of them killed by police and soldiers. Between January 1 and December 12, 1985, at least 10,836 people were detained, and 1,036 were still in prison at the end of that period. Under the state of emergency, large numbers of children have been detained. According to the reputable Detainees' Parents Support Committee, 23 percent of those in detention have been under the age of fifteen, some as young as seven years of age.

For South African blacks, the intensification of the conflict has sharpened debate on several long-standing tactical disputes.

One question that has bedeviled black politics for at least fifty years is the dilemma of whether or not to participate in government-sponsored political institutions. A total boycott of the system, for example, its schools and courts, is virtually impossible. On the other hand, bitter disputes continue over whether blacks should voluntarily participate in operating governmental organs.

The ANC itself in 1949 adopted a program of boycott of "all differential political institutions" but for pragmatic reasons did not consistently implement the policy. The UDF, as well as AZAPO and other groups identified with Black Consciousness, stigmatize as collaborationist those blacks who operate the nominally independent and other homelands and the local authority councils in urban African townships.

An abortive effort was made in 1983 to create a wide front of black leaders of the non-independent homelands, including Buthelezi, urban council representatives and a few church leaders, with the National Federated Chamber of Commerce as an interested observer. The proposed group was aimed at building support for a nonracial federation of South Africa that would bring the four nominally independent states back into the fold. The authoritarian president of the Transkei homeland, Chief Kaiser Matanzima, joined in the effort but withdrew under pressure from the South African government. And the unwieldy coalition proved incapable of mobilizing mass support throughout the country, especially in urban areas.

The only "collaborationist" groups now participating on a national level—that is, in the segregated chambers of the new Parliament—are a number of Coloured and Indian parties. The small minority of eligible voters who participated in the Coloured elections gave a dominant position in the Coloured chamber to the Labour Party and a few seats to the Democratic Workers Party, which is run by businessmen. The even smaller minority of voters who took part in the Indian election gave an edge to the National People's Party over its opposition, known as Solidarity, both led by businessmen.

Another tactical issue that has gained in importance concerns the abandonment of nonviolence. In planning the ANC's military wing in June 1961, Nelson Mandela declared that "fifty years of nonviolence had brought the African people nothing but more and more repressive legislation." By 1961, he said, "only two choices were left, submit or fight." The PAC reached a similar conclusion.

Yet, despite a commitment to "armed struggle," the ANC has considered sabotage and guerrilla attacks to be only a minor strand in a multifaceted strategy consisting mainly of politically inspired demonstrations, strikes and defiance. The ANC has welcomed consumer boycotts, for example, which have occurred in the past but have never before 1984 been as widespread or effective.

For years, ANC statements have envisaged the possibility of escalation to the stage of a "people's war," but only in 1985 was serious emphasis given to such a shift in priorities. ANC President Tambo stressed that this new policy represented a necessary response to the regime's own escalation of violence, since South African security forces were "killing children" and perpetrating "massacres . . . inside and outside the country." He stressed, however, that the ANC would not attack civilians unless they happened to be in military installations, and that, even in military zones, the ANC would not attack children.

Chief Buthelezi's position on violent tactics has shifted over time. Shortly after the 1977 crackdown, Buthelezi seemed to accept the necessity of international sanctions and violence to achieve change. His prevailing position now, however, is to reject "armed struggle" for pragmatic reasons, saying the time is not ripe. Buthelezi's professed strategy is to build "workers' and consumers' power" until there appears, one day, an overwhelming "groundswell" of black activism. In practice, however, Inkatha has never tested the strength of its following or demonstrated its power through action such as boycotts or civil disobedience, even as a means of winning additional support.

The use of violence against the regime is bound to become an increasingly important and emotionally contentious issue in South African life. Aboveground organizations, no matter how sympathetic to the ANC, attempt to avoid any appearance of advocating violence, although participants in meetings frequently sing, shout and chant their praises for antigovernment guerrillas. This has often been the case at UDF meetings.

According to recent opinion surveys, a growing number of South African blacks have come to accept violence as unavoidable if there is to be basic change. And, encouraged by the increasing legitimacy of "armed struggle" as a tool against the regime, young blacks have begun to use guns and throw grenades as well as rocks and stones. At mass meetings, young blacks frequently shout slogans urging the ANC to supply them with Soviet-made AK-47 assault rifles and sometimes are to be seen carrying wooden replicas of the rifle.

The role of whites, either as members or as organizational allies, is another important tactical issue. The ANC has always advocated a nonracial political system, although it did not open its own ranks to non-African members until 1969. In that year, it invited revolution-minded whites as well as Indians and Coloureds to join, and a number have done so. The ANC's National Executive Committee remained exclusively African until June 1985, when this limitation, too, was removed, and two Indians, two Coloureds, and one white were elected to the committee. The UDF, reflecting its sympathy for the ANC, has welcomed the participation of whites, and a few whites are prominent in its leadership.

A contrary point of view is taken by the Africanist or Black Consciousness organizations. The PAC, now of only minor importance, argues against the inclusion of whites in the liberation struggle. AZAPO, the principal Black Consciousness group inside South Africa, has criticized the involvement of whites in both the ANC and UDF, seeing them as representatives of the ruling class.

The role of whites in the labor movement is also a central issue in the lingering divisions that separate COSATU from the two other black trade union federations, the Council of Unions of South Africa and the Azanian Confederation of Trade Unions. Reflecting their ties to Black Consciousness, they stress the importance of developing black leadership. CUSA, representing a more moderate strain of Black Consciousness, has no problem with white assistance under black leadership or, in theory, with the election of white union members on the shop floor. AZACTU, on the other hand, leaves little room for whites in its organizational philosophy.

A fourth important tactical issue, closely tied to the question of white participation, involves the importance of class conflict as an element of the South African liberation struggle. Debate over this issue reaches back to the early years of this century, when the rise of an urban African proletariat encouraged definitions of the South African conflict as one of class rather than of color or nationalism. These two conceptions were to compete in the decades to come and have now begun to merge.

The ANC's Freedom Charter permits a broad range of interpretations. Based on notions of natural rights liberalism, the Freedom Charter envisages bourgeois democracy with a mixed economy and some socialism. It endorses the nationalization of mineral wealth, banks and "monopoly industry," and the redivision of land "amongst those who work it." In exile, the ANC's rhetoric has become more radical, but no program of future policies has been enunciated that supplants the Charter.

Communists allied to the ANC can accept the Freedom Charter as the key document during the first stage of the party's two-stage theory of revolution, in which national liberation must precede a working-class victory. Marxists who criticize the party from the left—notably four white members of the ANC who were expelled in June 1985— argue for a single stage of class struggle and working-class leadership to win popular ownership of the means of production. Others, such as Neville Alexander of the Cape Action League, share this view.

The Africanist faction of the ANC, which split off to form the PAC, rejected the ANC's decision to move toward cooperation with the Communist Party after it was banned in 1950. On the other hand, the mainly middle-class theorists of Black Consciousness have been reading and formulating a more radical analysis of South Africa's problems. Their leftward quest for a fusion of Black Consciousness and class consciousness has resulted in the description of the enemy as "racial capitalism." This concept appeared in the National Forum manifesto adopted in 1983. An amended version in 1984 has called for "worker control of the means of production, distribution and exchange." At the same time, there has been a heightening of interest, not confined to Black Consciousness, in the role of western capitalist states as underwriters and beneficiaries of the South African system. With this perspective, AZAPO members demonstrated against the visit to South Africa in early 1985 of Senator Edward Kennedy.

Chief Buthelezi has on occasion criticized the capitalist record but has moved toward a closer identification with capitalist interests. Praising free enterprise, he has recently suggested a reevaluation of the economic planks of the Freedom Charter.

The ongoing debate on these tactical issues reflects the long-standing diversity of black political opinion. But in recent years this diversity has increasingly given way to a widespread recognition of the African National Congress as the central focus of black political aspirations.

Assessments of support in a repressive police state are, at best, difficult to assemble. Yet the evidence of the ANC's popularity, especially among young blacks, is strong and growing.

The ANC symbolizes the historic struggle for equality. Other movements and organizations have risen and fallen, but it has endured. In exile, it has built organizational strength and won international legitimacy. In appealing for unity, it has been nondoctrinaire, making room for Christians, communists, liberal pragmatists, and members from all economic classes.

The blatant openness of support for the ANC is to be seen at mass meetings and funerals (although attendance has been severely curtailed since 1984), where ANC flags, colors, salutes, songs and slogans are often in evidence. The ANC has inherited some support almost by default as aboveground forces have been harassed and their leaders repressed. Some support may be symbolic, a manifestation of despair and frustration. Yet there is also an intensity of dedication, most vividly seen in the prison graduates who, after years of incarceration, return to the struggle either above- or underground.

The ANC faces problems of communication, control and discipline—problems which increased after South Africa's Nkomati Accord with Mozambique in March 1984 effectively severed infiltration routes through that country.[2] The logistical problems of transporting military equipment became less important, however, as the ANC's emphasis shifted to the problem of arming masses of people within South Africa—or assisting young activists in arming themselves. Young people are still leaving the country in small numbers to join the ANC, but ANC leaders are discouraging their departure, both because the camps are said to be full and because priority is now being given to the further development of underground structures and training within South Africa.

The UDF, which shares the ANC appeal, is the most popular aboveground opposition movement in the country. To a large extent, the largely middle-class leadership of the UDF has devoted its energies to skillful media campaigns at the national level. The state's repressive tactics have weakened the UDF, which has had little time since its inception to organize in rural areas and in some major regions, notably Natal and the Orange Free State. But it has sunk local roots in other parts of the country, and many of its affiliates have mobilized their followings by consumer, rent or school boycotts in small towns— particularly in the Eastern Cape. The effectiveness of the boycott of the Coloured and Indian Parliamentary elections in 1984 was due both to national propaganda and to local organization.

The size of the opposition that is politically sympathetic to the ANC is suggested if one links the UDF to the Congress of South African Trade Unions. It is important to emphasize that an opposition with popular support can present a sustained challenge to the regime only if it has built organizational structures with local roots. This is as true for the ANC, whose leaders continually stress the need to strengthen and expand its underground structures, as it is for aboveground organizations. COSATU has such strengths, and critics of the UDF argue that trade union experience should serve not only as an organizational model, but also as an example of democratic responsiveness to rank-and-file membership.

The difficulties African political leaders face in building organizational strength in a vast country under repressive conditions have been chronic for at least half a century. The Pan Africanist Congress is an example of a potentially powerful movement that was cut down within a year of its formation and that has been unable to develop organizational coherence even in exile. National organizations such as AZAPO, with a strongly intellectual leadership and much influence, fall far short of mass membership. National student organizations are also limited in membership by the fact that many youths are not in school; for them, local youth organizations have come into being. What is relatively new during the past decade, especially since the government's crackdown on Black Consciousness in late 1977, is the sprouting of community-level groups and the trend toward finding common ground with trade unions on local issues.

Ideological differences on the national level have sometimes been translated into intense conflicts in African townships. Occasional ugly and even violent clashes have occurred between UDF and AZAPO followers, sometimes involving thugs who are later perceived as political partisans. But leaders on both sides, charging that police "disinformation" has caused trouble, have sought to heal any rifts. They have appeared on platforms together and have sometimes campaigned alongside each other.

It is important to note that activists inspired initially by the Black Consciousness outlook and its values can move in different partisan directions. Some have become national officials of the UDF, and others, in leaving the country, have, for largely pragmatic reasons, moved into the ANC with little ideological inhibition. Moreover, many prominent black personalities—for example, the well-known Bishop Desmond Tutu—have credibility in both "Charterist" and Black Consciousness camps and devote themselves to furthering unity.

Chief Buthelezi remains a strong political figure within his traditional Zulu community, but his attempts to present himself as a possible alternative to the ANC have largely failed. A man of personal warmth, Buthelezi has a sensitivity to personal criticism approaching paranoia that has made it impossible for him to be a figure of reconcilation among blacks.

Critics on Buthelezi's left have seen him as acting on behalf of the government. His frequent characterization of the UDF as an advocate of violence—indeed, as "the terror wing of the ANC"—at a time when this was at issue in a treason trial of the UDF's major leaders was by many opposition activists seen as a traitorous act. His extensive travels abroad to visit such leaders as President Ronald Reagan and British Prime Minister Margaret Thatcher, and to argue against sanctions, have also been seen in this light. His reputation among blacks has also suffered from his arguments against stayaways, strikes and consumer boycotts—tactics Buthelezi claims can be effective only if accompanied by black intimidation and violence.

Some white liberals and progressives are apprehensive about Buthelezi's capacity for leadership and about the atmosphere of indoctrination and orthodoxy that he has encouraged in his political movement. Inkatha discourages dissent and retains the trappings of an authoritarian mass movement—enlisting its youthful members, for example, in paramilitary training.

Nevertheless, many liberals cling to the hope that Buthelezi might be a key element in the creation of a centrist coalition. In one such effort, Frederick van Zyl Slabbert, then leader of the Progressive Federal Party, and Buthelezi were the two main speakers in September 1985 at a meeting held to launch a National Convention Movement. The movement, however, was stillborn, due to both Buthelezi's prominence in the meeting and the absence of other popular leaders, who were in detention or on trial for treason at the time. And in view of the growing polarization of South African political life, the future prospects of such a centrist coalition, with the implication that the ANC is politically extreme, seem dim.

Meanwhile, there is much speculation that the government might adopt the "Natal option," that is, implement the recommendations of the "Buthelezi Commission." In

1982 this commission proposed the merging of KwaZulu and the rest of Natal into a "consociational" unit and the dismantling of apartheid under authority from the central government. Under the commission's plan, the legislative assembly would be elected by universal suffrage on the basis of proportional representation. Buthelezi presumably would become the leader of a nonracial Natal, but white and other minorities would have the power to veto majority decisions.

White commercial, industrial and agricultural interests support the proposal, arguing that existing government plans for the consolidation of the KwaZulu homeland would seriously disrupt the largely integrated economy of Natal. And if the government, in response to pressures for a dramatic breakthrough, were to adopt the commission's scheme, Buthelezi's prominence as a counterweight to the ANC would be boosted. Meanwhile, with acceptance in principle by the central government, a joint committee of the KwaZulu Cabinet and the Natal Provincial Executive has begun a piecemeal process of joint planning for both regions.

Opinion polls, despite their many limitations, confirm the relative importance of the ANC. Two examples among many may be cited. A detailed poll for the Johannesburg *Star* in 1981 asked Africans in Johannesburg, Durban and Cape Town how they would vote in a parliamentary election among candidates from the ANC, Inkatha, AZAPO and the PAC. The ANC emerged first in each city, in all the main African-language groups including Zulu and in all occupational groups except among the unskilled, where it was roughly equal with Inkatha. The more skilled or professional and the younger tended to be pro-ANC. The three leaders most preferred were Mandela, 76 percent, Dr. Ntatho Motlana (the pro-UDF civic leader in

Soweto), 58 percent, and Chief Buthelezi, 39 percent, with Mandela and Motlana outranking Buthelezi even in Durban. Two surveys in August and September 1985 showed 4.8 and 27 percent support for Buthelezi among Africans in Natal and 47 and 54.2 percent for Mandela; two other surveys each showed 6 percent support for Buthelezi among Africans in South Africa and 31 and 49 percent for Mandela.

In addition to such support among blacks, the ANC has received increasing recognition from South African whites. In 1981, the editor of *Beeld,* the most influential Afrikaans-language newspaper and the Transvaal mouthpiece of President Botha, compared the ANC's nationalism to the nationalism of the National Party and concluded: "The day will yet arrive when the South African government will sit down at the negotiating table with the ANC." In late 1984 *Beeld*'s deputy editor interviewed ANC officials in Lusaka and accompanied his series of articles with an editorial call for dialogue with the ANC. Talk of talks is usually conditional, but in April 1985 the student representative councils in the Afrikaans-speaking Stellenbosch University and Rand Afrikaans University came out in support of unconditional talks.

Discussion about possible negotiations between white leaders and the ANC has been fueled by rumors about the possible release of Nelson Mandela. As Christmas approached in 1984, President Botha offered to free Mandela if he would accept asylum in what was regarded as his homeland, the nominally independent Transkei. But Mandela refused.[2] Botha, he said, should himself "renounce violence . . . [and] guarantee free political activity so that people may decide who will govern them."

The specific motivations for Botha's offer of conditional freedom were unclear, but many possible explanations suggest themselves. Supporters of the government have—on the assumption that divisions exist between Mandela and the organization's left-wing exile leaders—privately speculated about the possibility of using Mandela's release as a tool to weaken the ANC. In addition, the government also has good reason for wishing to release Mandela before he dies or becomes seriously ill.

The unconditional release of Mandela has come to be seen as a litmus test of the government's readiness to talk with popular black leaders. A wide range of critics inside and outside the country link this to other steps that are essential in opening up the political process: releasing all political prisoners, legalizing the ANC and other banned organizations, giving amnesty to exiles, and rolling back South Africa's police state by repealing measures that date back at least to 1963.

The government has allowed selected visitors to meet with Mandela. Even more indicative of the ANC's growing importance have been recent private visits by prominent South Africans to ANC headquarters in Zambia—a journey that has taken on the character of a political pilgrimage.[3] The meetings produced world-wide publicity for the ANC, boosting its legitimacy, enhancing its appeal to some whites as well as blacks in South Africa, and infuriating the South African government.

Gavin Relly, chairman of the Anglo American Corporation, headed the first group of businessmen and journalists to visit Lusaka in September 1985. Relly, who had supported the new constitution, described the visit as "a function of frustration at the lack of political action on the home front."

Two delegations that went to Lusaka in March 1986 were of special significance. The first of some 20 members was headed by Enos Mabuza, chief minister of the Swazi "homeland" of KaNgwane. His group, he said, represented his political movement, Inyandza, rather than the homeland government. On his return, Mabuza praised the ANC's leadership. The visit was a blow to Chief Buthelezi since Mabuza's movement had been part of a loose alliance headed by Buthelezi.

Perhaps most important for the ANC was a two-day session with leaders of the Congress of South African Trade Unions. The delegation included Cyril Ramaphosa, whose National Union Mineworkers had elected Nelson Mandela as an honorary life president. Concerned by the ANC's cordial reception of the South African business delegation, COSATU officials who were committed to socialism and working-class leadership had wanted a face-to-face clarification of ANC policy, and were apparently satisfied by the meeting.

Opponents of white rule in South Africa face so many obstacles that an outside observer might conclude that revolution is impossible. Yet sophisticated black leaders express confidence that revolutionary change is not only possible but inevitable. And they define that change, at a minimum, as the the attainment of majority rule in an undivided and nonracial South Africa.

They are also in agreement on other matters. They have few illusions about the regime's political and military power and readiness to use that power ruthlessly. Nor do any of them, including the leaders of the African National Congress, believe that armed struggle alone can bring down the regime—although the perception that violence is a necessary strand of pressure is widespread and growing.

Militant black leaders have ideological differences that bear upon tactics, but they agree that nonviolent pressures of all kinds, internal and external, are crucial in making (as the ANC slogan has it) "apartheid unworkable and South Africa ungovernable." Black leaders are also more united than whites on their aims. To an extraordinary degree, the black struggle against the system of white domination is a nonracial struggle with white allies against a system rather than an antiwhite struggle.

White leaders of the regime, anxious about its lack of legitimacy, also recognize the importance of black allies. And their search for such allies may be aided by incremental reforms aimed at eliminating the most objectionable features of the apartheid system. But ending apartheid while maintaining white political control falls far short of the revolutionary changes that South Africa's black leaders now demand. The struggle for political power will continue and may be protracted. Although the identity and orientation of South Africa's leaders after liberation remain imponderables, the African National Congress will play a central role in the process of transition.

In assessing the trends of the current period, it is difficult for whites to look through the eyes of blacks. Whites who say that "time is running out" commonly refer with pessimism to the need for fundamental change before South Africa slides into full-scale civil war. Blacks also recognize the human costs and bitter legacy of such violence. But they and their white allies can also see that time is running out for an oppressive system, and they look forward with optimism, not pessimism.

NOTES

1. The Azanian Students Organization had its origins in Black Consciousness and retains "Azania" in its name, although

the ANC rejects it, arguing that any renaming of South Africa should be done by a representative body after liberation. "Azania," of obscure origin, was first proposed by PAC leaders in exile and has caught on inside the country, even among supporters of the ANC.

2. See pages 285–333.

3. Among others who traveled to meet with the ANC, in Zambia and elsewhere, were Progressive Federal Party leaders, a multi-racial delegation of Dutch Reformed Church ministers, students from the Afrikaans-speaking Stellenbosch University (whose travel plans were temporarily aborted by government opposition to the meeting), students from the white National Union of South African Students, clergymen led by an Anglican Archbishop, Catholic priests led by an Archbishop, and an official of the National Convention Movement.

THE AFRICAN NATIONAL CONGRESS: WAITING FOR THE DAY

Mark A. Uhlig

The exile headquarters of the African National Congress—South Africa's largest and best known rebel group—are located in the dusty, sunbaked city of Lusaka, the capital of Zambia. For security reasons, the group's offices are scattered among several sites—above a small store, in a wood-frame house. The main headquarters, an aging single-story structure surrounded by a high wall, opens unobtrusively onto a narrow, rutted alleyway just off the city's sweltering main street, Cairo Road. There, in a sparsely furnished meeting room, ANC President Oliver Tambo expressed confidence about the developing struggle within South Africa.

"The regime is on the offensive, we're on the offensive," he said with quiet satisfaction. "The regime has tried to divide us tribally, tried to divide us into communists and noncommunists, projected us as terrorists. But it hasn't succeeded. It hasn't succeeded because the people hate the regime so much that if the regime calls us terrorists, the people call us heroes. If the regime attacks us, in the eyes of our people this is only because we are being very effective."

Indeed, after nearly seventy-five years of opposition to South African racism, including more than twenty-five years in exile, the African National Congress has become a principal—perhaps decisive—element in South Africa's unfolding political drama. As the country's black townships have erupted in violence, the ANC has become a symbol of black strength, of black dreams of deliverance from white rule.

The government in Pretoria relentlessly denounces the ANC and has made it a crime to possess the group's publications, to quote its leaders or to do anything else that might further what it describes as the ANC's "terroristic aims." Yet increasingly the ANC's influence is impossible to ignore. Large demonstrations erupt at the funerals of ANC guerrillas in black townships. The group's colors and anthem have become emblems of black resistance and solidarity throughout the country and have been adopted in various forms by groups attempting to gain political legitimacy among blacks. Opposition leaders and businessmen have traveled to Lusaka to confer with ANC officials. And many whites as well as blacks admit that if free multiracial elections were held today, Nelson Mandela, the jailed ANC leader, would easily defeat any other potential candidate, white or black.

To a large degree, this success is the result of the ANC's dedicated efforts to put pressure on Pretoria through internal agitation, international lobbying and, since 1961, sabotage and other armed actions. Through decades of underground resistance, persistent diplomacy and guerrilla warfare directed from its remote outpost in Lusaka, the ANC exile leadership has built a growing network of support for its battle against apartheid.

But much of the ANC's new prominence is also an outgrowth of spontaneous changes that have occurred inside South Africa—changes that have little direct connection to the ANC or its platform. Important among these was the devastating police crackdown in the late 1970s that incapacitated much of the ANC's potential competition for black political loyalties, including the dynamic Black Consciousness Movement. More recently, the group has been a major beneficiary of the swelling tide of violent protest that has swept through the country's black townships—protest prompted not by ANC example or decree but rather by the government's own efforts to institutionalize white superiority.

As the power of the ANC has grown, the group and its program have come under increasing scrutiny from critics and supporters alike. For those opposed to the ANC, the question is whether the group's appeal can be effectively blunted through political manipulation, police repression or direct military action. For the ANC's supporters, it is whether and how the group's current popularity can be marshaled to defeat the regime despite the handicaps of exile. And for both, it must be asked whether even an organization dedicated to the violent overthrow of white rule will be able to channel and control the growing anger of South Africa's black population or whether confrontation will necessarily bring with it the mutual tragedy of an all-out race war.

Underlying the ANC's resurgent influence among South African blacks is the group's record, prior to 1961, of more than three generations of principled, nonviolent activism against apartheid. Founded in 1912, in the wake of Mohandas Gandhi's nonviolent campaign for Indian rights in South Africa's Natal region, the ANC won a broad following as the champion of peaceful opposition to government racism. A diverse coalition, it attracted multiracial support for its platform of equal rights and nondiscrimination.

Guided by a series of impressive leaders, including Mandela, Tambo and Chief Albert Luthuli, who won the

1960 Nobel Peace Prize for his ANC work, the group's nonviolent protests against apartheid reached a peak in the 1950s, when its program of civil disobedience won mass support from South African blacks. Strikes and demonstrations sponsored by the ANC repeatedly brought tens of thousands of protesters into city streets throughout South Africa. ANC meetings attracted overflow crowds, and British press reports of one ANC rally near Durban in 1958 estimated that it represented the largest public gathering ever held in a Commonwealth nation. Shaken by such successes, the government struck back with a campaign of official intimidation and police violence which set the stage for the military confrontation emerging today.

"When I started with the ANC in the 1940s," Tambo recalled, "we didn't think we would ever have to go for violence as opposed to nonviolence. Our obvious preference was for demonstrations, strikes. We called so many strikes! And the response was tremendous. Our people were very militant, but they were nonviolent.

"But at the climax of this period the situation just got out of hand for the government—they lost their nerve. We were unarmed, we were nonviolent, and they just slaughtered our people."

At Sharpeville, in March 1960, police killed sixty-nine unarmed demonstrators as they protested against laws requiring blacks to carry pass books. This, in Tambo's view, was "just the climax of a process that had been going on all the time. They were shooting at crowds and there was nothing we could do about it."

"When they began to call out the army to stamp out peaceful strikes, that marked the turning point," Tambo said. "Because after that, when we were confronted with the South African Defence Force, we knew that nonviolence had become meaningless. We couldn't take it any further. So we can't, if we have had the experience of the 1950s, we can't possibly see a solution which does not involve military struggle."

Banned after the Sharpeville incident, the ANC went underground and formed a military wing, Umkonto we Sizwe ("Spear of the Nation"), which launched a campaign of sabotage against government installations. In 1963 Umkonto's leaders—except Tambo, who had been sent to London to start the ANC's exile offices—were betrayed by an informant and captured in a farmhouse at Rivonia in the Transvaal, and through the late 1960s the group's visibility within South Africa waned considerably. Harsh police repression, aided by information from captured ANC membership lists, resulted in the arrest and indefinite detention of hundreds of ANC organizers. The ANC members who fled to join the exile group, moreover, found refugee life unexpectedly harsh.

"We plainly underestimated the staying power of the regime, as well as the problems of operating in exile," one veteran of that period recalls. "We had a lot of organizational work to do."

As the ANC concentrated on establishing itself outside the country, the focus of black opposition within South Africa shifted away from the mechanics of confrontation and toward the radical ideas of the groups in the Black Consciousness Movement. Black Consciousness leaders, who included such figures as Steve Biko and Barney Pityana, were generally too young to have developed strong contacts with the ANC before it was banned, and their harsh rejection of collaboration with whites brought their movement into sharp conflict with traditional ANC policies. The potential significance of this conflict was not lost on the white authorities in Pretoria, who initially allowed Black Consciousness activities an exceptional degree of freedom, both to counter ANC influence and to encourage an ideological counterpart to the government's own policies of racial separatism.

By the late 1970s, however, events both in and around South Africa worked to reestablish the ANC as the vanguard of South African opposition. Strengthened by growing diplomatic support and by the interest aroused by the deepening civil war in Rhodesia, the ANC was able to consolidate its exile presence and begin rebuilding its underground network.

More important, the racial tensions within South Africa, which had been heightened by Black Consciousness teachings, erupted in the bloody Soweto uprisings of 1976 and 1977, provoking a far-reaching police crackdown that decimated that movement and its leadership. The Soweto disturbances caused an unprecedented exodus of young black refugees, angry and impatient to fight back. Black Consciousness groups—never organized for practical resistance and now incapacitated by police repression—offered no real alternative to the ANC as a channel for effective action. ANC offices in Botswana, Mozambique and Zambia were consequently flooded with militant new recruits, many of them former followers of the Black Consciousness Movement.

The ideological ferment that characterized the Black Consciousness period had an indirect impact on ANC thinking, accelerating the growth of radical thought within the ANC exile community and giving intellectual depth to left-wing alliances it had already formed.

The general directions of ANC political doctrine were established during the tumultuous period of the 1950s, when ANC leaders decided to accept the support of members of all races, as well as the South African Communist Party, in forming the broadest possible base of opposition against the Nationalist government. The coalition which resulted, the Congress Alliance, produced an original populist manifesto, the Freedom Charter, which remains the principal definition of ANC aims.

The broad language of the charter reflected the ANC's commitment to diversity, leaving room for a range of ideological interpretations and political beliefs. Calling for universal suffrage, racial equality and personal freedoms, it could hardly be construed as revolutionary by western democratic standards. Its mild references to land reform and to redistribution, too, are hardly surprising in a country where existing racial legislation restricts 72 percent of the population to 13 percent of the nation's land.

As the ANC has developed in exile, however, several factors have worked to promote a leftward drift in the political thinking of many of its members, encouraging an increasingly radical interpretation of the charter's language. Emphasizing the economic roots of South African racism, this school concentrates on the poverty and exploitation of black workers and interprets the ANC's struggle as following the pattern of Marxist class conflict.

One element influencing this shift has been the logistical assistance Soviet-bloc nations have provided to help support the ANC's growing exile presence. Since 1960, the size of the ANC's exile community and the scope of its activities have grown rapidly, and its need for material assistance has kept pace. In addition to its Lusaka headquarters, the group maintains a far-flung collection of camps and facilities, including farms in Zambia, a large communal settlement and secondary school in Tanzania and military training facilities north of the Angolan capital of Luanda. The organization also maintains diplomatic representation in more than thirty capitals worldwide.

Tambo, who led the group's early fund-raising efforts, recalled his experiences in attempting to win support for the ANC's burgeoning exile community: "I left South Africa in 1960. It was in the United States that I went first to ask for assistance and to address meetings—addressing Americans, asking them for support. But we received no real response. I only went to the Soviet Union in 1963, and when I got there, in the first instance, I said we needed some funds. They gave us some. I'd never handled so much money before—it was only $20,000. I went to China after that, and they gave us money. We asked for it. They didn't come and say, 'Do you want money?'—we asked for it, we needed it."

The influence of such logistical ties has been amplified by the growing number of ANC members who have been trained in Soviet-bloc nations and are now returning to ANC leadership positions. The movement is invited to place more than 300 students a year in Soviet-bloc universities, and returning students have had an important intellectual influence among their peers.

Of clear importance, too, is the outward respect shown to ANC leaders by their Soviet counterparts. "If we want to go to Moscow," an older ANC member explained, "they will meet us at the airport. If we want to go to New York, we will have to beg for a visa, if we can get one at all. A lot of it is as simple as that."

Over time, the influence of Soviet-bloc dogma and procedures has become clearly visible in many dimensions of ANC life, particularly in formal leadership structures, which are notable for their redundant layers of Soviet-style bureaucracy. ANC recruits (and ANC sympathizers within South Africa) address one another as "comrade," and ANC publications and other official pronouncements, many of which are produced in East Germany and other Socialist-bloc nations, are heavily larded with the political vocabulary of Soviet-style "anti-imperialism." Soviet influence is particularly strong within the ANC's military wing, Umkonto we Sizwe, which receives the bulk of its weaponry and military training from Soviet-bloc sources.

The shift toward radicalism was accelerated sharply by the influx of young recruits that followed the Soweto uprisings in 1976–77. "At base, it is less a question of ideology than of experience," said Mfanafuthi Makatini, a longtime ANC official who now heads the movement's diplomatic section. "When we first marched in the early 1950s, we were charged with batons. But when [young blacks] first tried to march in Soweto they were shot down in the streets. You don't come away from that as a moderate."

The radicalism of the Soweto recruits has worked to crystallize emerging generational differences between ANC members, particularly with regard to international politics and, in particular, policy toward the United States. The older group, including Tambo and many other longtime ANC officials, reflects the strong admiration that many senior ANC members still hold for western—and specifically American—legal history.

"When we grew up," Tambo said, "we were fascinated by the history of the United States. Looking at life against the backdrop of our own experiences, we were fascinated. And we thought that if there was any country which would understand our position, it was the United States. There was the South, there was the Civil War, and then there was the civil rights movement. There were laws against racism, which they enforce. It is the opposite in South Africa—the laws dictate racism, they punish people who are not racists."

The energetic radicals of the Soweto generation, by contrast, found in the Reagan administration's policy of "constructive engagement" confirmation of Marxist predictions regarding America's economic stake in the exploitation of South African blacks. For that reason, many young ANC members tend to see the United States as a self-defined enemy of their cause and view U.S. policy with a mistrust that is quickly hardening into hatred.

"What do you expect us to think?" asked Welile Nhlapo, the grimly professional former Black Consciousness leader who directs the ANC youth section. "The United States has an unbroken record of support for the racist regime, not just in terms of its commercial interests, but in Angola, Namibia. And as our people have died and suffered, Washington has just moved closer to the regime —a racist regime that is despised around the world. Under Reagan, this situation has got much, much worse—we will not forget that. As far as the position of the U.S. is concerned, our expectations are very low."

The South African government has made much of the ANC's ties with the banned South African Communist Party and the Soviet-bloc nations and emphasizes both in its efforts to maintain U.S. support for the white government.

Particularly when invoked with respect to U.S. concerns about maintaining access to South Africa's strategic mineral resources, the vision of "losing" South Africa to a Soviet-supported takeover has found a ready audience among American conservatives. After viewing documents supplied by South Africa and hearing testimony of communist subversion that included lurid tales of sexual coercion and psychological abuse of ANC recruits by Soviet agents, the Senate Subcommittee on Security and Terrorism, led by conservative Senator Jeremiah Denton of Alabama, declared that the ANC has "been deeply infiltrated by those who seek to advance the imperialistic ambitions of the Soviet Union" and thus works "to the obvious detriment of the peoples of the southern African region, not to their advantage."[1]

Among the Western allies, the United States is by far the most estranged from the ANC and its growing influence. The West German government made informal contacts with the ANC during the 1970s, and the movement was later officially invited to open an office in Bonn. This office continues to have good working relations with the conservative Kohl government, and West German foundations now provide scholarships and other aid for some 120 ANC students attending universities in that country. French contacts with ANC officials have also intensified recently, and the ANC also receives support from several British humanitarian relief groups.

As international condemnations of apartheid have intensified, the sources of ANC support have broadened considerably, particularly for humanitarian purposes. The ANC has cultivated especially close ties with the Scandinavian nations, which together provide a majority of the group's outright cash assistance. In addition, it receives funds from the governments of Austria, Italy and a broad cross section of Third World nations. The United Nations and its related agencies provide the ANC with more than $10 million in refugee funds annually, and the movement also receives aid from a range of nongovernmental organizations, including Oxfam, the World Council of Churches, the United Church of Canada, the British Council of Churches, various Catholic aid agencies and Scandinavian charities.

Since 1976, the scope of ANC military operations has grown substantially, and an estimated 6,000–10,000 ANC fighters are now undergoing training at bases in Angola as well as in a number of Eastern Bloc nations.

"Our problem," one ANC official says, "is not recruiting new fighters. The regime's policies take care of that for us. The problem is convincing those who are arriving from South Africa that there is more to this than simply grabbing a gun and going back to kill the people who have been stepping on them."

The post-Soweto recruits, together with a growing number of former ANC activists who have completed long sentences in South African prisons and are returning to the movement, have been responsible for a new military assertiveness that has produced significant results. ANC guerrillas have carried out frequent and increasingly sophisticated attacks against South African government installations, including the bombing of the country's central oil-from-coal processing complex in 1980 and the Koeberg nuclear power facility in late 1982. The most dramatic and violent ANC attack to date took place in May 1983, when a car bomb planted by ANC members exploded outside South African Air Force headquarters in Pretoria, killing nineteen people, including eight blacks.

The Pretoria bombing was the first ANC attack to produce serious civilian casualties, and it fulfilled growing expectations among analysts both within South Africa and abroad that a major escalation in ANC violence was imminent. In talks several weeks before the attack, Tambo warned that such a development should surprise no one.

"We have avoided civilian casualties because we don't think that individual people are to blame for apartheid," he said. "We're not fighting civilians—we're not even fighting whites. We're fighting a system. But it's an armed struggle—it's bound to develop into quite a war, and the civilian population will be affected.

"In any event, I think one really ought to be careful about the use of the word 'civilian' in relation to what the African National Congress is doing, because that risks committing the error of treating [black] Africans as if they are not civilians—as if they are not civilians because they are being killed all the time. [Black] civilians have always been the targets of armed violence by the regime. The regime has been killing us anyway, but somehow the question only seems to be important when those civilians are likely to be hurt by the ANC.

"Our violence, compared to the regime's violence, physically, is minimal—minimal. Sharpeville, Soweto, hangings, shootings by the police—the number of people they have killed! When the police shoot down children, they're shooting down civilians, and they have no qualms about it. From that point of view, the ANC has been remarkably restrained, because the shooting down of children has become routine in South Africa—the regime has made it routine."

Although some senior ANC leaders have distanced themselves from immediate responsibility for the Pretoria bombing, it was nonetheless significant both for what it showed about the development of ANC tactics and as an ANC judgment about the mood of South African blacks. Throughout its period of armed opposition, the ANC has taken care to preserve its prestige among blacks by choosing its targets carefully and by avoiding civilian deaths. This restraint has clearly slowed the growth of its military activities, but, combined with the organization's long early record of nonviolence, it has helped to establish a strong sympathetic following for the ANC among South African blacks—who themselves are likely to suffer the most from violence in any civil war.

The willingness to risk civilian casualties in the Pretoria

attack demonstrated the ANC's increasing confidence in the strength and militance of its popular support—a belief that was borne out by black reactions to the bombing itself. Although the bombing was characterized in western press reports as an unprovoked increase in ANC violence, few black leaders criticized it as excessive, and many blacks said they expected such an escalation as a logical and necessary retaliation for the regime's harsh series of "punitive" raids and assassination attacks against suspected ANC officials and hideouts in neighboring nations.

The government has shunned few if any tactics in its war against the ANC and has left a trail of blood which even its supporters have found difficult to defend. Pretoria's stepped-up counterinsurgency campaign has included shootings and parcel-bomb assassinations of ANC leaders in Zimbabwe and Mozambique, as well as two major cross-border attacks against the homes of South African exiles in Mozambique and Lesotho. In the latter attacks alone, indiscriminate South African rockets and gunfire killed fifty-four persons, most of them asleep in their beds and many of them refugees with no demonstrable connection to the ANC. As if to prove its point, moreover, the government responded to the Pretoria attack with an air strike on Maputo which killed or wounded at least twenty more people, most of them Mozambican citizens, in a factory and residences unrelated to the ANC.

Ironically, it was neither the increased radicalism of ANC cadres nor the growing scope of ANC military attacks that was to finally push South African blacks into a new era of revolt. Rather, that job was done by the white government itself, in its efforts to divide black opposition through the promulgation of its new constitutional "dispensation."

"The introduction of the new constitution—or, more

precisely, the amended apartheid constitution—meant that the South African regime was introducing into the discussion the question of what kind of political system the people want," observed Thabo Mbeki, an ANC spokesman and son of Govan Mbeki, a longtime ANC leader who has been imprisoned for more than two decades. "In that sense, they themselves were raising the level of the debate and raising the focus of the struggle away from issues like rents, bus fares, education—the elements of the apartheid system—and toward the question of what kind of South Africa we want, of what the political physiognomy of South Africa should look like. All of the different elements of the population then became active on this central question of the nature of political power, and that was a decisive difference."

The growth of popular black opposition to the government's new constitutional scheme provided the ANC with the opportunity to link its exile efforts with an important stream of legal, aboveground opposition for the first time since the ANC's banning in 1960. The principal organization that emerged, the United Democratic Front, scrupulously avoided any demonstrable connection to the ANC, but its sympathies were clear from the start. The UDF named several key ANC figures, including Nelson Mandela, to its list of "patrons," and and the ANC has been vocal in its support of UDF activities.

"In a lot of the urban African townships, there is no system of local government," one senior ANC official told me. "The affiliates of the UDF have thus been able in effect to take over the administration of a number of townships because clearly they are the genuine representatives of the people and are accepted as such."

Another largely independent development which redounded to the benefit of the ANC was the dramatic growth of the black labor movement, culminating in the formation of the Congress of South African Trade Unions in December 1985. Again, no direct connections exist between the COSATU leadership and the ANC, and disagreement exists within the labor movement about the wisdom of using job actions as a tool of broader political change. COSATU officials, however, have made no secret of their sympathies, and some, like COSATU president Elijah Baraji, belonged to the ANC before it was outlawed. The growth of the labor movement fulfills a longstanding ANC ambition to build a broad antigovernment coalition based on working-class interests and has provided an important aboveground structure through which eventual pressure for change may be coordinated.

The formation of the UDF and the growth of sympathetic labor organizations might have been less important were it not for a third major factor, the wave of violent protest that has swept through South Africa's black townships since the promulgation of the new constitution in September 1984. The scope and ferocity of this reaction have confirmed ANC expectations regarding popular support for violent resistance to the regime and, indeed, outpaced the ANC's own plans for escalating the fight against apartheid.

The growth of township violence has quickly heightened perceptions of the ANC's importance among blacks and whites alike. By lending new legitimacy to the use of violence against the regime, it has strengthened the ANC's claim to leadership within the black community and focused new popular attention on the ANC as the only organization that is capable of channeling spontaneous uprisings into a tool of meaningful change.

Displays of black support for violence against the regime have become commonplace, often taking the form of songs and chants which appeal openly to ANC leaders to come and liberate the land:

"Tambo, Tambo is in the bush,
Yes, what is he doing there?
He is teaching soldiers . . .
How would it be when we sit with Tambo,
Seeing the Boers falling?"

This kind of radicalization of popular opinion has been particularly important in strengthening the ANC's appeal relative to more conservative black political figures such as Zulu Chief Mangosuthu Gatsha Buthelezi, who heads the Natal-based Inkatha movement. And it has been reinforced by the increasingly open support the ANC has received from such respected black moderates as Nobel laureate Desmond M. Tutu, the Anglican Bishop of Johannesburg. Visiting the United States in early 1986, Tutu urged western governments to support the goals of the ANC and chastised the Reagan administration for its policy of "constructive engagement" with Pretoria. The ANC's importance within the black community has been reflected at the local township level. Before deciding upon ways to end a boycott that was keeping their children from attending school, for example, a committee of parents from Soweto traveled to Zimbabwe to seek advice from ANC representatives there.

While blacks are looking to the ANC to escalate the struggle against Pretoria, growing number of whites have also begun to turn to the ANC as the only group capable of controlling black violence and of serving as a credible spokesman for black interests in a negotiated solution that might resolve the country's problems short of an uncontrolled black-versus-white bloodbath.

Perhaps the most important indication of this emerging attitude came in the fall of 1985, when two high-level white delegations traveled to Zambia to meet with ANC leaders. The first visit, held on September 14, 1985, at a game lodge maintained by Zambian President Kenneth D. Kaunda, brought Tambo and other ANC leaders together with several of South Africa's most prominent white businessmen and journalists, led by Gavin Relly, chairman of the Anglo American Corporation, the major South African mining and industrial conglomerate. The second, held in Lusaka, was led by white Progressive Federal Party leader Frederick van Zyl Slabbert and other liberal political leaders.

The two meetings coincided almost precisely with a comparable breakthrough in ANC relations with the United States. Reversing its longstanding refusal to accept the ANC as a legitimate participant in discussions about South Africa's future, the State Department in late August 1985 publicly urged Pretoria to open talks with ANC leaders. "The ANC we look at as obviously one of a number of important political parties in this situation," one high State Department official told reporters. "I mean, for us to say the government shouldn't talk to the ANC would be madness."

During an interview with reporters and editors at *The New York Times* in October 1985, Secretary of State George Shultz explained the thinking behind the decision to press for negotiations. "Apartheid is through," he said. "It doesn't matter whether you think apartheid is a good idea or not, it's going to disappear. Now the question is, how do you manage the transition? That's the problem psychologically we would like the South Africans to address, because if they address it even now, there is a real chance of doing so, through a process of discussion and negotiation. If it isn't addressed, we can have a cycle of continued violence and at least one can readily imagine this blowing up into a really violent upheaval."

The change in U.S. attitudes toward the ANC was made even less ambiguous in March 1986, when Assistant Secretary of State for African Affairs Chester Crocker, testifying before Congress, agreed that ANC guerrillas could be considered to be "freedom fighters," although administration spokesmen moved quickly to retract Crocker's statement.

Collectively, this broad set of changes has served to give the ANC greater credibility and prominence, both inside and outside South Africa, than it has ever enjoyed before. Yet, as the conflict escalates, it remains unclear how that prominence may be translated into concrete political or military gains. The passage of time, moreover, which has for so long worked in favor of the ANC's effort to build support for "armed struggle," may soon begin to work against the ANC and its program, as black anger and frustration grow beyond the control or direction of any organized leadership.

The recent period has clearly enhanced the ANC's credibility as a potential participant in any negotiations on power-sharing or other talks aimed at deciding South Africa's political future by nonviolent means. Indeed, the rapid growth of the ANC's strength relative to that of other potential black leaders has made it almost impossible to imagine any effective framework for negotiations that would exclude the ANC.

Yet there is no indication at this point that the white government has any interest in pursuing serious negotiations with major black leaders. And there is still less reason to believe that enough common ground exists between the two sides to make such talks worthwhile if they were to occur. The widely hailed meetings between ANC leaders and liberal white business and political delegations, for instance, took place in an atmosphere of mutual accommodation and goodwill that is unlikely to be duplicated in any official context. Yet even those talks appear to have produced only the broadest of agreements, with little meeting of the minds on key substantive issues such as one-man-one-vote and nationalization of major industries. "A fuller understanding of each other's attitudes was achieved," read the self-consciously diplomatic assessment released by the Anglo American Corporation.

For many ANC officials, the meetings were less important as an opportunity for dialogue than as a demonstration of their organization's growing strength. "The meetings were an affirmation of the fact that big business in South Africa and the official opposition needed to act to bring about change," said one official. "It was self-interest that drove Gavin Relly to Zambia. Let's face it, big business is worried."

And most ANC leaders remain skeptical about the value of negotiations at this stage in the conflict. "Our target is not negotiations," said Tambo, "it is the end of the apartheid system. There can be no compromise about that." The ANC leadership has insisted, in particular, that talks cannot even be considered until the South African government releases Nelson Mandela and other jailed ANC leaders.

In the absence of direct negotiations, the ANC's growing political strengths can be brought to bear against the regime in the form of boycotts and strikes. And the potential importance of such actions has been expanded enormously with the establishment of coordinated federations such as the United Democratic Front and, in particular,

COSATU. ANC officials have long emphasized this sort of activity as a main element in the organization's strategy for liberation, and there seems little doubt that it will become an area of increasing difficulty for the regime.

In this area, however, the ANC faces important problems, not only in terms of protecting internal organizational structures from police repression but also in exerting leadership and coordination over diverse and often self-interested groups. The problem of police repression has been self-evident during the most recent period, as thousands of UDF organizers and suspected ANC recruiters have been arrested and detained under sweeping emergency powers. For labor unions, the analogous risk has been that of mass dismissals, a tactic that has been used successfully by management in quashing several attempted job actions since September 1984. Although the political activism of trade union leaders has been strong and growing, the vulnerability of black workers to such penalties has heightened debate within the union movement about the wisdom of using job actions as a tool of broad political change, seriously complicating ANC efforts to exert direct influence upon the government in this fashion.

The strongest tool available to the ANC is that of escalating the level of violent resistance. And the ANC has shown its willingness to accommodate and capitalize upon popular black anger by sponsoring a rising level of violence against the apartheid system. But this most potent form of antigovernment protest carries with it difficult tactical choices that may well be decisive in shaping the kind of country a future ANC government may inherit.

The most immediate difficulty with an escalation of the armed struggle lies in the ANC's own failure to pose a serious guerrilla threat to the white regime. After nearly twenty-five years of armed resistance with significant military assistance from the Soviet Union and its allies, the ANC has proved its ability to carry out harassment attacks against symbolic targets and even, as in the case of the Pretoria bombing, to inflict serious damage to selected targets. Beyond that, however, the ANC has shown little serious military capability. In contrast to popular resistance movements in Latin America, Southeast Asia and elsewhere in the developing world, the ANC has been unable to establish a clear military presence in any nation bordering its own. Rather, it has been restricted to sending infiltrators into South Africa in small groups of three to five, and has yet to confront the South African Defense Forces in any direct combat, leading one observer to call it "one of the world's least successful 'liberation movements.' "[2]

This record of military ineffectiveness is due largely to the ANC's own self-imposed limitations on violence against civilians. For many years, ANC leaders have taken pride in their organization's refusal to engage in careless or indiscriminate violence aimed at sowing terror in the white population. "If we wanted to, we could hit buses, trains, shopping centers," said one ANC official. "But we are not terrorists. We are not fighting a race war. It is precisely against that kind of racial definition that we are doing this."

ANC leaders have also consistently attempted to deemphasize the role of military action in their strategy for ending white rule, going out of their way to portray the ANC's military efforts as an exercise in "armed propaganda" rather than guerrilla war and emphasizing that violent resistance constitutes only "one strand" in a fabric of resistance that stretches from civil disobedience to strikes to armed conflict.

Principles aside, the ANC's poor record of military accomplishment may also be seen as a significant reflection of the strength of the South African Defence Forces and the enormous difficulties that face any effort to weaken the white government by direct military means. In attempting to bring down apartheid through direct military pressure, the ANC would be playing against Pretoria's strongest suit, and, by all indications, the white regime has many cards left to play.

Forced by international boycotts to develop its own, self-sufficient arms industry, Pretoria can draw upon a staggering array of locally produced weapons ranging from armored cars and tanks to a new helicopter gunship specifically designed for counterinsurgency missions. Every indication, moreover, suggests that its willingness to attack suspected ANC installations and bases will only increase as the ANC's popularity grows.

On June 15, 1985, South African commandos crossed the border into Botswana in a surprise nighttime attack against what Defence Force commander Gen. Constand Viljoen termed "a nerve center of the ANC machinery." The raiders killed sixteen persons, including a six-year-old girl and two Botswanan nationals, at ten different offices and homes involved in the attack. Six months later, on December 20, South African troops descended upon suspected ANC safe houses in Lesotho, killing nine persons. In the wake of that raid, the South African State Security Council warned that "all the peoples of southern Africa will pay a heavy price" if they continued to allow ANC guerrillas to operate from their territory.

Such direct attacks have been only one part of a broad-based military and diplomatic strategy aimed at denying the ANC facilities and infiltration routes in neighboring black states. This effort reached a high point in March

1984 when Pretoria, through military support to antigovernment guerrillas in neighboring Mozambique, pressured the Mozambican government to sign the so-called Nkomati Accord, a nonaggression pact that obliged Mozambique to close its borders to the ANC. Similar agreements were reached with Swaziland and Lesotho, and all three countries expelled suspected ANC members and officials who were living on their territory, severely restricting the ANC's ability to mount significant cross-border guerrilla operations into South Africa.

In the face of such overwhelming military strength, the ANC has placed increasing emphasis on what might be called nonmilitary violence—that is, an escalation of popular unrest through the provision of guns and explosives to township residents with the hope that the ensuing destruction will force the collapse of order and the demise of the white regime.

"The general orientation of the armed struggle up to this point has been what we have called 'armed propaganda,' " Mbeki observed. "Now it is necessary to move beyond that point, it is necessary to move to what we call 'people's war.' We're saying this now because in fact there is not only a mass popular opinion in favor of armed struggle—there is a mass popular willingness to carry it out."

In part, this change has been deliberately fostered by the ANC as a means of confronting Pretoria with a violent challenge that cannot be readily defeated by conventional military means. In response to the promulgation of the new constitution, with its corresponding plans for new black political institutions at the local level, the ANC announced its commitment to a campaign of violence aimed at making "apartheid unworkable and South Africa ungovernable." That strategy may be seen to have played a role in encouraging the especially brutal violence that has been focused against black town councilors and others perceived to have collaborated with the regime.

At the same time, the shift toward a "people's war" can also be read as an acknowledgement that black anger and frustration have grown beyond the control of any external leadership and that the ANC is now following, rather than leading, the move toward violence. Most of the unrest that has shaken the black townships has erupted spontaneously, with no apparent guidance or instigation from the ANC or any other organized sponsor. "The revolution isn't being spearheaded by trained ANC fighters," said one observer. "It is being led by unarmed children facing down tanks and Casspirs [armored cars] with rocks and slingshots."

In order to accommodate the rising fever of unrest and to avoid jeopardizing its position of leadership among blacks in the townships, the ANC has thus been forced repeatedly to raise the stakes of the armed conflict, even at the risk of igniting an uncontrollable race war. Meeting in Lusaka in June 1985, the ANC's National Executive Committee announced its determination to "intensify the struggle at any cost," and Tambo warned reporters that it would be increasingly difficult for the group to "distinguish between hard and soft targets" in future military operations.

The implications of this new policy were underscored three months later, when, in a dramatic departure from previous strategy, the ANC urged its followers for the first time to attack white areas. "The whites of this country now have to be rudely awakened from the dreamland that they have closed themselves into," declared the ANC's broadcasting arm, "Radio Freedom," which transmits to South Africa from facilities in Addis Ababa, Ethiopia.

"We have now to take the battle right into their homes, into their kitchens and bedrooms."

The ANC leadership has adjusted its military tactics in order to accommodate its supporters within South Africa who are increasingly adamant in demanding weapons to confront the white regime. "There will be an increasing use of hand grenades," said one ANC official. "Hand grenades are classic weapons of people's war because they are easy to carry, easy to train on. They don't need specialized military units. They are immediately accessible to the same people that have been throwing stones—they can be throwing hand grenades literally the same day. That's what you're going to see more of."

The implications of this change in strategy are likely to be profound, not only for the ANC and its supporters but also for the broader development of South African politics. By expanding the definition of combatants to include township protestors and by adopting street violence as a tool of political struggle, the ANC has put at risk many of the fine distinctions that it has for decades paid dearly to preserve: the distinctions between military and civilian targets, between impulsive violence and principled resistance, between a race war and a struggle for national liberation.

ANC leaders express confidence that they have not abdicated control of their struggle to mob rule. "The people in the townships know what we are doing," said one official. "We are not dealing with a population that has come out of the political void."

But they point out that, against the rising tide of black anger and radicalism, the ANC cannot dictate the terms of its struggle. And they recognize that, in a protracted fight to the finish, it will be increasingly difficult for either side to control the direction of events.

"The greatest danger we face," said Thabo Mbeki, "is the continued stubbornness on the part of the Botha regime. In the end, none of us will have any choices, really. An escalation of the conflict will force any thinking person to look for ways to resolve the situation. To that extent, we must depend upon the rationality of the white population. We must demonstrate to them that there is a crisis in the country. And if whites are concerned about security, they must be convinced that their security can only be guaranteed in a united, nonracial, and democratic South Africa."

NOTES

1. U.S. Senate, Subcommittee on Security and Terrorism, "Soviet, East German and Cuban Involvement in Fomenting Terrorism in South Africa," 97th Congress, 2nd Session (Washington, D.C., GPO, 1982), p. 24.
2. Joseph Lelyveld, "Black Challenge to Pretoria," *The New York Times,* October 12, 1983, p. A-8.

THE BLACK TRADE UNION MOVEMENT

Steven Friedman

Steven Friedman is a special research fellow at the South African Institute of Race Relations in Johannesburg. He formerly covered labor issues for the Rand Daily Mail, *and is the author of* Building Tomorrow Today, *a history of the black trade union movement in South Africa.*

L abor journalists used to call it the "Solidarity syndrome." In late 1980, political commentators and journalists discovered South Africa's black trade union movement and began to beat a path to its door, seeking similarities between it and Poland's Solidarity. When they found that the unions were not about to overthrow apartheid, they soon turned their attentions elsewhere.

Today, the syndrome lives again. In December 1985, the unions formed a new superfederation, the Congress of South African Trade Unions (COSATU), which represents some 500,000 workers, a dues-paying membership far in excess of any of the militant antiapartheid political groups. Its president, mine clerk Elijah Barayi, immediately committed it to campaign against racial laws, and once again the unions were seen as a central threat to white supremacy.

As in 1980, this development highlights a truth but distorts it, too. The growth of the union movement is an important political development with implications for the style, tactics and goals of black efforts to win change. The way in which the government was forced to accommodate the unions also says much about reform in an apartheid society, and changes in the mines, shops and factories are increasingly seen by some white reformers as a model for wider political change.

But the union movement cannot of itself end apartheid. Its more experienced leaders do not expect it to, and, if black activists or political observers look for it to lead a challenge to white power, they will again be disappointed. Unionized workers may well play a vital role in change, but, paradoxically, they are likely to do this only if their unions do not mount the frontal assault on white power that black nationalists expect and white supremacists fear.

Little more than a decade ago, black workers were powerless, subservient cogs in the white industrial machine. A rigid racial policy barred them from taking part in the economy, except as unskilled laborers. The law excluded them them from skilled jobs and so they had little bargaining power: because workers had no skills, employers could fire them when they organized and replace them quickly. The pass laws barred many black workers from the cities unless they worked for a particular employer, and to lose a job often meant losing the prospect of finding another. Black unions were not outlawed, but the law did not guarantee them bargaining rights: employers ignored them and arrested their members if they struck.

But in the late 1960s employers found they could not meet their labor needs in a growing economy if they relied only on non-black workers. They began using blacks in more skilled jobs which other races would not accept, and the government began to encourage them to train blacks. While black workers still could not compete with other races for jobs—they could fill only those which other nonblacks vacated—this was a first recognition by the white establishment that black workers were no longer dispensable.

In 1973 the white establishment was jolted when tens of thousands of black workers in the port city of Durban struck in support of wage demands. The strikes spread to other cities, and the year saw more labor unrest than any other since the Second World War. Previously, employers would simply have fired the strikers and the police would have arrested them. This time, however, most employers offered the striking workers small wage increases and the police did not act against them. The then-prime minister, John Vorster, castigated employers for paying poverty wages and urged them to see their black workers as "human beings with souls."

Since black workers had become more important elements in the nation's labor pool, their strikes could no longer simply be crushed. In an attempt to prevent fresh unrest, the government and employers encouraged black workers to use workplace committees to express grievances. The committees were weak and ineffective, as they were firmly controlled by the employers and were seen as a substitute for, not a precursor to, full-fledged unions. But they offered trade unionists and black workers an opening which they soon exploited.

The strikes also prompted the rebirth of black unionism. Black workers had been forming unions since 1919, but successive waves of labor organization had been crushed. In the early 1970s a small group of unionists and student activists had begun to organize black workers again, but they had little impact: the 1973 unrest was a spontaneous reaction to the workers' economic plight, not a sign of organization. Still, it gave workers new confidence, and thousands began joining the new unions, particularly in Durban. The unions recruited some 40,000 members in a matter of months, only to decline swiftly in the face of a recession and police action against unionists. For the rest of the decade, the new union movement struggled on in virtual obscurity. Despite their shock at the appearance of the 1973 strikes, employers and the government still sought to thwart black unionism: employers repeatedly fired unionized workers, and the government used security laws against unionists and encouraged employers to resist the unions. The unions suffered repeated setbacks and numbered their members in hundreds, not thousands.

But it was in this lonely period that today's union movement was forged. The small worker organization bodies that were formed then later became the nucleus of union groups—the Federation of South African Trade Unions (FOSATU), the Council of Unions of South Africa (CUSA), the General Workers Union (GWU)—which led worker actions in the 1980s.

The unions were too weak to recruit a mass following, so they concentrated instead on making gains in individual factories. Because they had no legal rights, their only resource was the unity and commitment of their members. The unions told workers they could advance only through collective efforts and began to train them in the leadership skills they would need to resist their employers' attempts to break the union movement. Because the strategy relied on worker unity, factory leaders would have to be controlled by their followers, and union officials stressed grass-roots democracy as much for its tactical as for its moral value.

The unions also could not afford the luxury of shunning compromises if accepting them would produce practical gains. The workers' chief impediment was their powerlessness, which they could break out of only if they made gains and so came to believe in their ability to change the factory world. Unions were always ready to accept small gains which fell short of what workers wanted or needed, for these gave their members new confidence and an appetite for bigger victories. While they rejected the concept of the workplace committees, they used the committees because they gave unionized workers some freedom to organize without the threat of employer reprisals. This tactical flexibility would enable the unions later to exploit government concessions designed to stunt worker organization, using them instead as a tool to strengthen the unions.

A new style of black organization thus began to grow in the factories. It stressed tight grass-roots organization and democracy—and stressed also that compromises were advances rather than defeats. For decades, powerless blacks had not believed that they could change their world, and they had longed for some political messiah who could do it for them. The unions, in contrast, told workers they could take charge of their own lives and working conditions.

It was this style that enabled the unions to make dramatic gains in the early 1980s, once they were given the formal right to bargain. It helped them transform a government/employer attempt to control them into a channel for worker power; later, it influenced their unique approach to political organization.

Throughout the 1970s, the government and employers tinkered with the committee system in an attempt to neutralize black unionism but failed to eliminate the movement. The skills shortage grew; black workers became less dispensable and gained new skills which made it more difficult for employers to fire them. A handful of foreign-owned companies, responding to pressure in their home countries, began to bargain with the unions, giving them a permanent base in some factories. By 1979, the government was forced to accept the inevitable: it adopted the report of an official inquiry, the Wiehahn Commission, which urged that racial job bars be scrapped and that black unions be granted legally sanctioned bargaining rights.

But this reform, too, sought to control black worker power. The unions would enjoy official bargaining rights only if they registered with the government. Registered unions had to accept some government control and were barred from political involvement. They would have to bargain through official industrial councils which seemed designed to cut them off from their factory power base. They could strike only if they followed cumbersome procedures that made legal stoppages difficult or impossible. The reforms thus allowed unions to operate but denied them real power.

Over the next three years the unions turned the reform strategy on its head. Some, such as the General Workers Union, which had its power base in Cape Town's harbor, and the Food and Canning Workers Union, refused to register with the government, but they advanced despite this. Later, a new breed of militant unions such as the South African Allied Workers Union (SAAWU), also shunned registration and won a large following. Some, like those in FOSATU, an alliance of unions in key industries such as the metal, motor, textile and chemical sectors, did register but continued to build the factory power the reforms seemed designed to prevent. Almost all the unions shunned the industrial councils and demanded factory bargaining rights, and workers ignored the antistrike laws. Instead of controlling workers, the reforms ushered in a period of sustained factory unrest: by 1984, in the midst of a crippling recession, official strike figures broke the record set in 1973. The factory organization and the tactical suppleness the unions had developed in the 1970s allowed them to make these gains.

Both the government and employers attempted to roll back the tide. Many employers refused to deal with unions that did not register or insisted that unions could have no bargaining rights in the factories. The police acted repeatedly against unionists and striking workers. Many unionists were detained without trial, and strikers were arrested. But soon employers began to give way and to bargain with the unions in their factories. The government could not prevent them from doing so without undoing the reforms, and so it was forced to allow the unions to grow.

The unions used their new power to gain something that blacks had always been denied: a share in decisions that affect their lives. First, they challenged the employers' right to set their pay alone. They demanded a "living wage," and, after some bitter factory battles, many employers were forced to concede it. Then, as the economy declined, they fought arbitrary firings. In the 1970s, tens of thousands of black workers were fired and banished to jobless rural backwaters on a day's notice, some simply because they were worker leaders. Then many employers found they could fire workers only if they applied standards demanded by the unions: job preference for longer-serving workers, compensation for fired workers and the like. These initial gains prompted demands for even greater decision-making, and unionized workers sought— and sometimes won—a say in areas where employers had taken unilateral decisions for decades, such as health and safety or working-women's rights.

To many outsiders, this change did little to dent apartheid. African workers might have won some factory rights, but they were still subject to unfettered white power outside the workplace. The unions might be strong in many factories, but they lacked industry-wide and national influence. They had won rights for only a fraction of working blacks and could not aid the millions of unemployed.

But the change was profound. Blacks not only had won a say in the decisions which had always been the sole preserve of whites, but had done so through the collective efforts of ordinary black people rather than by following a few high-profile leaders. They had developed a new kind of black leadership: workers with little formal education were now bargaining with sophisticated white managements—and often outmaneuvering them. They relied on grass-roots support, thus rendering themselves less vulnerable to government action, and on compromise.

Inevitably, the achievement of new influence inside the factories prompted workers to demand a say outside the workplace as well. The newer unions, such as SAAWU, had seen themselves as vehicles for antiapartheid action from the start. While they later declined as state action crippled them and their factory base proved fragile, their initial success helped impel the unions in a more overtly political direction. The unions that had weathered the storms of the 1970s had avoided political action, partly because they felt they were too weak to undertake it. Now they, too, began to consider it. But they insisted that they carry over the principles and tactics they had learned in the factories to the battle outside them.

In 1982, FOSATU, the biggest of the older union groups, said it would launch political campaigns, but only if they had been endorsed by its members, if workers could control their direction and retain their independence. It and many of the other older unions would not join political movements, as SAAWU and other new unions soon did, for this meant, FOSATU leaders said, surrendering the workers' right to set their own political agenda.

Over the next two years, these unions challenged the government's new racial constitution and the pass laws, and their members began to play a role in community politics too. But they did not do this at the expense of their factory base, which had always been the source of their strength. They did not have the muscle to move the government, but they could use factory power to pressure employers into conveying black demands to the government, and this they tried to do. They also retained their independence, refusing to join the United Democratic Front and other political movements that emerged in 1983.

But the unions did encourage their members to join community groups, and this had an inevitable impact on the style of black politics. Because blacks have always been denied the right to organize freely, their political movements have often been dominated by a few high-profile leaders who did not develop a grass-roots base. Because the prospect of any accommodation with the white establishment has always seemed so remote, black political leadership has had little patience with compromise and has sought to mobilize the black population behind "maximum demands" which they did not have the power to win, thus forfeiting the short-term gains which would have helped to build their followers' confidence.

Now workers began to demand the same control over their community organizations as they had over their unions—and pressed those organizations to adopt the same strategies that had won the unions their gains. Where unionized workers dominated township politics, in areas such as the East Rand, the industrial area to the east of Johannesburg, or parts of the Eastern Cape province, community groups began to move closer to the "mandate and negotiation" politics the unions favored.

It is significant that union members sought to influence community groups, for this acknowledged that unions could not in themselves lead the fight for change; their goal was both less and more ambitious. Unions still insisted that their chief role lay in the factories where they could build the skills and confidence that the workers needed to fight for political change. The training this provided could allow them to play a role in the political groups which were better equipped to challenge apartheid directly. But their strategy also sought not only to strengthen the fight against apartheid but to influence its strategies and goals, and hence to determine the kind of society that would emerge when racial supremacy ended.

From the outset, the unions have been committed to more than simply replacing the white government. Their goal is to win rights for their worker members, and this implies full social as well as racial equality, not a society in which a white elite is replaced by a black one. Workers, the unions argue, should influence political groups not only to insure that the tactics of those groups are more effective and that they recognize worker needs, but also to insure that the values which have guided the union movement, in particular the stress on grass-roots democracy, are carried over into a new society. Unions cannot be "laboratories for revolution," for they are open, legal organizations; nor can they be political parties, for their members have a variety of political views. But they can be "laboratories for democracy," training grounds in a type of grass-roots democratic politics that could not only challenge apartheid but help shape the society that replaces it.

This strategy is ambitious; indeed, some argue it is unattainable, because it seems to fly in the face of both recent black political tradition and daily black experience. It stresses democracy in a society in which blacks have always been denied any democratic experience and in which demagoguery, whether white or black, almost seems part of the natural political order. And it urges workers to see themselves as workers first and black second, in a society in which their powerlessness has always seemed to stem from their blackness, not their position in the economy.

Inevitably, the unions' political stance faced severe stresses as township ferment began to grow in 1984 and 1985. In some areas, such as the Eastern Cape, FOSATU unionists maintained their independent stance, only to seem to lose ground to the political groups. In others, such as the East Rand or Natal, where the Durban strikes had ushered in the new era, they moved closer to the ability to mobilize their members. In November 1984 at least 300,000 workers took part in a work stayaway organized by FOSATU leaders on the East Rand—but did so, their critics charged, at the cost of the principles the unions had long embraced.

Now, critics argued, union leaders no longer sought worker mandates before endorsing political campaigns. They no longer sought compromises and winnable goals, and so they failed to take their followers with them. The unions were thus no longer placing their unique stamp on antiapartheid politics; they were in danger of becoming mere adjuncts of nationalist political groups and, perhaps, of losing their factory base.

The establishment of COSATU confirmed these trends. It was planned as an alliance of the unions that favored independent worker politics—FOSATU and other graduates of the 1970s, together with the country's biggest union, the National Union of Mineworkers. It was designed to give the unions' political strategy a national base. But the climate of the times seemed to overtake it. By the time it was launched it not only included SAAWU and ten other unions that had joined the UDF, but its leaders, such as Barayi and general secretary Jay Naidoo—formerly secretary of FOSATU's food union—seemed closer to the style and goals of the political movements than to the union tradition. Barayi began his tenure with a call for a mass passive resistance campaign against the pass laws, a call that had not been endorsed by union members. The new federation's officials soon began appearing at political rallies organized by the UDF. The goal of independent worker politics appeared to have receded.

If it has, the unions, rather than apartheid, may well be the loser. The unions are a power in many factories and industries, but they have not yet developed the national muscle that would enable them to challenge the government. They have proved the value of tight grass-roots organization, but, if they opt for mass protest politics, they are certain to sacrifice elements of that organization—and to be weakened in the process.

But it is far too early to begin writing obituaries for the unions' unique attempt to inject a new dimension into black politics. Their bargaining rights are only six years old, and many workers are only now beginning to apply the new style of organization in the factories. It may be years before "mandate politics" becomes so ingrained that it can mount an effective challenge to the populist style of many black nationalist groups.

Its prospects depend partly on imponderables: If black nationalists gain power within, say, five years, the unions' style of politics may well prove too new and partial a phenomenon to influence the new society. If, as seems more likely, the battle for political power is protracted, organized workers could have a decisive impact on the nature of change. "Workers who have been wielding power in the factories for twenty years won't surrender it to any government, black or white," says one unionist.

But the unions' ability to influence events depends also on the response of the white establishment to black demands. Mandate and compromise can thrive only in a climate of reform, one in which free organization is allowed. If it is not allowed, politics assumes less manageable forms and demagoguery flourishes, as events in beleaguered black townships have shown. The more the authorities allow free black political organization, the more will the style of politics the unions have pioneered be able to shape the course of events.

Free political activity may not be enough. Much of the township ferment has been fueled by the young unemployed, who know that a white economy which relies increasingly on machines rather than workers will never offer them jobs in their lifetimes. In the countryside and in some cities, black unemployment is so widespread that workers, unionized or not, are increasingly a minority: the attractions of patient organization and compromise are hardly apparent to the jobless. Unless a sustained job creation program and vastly increased black participation in the economy begin to reverse this tide, the politics of mandate and negotiation will not take root outside the factories.

The unions' growth is not only a challenge to white power; it also provides the white establishment with the prospect of a relatively peaceful transition to an egalitarian society. Only if whites grasp the opportunity will South Africa have a chance of escaping the cycle of violence that now grips it.

AN INTERVIEW WITH NELSON MANDELA

Lord Nicholas Bethell

Lord Bethell is a member of the British House of Lords.

I waited for Nelson Mandela in the Governor's office in the maximum security block of Cape Town's Poll-smoor Prison. Senior officers in yellow khaki uniforms with gold stars on their epaulettes, some with peaked caps pulled over their eyes like Guards sergeant majors, scurried in and out talking excitedly in Afrikaans. At last, three men entered the room and one came towards me. "How do you do?" he said. I greeted him in return. "You must be related to Winston Churchill," he went on, hinting presumably at my need to lose a few pounds in weight. "Anyway, I'm very pleased and honored to receive you."

He was anxious to put me at my ease, and he invited me to sit down at the desk where I was ready to make my notes. It was a second or two before I realized that this was the man I had come to see.

A six-foot-tall, lean figure with silvering hair, an impeccable olive-green shirt and well-creased navy blue trousers, Mandela could almost have seemed like another general in the South African prison service. Indeed, his manner was the most self-assured of them all, and he stood out as obviously the senior man in the room. He was, however, black. And he was a prisoner, perhaps the most famous prisoner in the world, the man they write songs about in Europe and name streets after in London, the leader of the African National Congress, a body dedicated to the destruction of the apartheid system, if necessary by force.

He is the black man's folk hero, his fame made all the greater by the fact that he has been out of sight behind prison bars for nearly twenty-two years. All this time virtually no one other than his lawyers and his immediate family have been permitted to see him or talk to him. Newspapers have speculated about the harshness of his prison regime, about his political views and his chances of release. Our meeting gave me the chance to set the record straight for the first time on all these points.

"In my first ten years on Robben Island," Mandela recalled, "conditions were really very bad. We were physically assaulted. We were subjected to psychological persecution. We had to work every day in the lime quarry from 7 A.M. to 4 P.M. with a one-hour break, wearing shorts and sandals, with no socks or underwear and just a calico jacket. It was hard, boring, unproductive work, and on rainy days in the winter it was very cold.

"The guards pushed us all the time to work harder, from dawn to sunset, and we could get solitary confinement if they thought we were slacking. The diet was maize porridge for breakfast with half a teaspoon of sugar, boiled grain for lunch, with *puzamadla*—a drink made out of maize that is, to put it mildly, an acquired taste—and porridge with vegetables in the evening. There was a lot of tension between guards and prisoners."

Helen Suzman, who has campaigned for the black man's rights throughout her thirty-two years in the South African Parliament, remembers with horror her visits to Robben Island in the 1960s. "Guards with Alsatian dogs on leads, and sometimes with swastikas tattooed on their wrists, would drive the men to work," she told me. "I remember one prisoner complaining to me that he had been assaulted. I was noting down the details when the guard in question came running up saying, 'Ah, it was really nothing, Mrs. Suzman, it was only a kick up the arse.' "

Then around 1974 there were dramatic improvements in the treatment of "security prisoners," as those convicted of threatening South Africa's system are known. This is confirmed by Helen Suzman, by Red Cross officials in Geneva, who today describe Mandela's treatment as "broadly satisfactory," and by Mandela himself.

"Things can now be made significantly better by dismantling the whole South African system," he told me. "For instance, it would be good if some of the country's senior prison officers were black as well as white. But how can this happen under apartheid?"

"I am in good health. It is not true that I have cancer. It is not true that I had a toe amputated. I get up at 3:30 every morning, do two hours' physical exercise, work up a good sweat. Then I read and study during the day. I get the South African newspapers as well as the *Guardian Weekly* and *Time* magazine. We have a radio in the cell —VHF only, unfortunately, so that we can only get South African stations, not the BBC. I cultivate my garden. We grow vegetables in pots—tomatoes, broccoli, beans, cucumbers and strawberries."

He gestured expansively to his right: "The major, here, has been tremendously helpful. He is really an excellent gardener." The major in question, Fritz van Sittert, who guards Mandela and his cellmates[1] and was detailed to supervise our meeting, did not react or even utter a word throughout the entire two hours. We spent the time, just the three of us, in the functional office with its G-Plan furniture, dominated by a large glass-topped desk and overlooked by a picture of State President P. W. Botha wearing a silver order and an orange sash. The major was there not to censor the conversation, which was unhindered, but to make sure that no document or other object passed between us.

I had been asked, for instance, to obtain Mandela's signature on a paper authorizing his name to go forward in the election of the rectorship of Edinburgh University. He was not allowed to sign the paper, but he agreed verbally to be a candidate. "I am very flattered. I am a politician and of course I like to win elections, but in this case it is such a kind gesture that I really don't mind if I win or lose."

Mandela had kind words, too, for Pollsmoor's Governor, Brigadier F. D. Munro. "The brigadier does his best to solve our little problems. But, poor man, he has very little authority. Everything concerning the six of us he has to refer to Pretoria. For instance, a year ago my sister died and I wrote to my brother-in-law about her funeral. They blocked the letter. Why? I suppose because he is a policeman in Transkei and they don't want me to make contact with him. His name is Russell Piliso. They also blocked my letter to Bishop Tutu congratulating him on winning the Nobel Prize. A few days ago a friend of mine here received a letter completely cut to ribbons. It's not the poor brigadier, it's the politicians. Still, conditions here are quite reasonable, better than on the Island. The food is good and there are no problems with the staff, racial or otherwise."

It was to enable me to confirm the conditions of Mandela's imprisonment that the South African Minister of Justice, H. J. Coetsee, authorized my visit, making it clear that I would not be allowed to bring press or television with me. Coetsee wanted the point to be made that Mandela was in good health and being well treated. And I can confirm that, generally speaking, that is the case. Even so, it was an unusual concession to a foreign parliamentarian.

Pollsmoor consists of a dozen long buildings built in the 1970s, each one a separate unit. It looks from the outside like a huge, gloomy campus of a comprehensive school or red-brick university. "This is the white women's section. This is the Coloured men's section," explained the Deputy Commissioner of Security, Major General "Bertie" Venter, as we drove past the main barrier along roads lined with grass and flower beds, toward the Governor's dining room. Over lunch—steak and chips cooked and served by convicted men—the Commissioner of Prisons, Lieutenant General "Willie" Willemse, presented his case that South African conditions are up to North American or West European standards. Each man, black or white, receives a minimum of 10,571 kilojoules per day. Prisoners have decent clothes, family visits, recreation and the possibility of parole. "If only people abroad knew the facts," he said, "we in South Africa would not be so harshly judged."

Mandela's quarrel with South Africa is not one of prison conditions, however. "Things get exaggerated because of lack of communication," he told me. "A little time ago I was wearing size eight shoes. Once they gave me size nine. It was okay, but they bothered me for a bit, and I mentioned it to my wife. She was upset and there was a fuss in the press. They even mentioned it in the song 'Free Nelson Mandela.' I was sorry for all the trouble caused. If I'd had a phone I'd have called her up and said, 'Don't worry, my dear, it's all right,' only I didn't have a phone and that's the sort of thing that happens.

"I wish that the senior men who make the real decisions

would come and see us. Louis Le Grange, when he was Minister of Justice, and Commissioner Steyn used to come at least every year. Now the minister and commissioner don't come. It is worrying, because when the top men stay away it sometimes means a move toward a tougher policy. And if they came we could discuss our little problems, and I am sure we could convince them.

"My other complaints are about cell conditions. There is a damp patch on the wall. There must have been a fault in the way it was built. And it is wrong for the six of us to be segregated from all the other prisoners. We would like more companions. But I have not asked for more to be brought here, as I am not sure that the other political prisoners on Robben Island—there are 230 of them— would like the regime here.

"I would like greater privacy, too, for my studies. In fact, our basic demand, which we made in 1969, is for political status, for instance, the right to keep a diary and to be visited by the family. I mean the African family, not just wives, brothers and children, which is the family in the European sense."

The problem is, therefore, not one of brutal prison conditions. It is that Mandela and his friends are in prison at all. Mandela and other top ANC officials have spent eighteen years on Robben Island and three in Pollsmoor—all for no worse a crime than conniving at the destruction of property. It is a punishment that far exceeds the offense, even if one ignores the argument that they had every right to use force against apartheid, deprived as they were of the right to vote, to stand for election or to reside where they wish in their own country. They are in prison now, it is clear, not as an act of justice or punishment, but because it does not politically suit the South African state to release them.

The problem is that Mandela still supports the armed struggle. This is why some human rights bodies—for instance, Amnesty International—will not campaign for his release. Also, his case does not appeal to the Parole Board, since he shows no repentance for his past actions. Rather, the contrary: he makes no secret of his wish to return to the fray. This provides the authorities with the ideal pretext for not putting his name forward to State President Botha for clemency.

"The armed struggle," Mandela told me, "was forced on us by the government. And if they want us now to give it up, the ball is in their court. They must legalize us, treat us like a political party and negotiate with us. Until they do, we will have to live with the armed struggle. It is useless simply to carry on talking. The government has tightened the screws too far.

"Of course, if there were to be talks along these lines, we in the ANC would declare a truce. This is what SWAPO[2] did in Namibia. But meanwhile we are forced to continue, though within certain limits. We go for hard targets only, military installations and symbols of apartheid. Civilians must not be touched.

"This is why I deeply regret what happened in Pretoria on May 23, 1983. A bomb went off and more than a dozen civilians were killed. Something must have gone wrong with the timing. It was a tragic accident. On the other hand, the incident that took place in Vryheid [in Natal] a few weeks ago, when a South African lieutenant was killed, was quite justified. Some ANC members were in a house and the security forces came looking for them. We have reason to believe that their policy now is to shoot to kill rather than try to arrest our men. So they opened fire in self-defense and the lieutenant was killed, as were several of our soldiers.

"We aim for buildings and property. So it may be that someone gets killed in a fight, in the heat of battle, but we do not believe in assassinations. I would not want our men to assassinate, for instance, the major here. I would only justify this in the case of an informer who was a danger to our lives. And all this can end as soon as talks begin. It would be humiliating, though, for us simply to lay down our arms."

It is this "humiliating" condition that the South African government requires and that blocks any progress toward a political settlement and Mandela's release.

Louis Le Grange, now South Africa's Minister of Law and Order, told me his government is "not so weak as to agree to talks with the ANC at the moment. But if they will forego the armed struggle and enter the political arena we will talk to them. As for Mandela, if you ask me whether I should recommend his release so that he can carry on where he left off, I say no. I can't give such advice unless he gives some assistance through his own attitude. Things are at a sensitive stage in South Africa. We have changed our constitution and are contemplating further changes. So we must have proper law and order. As things are, Mandela's release would invite a lot of problems and trouble."

Justice Minister Coetsee, while agreeing that "objectively speaking, it would be better if Mandela were not in prison," also made it clear that, for the moment, reasons of state prevent his release.

The authorities may have recently tried to find a way out of this impasse. Mandela has been told by his wife Winnie that his nephew Chief Kaiser Mantanzima would give him sanctuary in the semi-autonomous black "homeland" of Transkei if Mandela would give up political activity. But "I completely rejected the idea," Mandela told me. "I have served twenty-two years in prison for fighting against the policy of Bantustans. There is no way that I could then go and live in a Bantustan. I would also reject an offer to go abroad. My place is in South Africa and my home is in Johannesburg. If I were released, I would never obey any restriction. If they confined me, for instance, to the Cape area, I would break the order and walk to my home in Soweto to be with my wife and daughter. I would only leave my home if the ANC leadership ordered me to do so."

Meanwhile, Mandela wants to see the ANC develop as a widely based national movement. "Personally, I am a Socialist and I believe in a classless society. But I see no reason to belong to any political party at the moment. Businessmen and farmers, white or black, can also join our movement to fight against racial discrimination. It would be a blunder to narrow it.

"I appreciate the Soviet Union only because it was the one country that long ago condemned racialism and supported liberation movements. It does not mean that I approve of their internal policy. I was grateful, too, by the way, to Emperor Haile Selassie of Ethiopia, who received me in 1962. He was a feudal ruler, but he supported our movement, and I was grateful to him. Britain, too, has helped us, under Mrs. Thatcher as well as under socialist governments, by condemning apartheid on principle. We may have different views about the methods that should be used, but the most important thing is to condemn apartheid outright. And this, as I understand it, is what your prime minister does."

Our talks drew to a close, and Brigadier Munro invited me to visit Mandela's cell in the isolated wing of the long, low buildings. So we walked in slow procession up flights of stairs and around corners, with Mandela leading the way as if showing me around his home. He did not open doors for me; this was done by sergeants with heavy keys after much saluting and clanking. Always, though, Mandela was the one who showed the way, inviting me to go first through every door and plying me with questions on Britain and the world, anxious, apparently, to supplement the information he gets from the radio and press he has in his cell.

Did I think that Gorbachev's recent visit to England would relax East-West tensions? What were my hopes for the Shultz-Gromyko talks? Would the Liberals at last make a breakthrough in British politics? What was Mrs. Thatcher's secret of success? Who was now leader of the Labour Party?

And so we reached the "Mandela enclosure" on the third floor, a large room with beds, plenty of books and adequate facilities for washing and toilet. The cell door is open almost all day. The prisoners have access to a long, L-shaped roof yard surrounded by high white walls. As well as the vegetable pots there is a ping-pong table and even a small-scale tennis court, apparently unused.

Mandela proudly showed me his vegetables, like a landowner showing me his farm. As for the yard, he wished only that it was less monotonously black, white and grey. As a rural man, he longed for green, and he understood, he said, what Oscar Wilde meant by "the little tent of blue that prisoners call the sky."

He showed me the damp patch on the cell wall and introduced me to his cellmates, who apologized for being informally dressed. He explained who I was and briefly what we had been discussing. In spite of the brigadier's mild protests, he then showed me the letter that had been so badly savaged by the censor. And he joked as we prepared to leave, "Aren't there any other complaints? Doesn't anyone want to go home?"

And so we walked the last few yards toward the end of the enclosure. And I prepared to say goodbye to this remarkable man whom I have begged the South African government to release, on humanitarian grounds if for no other reason. A sergeant opened the grey, heavy steel door. Mandela said, "Well, Lord Bethell, this is my frontier and this is where I must leave you." We shook hands and I told him I would be writing. I walked through all the other steel doors, down the stone staircases, out through the front door into the fine Cape summer, feeling poorer for being so suddenly deprived of this man's exhilarating company.

NOTES

1. Mandela cellmates include Walter Sisulu, Ahmed Kathrada, Raymond Mhlaba, and Andrew Mlangeni.
2. The South-West Africa People's Organization is an armed guerrilla group fighting South African rule in Namibia, also known as South-West Africa.

BLACK VOICES

Nelson Mandela

Nelson Mandela, leader of the banned African National Congress, has been imprisoned in South Africa since his conviction on charges of sabotage in 1963. In early 1985, State President P. W. Botha offered to consider releasing Mandela from prison if he would agree to renounce violence as a means of opposing the South African government. Mandala's response to this offer was made public in a speech read by his daughter Zinzi at a rally in Jabulani, Soweto, on February 10, 1985. The full text of her speech follows.

On Friday my mother and our attorney saw my father at Pollsmoor Prison to obtain his answer to Botha's offer of conditional release. The prison authorities attempted to stop this statement being made, but he would have none of this and made it clear that he would make the statement to you, the people.

Strangers like [Lord Nicholas] Bethell from England and Professor [Samuel] Dash from the United States have in recent weeks been authorized by Pretoria to see my father without restriction, yet Pretoria cannot allow you, the people, to hear what he has to say directly. He should be here himself to tell you what he thinks of this statement by Botha. He is not allowed to do so. My mother, who also heard his words, is also not allowed to speak to you today.

My father and his comrades at Pollsmoor Prison send their greetings to you, the freedom-loving people of this, our tragic land, in the full confidence that you will carry

on the struggle for freedom. He and his comrades at Pollsmoor Prison send their very warmest greetings to Bishop
Desmond Tutu. Bishop Tutu has made it clear to the
world that the Nobel Peace Prize belongs to you, who are
the people. We salute him.

My father and his comrades at Pollsmoor Prison are
grateful to the United Democratic Front, who without
hesitation made this venue available to them so that they
could speak to you today. My father and his comrades
wish to make this statement to you, the people, first. They
are clear that they are accountable to you and to you
alone. And that you should hear their views directly and
not through others. My father speaks not only for himself
and for his comrades at Pollsmoor Prison, but he hopes
he also speaks for all those in jail for their opposition to
apartheid, for all those who are banished, for all those who
are in exile, for all those who suffer under apartheid and
for all those who are oppressed and exploited.

Throughout our struggle there have been puppets who
have claimed to speak for you. They have made this claim
both here and abroad. They are of no consequence. My
father and his colleagues will not be like them. My father
says:

"I am a member of the African National Congress. I
have always been a member of the African National Congress, and I will remain a member of the African National
Congress until the day I die. Oliver Tambo is much more
than a brother to me. He is my greatest friend and comrade for nearly fifty years. If there is any one amongst you
who cherishes my freedom, Oliver Tambo cherishes it
more, and I know that he would give his life to see me free.
There is no difference between his views and mine.

"I am surprised at the conditions that the government
wants to impose on me. I am not a violent man. My

colleagues and I wrote in 1952 to Malan asking for a round-table conference to find a solution to the problems of our country, but that was ignored. When Strijdom was in power, we made the same offer. Again it was ignored. When Verwoerd was in power, we asked for a national convention for all the people in South Africa to decide on their future. This, too, was in vain.[1]

"It was only then, when all other forms of resistance were no longer open to us, that we turned to armed struggle. Let Botha show that he is different than Malan, Strijdom and Verwoerd. Let him renounce violence. Let him say that he will dismantle apartheid. Let him unban the people's organization, the African National Congress. Let him free all who have been imprisoned, banished or exiled for their opposition to apartheid. Let him guarantee free political activity so that people may decide who will govern them.

"I cherish my own freedom dearly, but I care even more for your freedom. Too many have died since I went to prison. Too many have suffered for the love of freedom. I owe it to their widows, to their orphans, to their mothers and to their fathers who have grieved and wept for them. Not only I have suffered during these long, lonely, wasted years. I am not less life-loving than you are. But I cannot sell my birthright, nor am I prepared to sell the birthright of the people to be free. I am in prison as the representative of the people and of your organization, the African National Congress, which was banned.

"What freedom am I being offered while the organization of the people remains banned? What freedom am I being offered when I may be arrested on a pass offense? What freedom am I being offered to live my life as a family with my dear wife who remains in banishment in Brandfort? What freedom am I being offered when I must ask for permission to live in an urban area? What freedom am I being offered when I need a stamp in my pass to seek work? What freedom am I being offered when my very South African citizenship is not respected?

"Only free men can negotiate. Prisoners cannot enter into contracts. Herman Toivo ja Toivo,[2] when freed, never gave any undertaking, nor was he called upon to do so.

"I cannot and will not give any undertaking at a time when I and you, the people, are not free.

"Your freedom and mine cannot be separated. I will return."

ANC "Radio Freedom"

The African National Congress broadcasts regular antigovernment messages to South African audiences from transmission facilities in Addis Ababa, Ethiopia, under the title "Radio Freedom." The following text was transmitted in English at 7:30 p.m. Greenwich Mean Time on September 2, 1985. The broadcast, which was monitored through the facilities of the British Broadcasting Corporation, was entitled "Let Us Take the Battle to the Enemy's Backyard."

Compatriots, the entire of black townships of our country, from the northern Transvaal down to the Cape, are being engulfed by the flames of the revolution. The battle has now even spread to the rural and remote parts of our country. Daily, the confrontation between our heroic and death-defying people and the repressive forces of the apartheid regime, its troops and police, has continued unabated. More than 700 lives of our people have now been lost in this period of over one year, most of them the victims of the bullets of the apartheid killers.

All these months long, the battlefield has been confined to the areas where we, the oppressed black people, live, safely far away from the white areas of the country. Throughout this period, the majority of the white population of this country have learned of the bitter confrontation only through their television screens while sipping their drinks comfortably in their cozy homes. They have been channeled by the severely controlled propaganda of the racist regime and have also chosen on their own to be oblivious to the turmoil continuing just in their backyards.

The time has come, countrymen, when the oblivion has to be ended. The whites of this country now have to be rudely awakened from the dreamland that they have closed themselves into. The false myth that the fascist Botha-Malan regime has been lulling them with and deluding them into believing, that it can successfully secure them away from the flames of revolution that are sweeping this country, must now be shattered. We have now to take the battle right into their homes, into their kitchens and bedrooms.

Evidently, it was with this very same false sense of security in mind that the fascist Botha could afford, only a few days ago, to shout arrogantly from the rooftops, in defiance of the whole world, that the white domination will never be ended in this country. He was, of course, [words indistinct], which is always in the bedrock and rear base of his criminal apartheid system. No wonder they cheered him so much. They were able to do so precisely because they have not as yet felt the heat of battle. To them, business still continues as usual and things are still normal as long as Botha says so.

Now is the time, countrymen, to crush all that myth. As the president, comrade Oliver Tambo, called on us, it is our task, all of us, patriots of our land, to crush that false sense of security. It is our task to bring sense into the minds of the hidebound white supremacists of this country, to make them realize that they cannot continue supporting and abetting and applauding a regime that can only succeed in nothing else but to lead them into a catastrophe.

The supreme task, countrymen, as the president has said, lies not only on our shoulders, the oppressed black people, who continue to perform heroic feats in the dusty streets of our townships, but it is equally the task of all our white democrats who are genuinely committed to the realization of the future democratic and nonracial South Africa. Together we must now devise ways of carrying the battlefield right into the enemy's rear base, the white areas of the country.

Secondly, the black people alone cannot continue being the one who pays the supreme price for their determination to see the collapse of this regime. Those who gained the privileges of its continued existence must also pay for their optimism. They must now feel the pain of maintaining this most hated criminal regime. So far it has only been their sons in the police and so-called defense force who have been feeling the brunt of the civil war in the country. Now is the time that those who pay for their continued stay in our townships, those who even afford to demonstrate in support of the massacres that these hooligans have been committing in our townships, must also feel the same pain that our mothers and fathers, our brothers and sisters have been feeling all along.

We will be doing this not because we love bloodshed, countrymen, but because Botha and his fascist clique must take the blame for these inevitable consequences. Certainly we, for our part, would be less than human if we were to sit back on our laurels and accept that we should continue to be oppressed, exploited and massacred by a regime that enjoys the support of a minority. We have long warned against such an eventuality, but the white population of this country has all along chosen to close its ears, and instead continues to support this most conservative and reactionary regime.

We hope, even at this late hour, many will heed our call to abandon Botha and his sinking ship and join the mass of the oppressed people in their just struggle to bring about genuine democracy and peace in our country. The time for vacillation is long over. There is no middle road. The battle lines were long drawn up. Confrontation has now to be inside the enemy's rear base, right in the white areas.

Chief Mangosuthu Gatsha Buthelezi

Chief Gatsha Buthelezi, a hereditary leader of South Africa's Zulu population, is chief minister of the KwaZulu homeland area and president of Inkatha, a Zulu-based social and political organization. The following text has been adapted from remarks made by Chief Buthelezi at a luncheon sponsored by the Manhattan Institute for Policy Research in New York City on November 4, 1985.

The unwritten story of South Africa is the intriguing story of the birth of a new society. A great deal is written about black South Africans' rejection of apartheid, but the process by which blacks formulate tactics to combat the system is hardly ever told. The horrors of apartheid are far more frequently reported than is the slow progress which South Africa is making toward normalizing itself as a western industrial state. The vested political interests of the South African government, as well as those of the groups which are involved in the struggle for liberation, lead to serious distortions concerning what is actually taking place in South Africa. On the one hand, the South African government presents the country as one in which meaningful progress is being made through the implementation of its own policy. On the other hand, the African National Congress mission in exile presents an image of total black rejection not only of the South African government and its policies but also of the entire South African way of life. Apartheid, however, is not synonymous with the South African way of life. I am talking about a way of life based on democratic institutions and a market economy.

Generally speaking, the picture now being painted of South Africa is one in which the government is seen as the bad guys, and where sentiment and support for the ANC mission in exile is regarded as a litmus test for the credibility of black political leaders. The West must understand that the struggle currently taking place is directed not only at eradicating apartheid but also at replacing it with a free and open society. It is the techniques and strategies black political leaders adopt that will make or break the vision that so many of us have of a Western-oriented political democracy.

South Africa's present adult population and the newly emerging generation of young people share a common anger in their rejection of apartheid and their commitment to the struggle for the liberation of our country. Black leaders who do not give people scope to express that righteous anger will not survive for any length of time. That anger can be employed to drag down South African society along with apartheid, or it can be employed to integrate blacks on an equal footing into an affluent society which up until now has been the exclusive province of whites.

Foreign analysts must ask, "What forces are at work in stable, industrialized Western countries which preserve decent standards of behavior?" I would suggest that certain critical factors in that regard are the willingness of people to accept the rule of law, to honor contractual agreements and to establish governments that operate within the framework of public opinion. We stand in a very real danger that the current power struggles in South Africa, which are ever increasingly between black radicals and moderates, will erode precisely those underpinnings of a free society.

As the politics of coercion is used by blacks against other blacks, and as blacks, as a whole, lose faith in the notion of democratic opposition, the danger grows that our post-liberation government will not be a democratic one. The lesson of African history is that the way a country brings about its liberation will determine the kind of government it has after liberation. Many of the victories against colonialism in Africa have tended to produce post-liberation military governments. The lack of a democratic dialogue between groups during the liberation struggle made it impossible for people to live within an idiom of political democracy after liberation. We in South Africa need to be aware of this truth.

One of the most hideous crimes apartheid has committed against black South Africans has been its destruction and suppression of black political institutions. The banning of black leaders and organizations, the Improper Interference Act, which for decades prohibited racially mixed political parties, the curtailment of freedom of movement and freedom of speech, and the horrendous use of police informers and phone taps have all impaired black

South Africans' ability to handle differences of opinion in matters of crucial importance.

Inkatha, of which I am president, is one of the few black political organizations in South Africa which is membership-based and constituency-oriented. Inkatha has been in existence for ten years and is now the largest membership-based organization in the country. It has over one million paid members and a structure which includes local and regional branches. It is intensely democratic in nature. Its leaders are elected at general conferences, and they are responsible to those constituencies. There is a yearning in South Africa for this kind of organization. Ordinary people want to feel that they are involved in decision-making and can censure or approve of the behavior of the leaders. Unfortunately, Inkatha is alone as a democratic institution in providing this outlet for blacks. I long for the day when leaders like Nelson Mandela and Oliver Tambo can present their appeals to South Africans and stand accepted or rejected by public opinion. That is how democracy operates.

In a democratic society, individuals are socialized into becoming useful citizens. The politics of violence is now attempting to socialize black South Africans into a rejection of the norms and values of a stable society. This is the crime of apartheid, and it has now become a crime in which black organizations themselves are beginning to participate. The ANC mission in exile has ceased to tolerate those in their midst who disapprove of their tactics. Black town councillors in many parts of the country have been murdered as collaborators with the South African government, and black policemen and their families have been burned alive. The ANC mission in exile is determined to make the country "ungovernable" through the employment of violence. The problem with that strategy is that it will make the country ungovernable for any future regime—black, white or mixed.

South Africa will be destroyed by black politicians unless they can gather together all of the positive forces for change without destroying the fabric of human decency. In the end, only those organizations working to normalize South Africa as a civilized Western democracy with a market economy can save South Africa from both apartheid and the impending crisis. I emphasize a market economy and free enterprise because I do not see any other system devised by human beings which is such a potent force for development. In a country where over half the population is fifteen years old or younger, we desperately need the jobs which free enterprise can create.

This is not an academic issue. Some people say that black South Africans must pay a price for their liberation. As a historian, I too realize that a price must be paid. I know that my people are prepared to suffer. Yet they are not prepared to suffer futilely. I reject the view that you punish white racists in South Africa by killing black people. There is a great yearning for a normalized society by the vast majority of South Africans of all colors. It is suicidal for blacks to believe that they can simply wipe the slate clean.

Oliver Tambo said in a recent interview that he is going to nationalize industries in South Africa and that we must all look forward to a socialist future. He wouldn't mind ruining the economy of the country. He says that we will have to build on the ruins.

It is against that kind of thinking that I appreciate Prime Minister Margaret Thatcher's courageous stand at the recent Commonwealth Conference, where she rejected apartheid but also rejected the notion that violent tactics can author decent societies. In the same way, I appreciate the way in which President Reagan handled the tremendous pressures that were exerted upon him to apply damaging sanctions against South Africa. The effect of economic sanctions would be disruptive not only of apartheid, but disruptive of the whole process on which a new democratic future for South Africa depends.

Cyril Ramaphosa, Congress of South African Trade Unions

Cyril Ramaphosa is General Secretary of South Africa's National Union of Mineworkers. The following is adapted from his address at the inaugural session of the Congress of South African Trade Unions at the University of Natal, November 29, 1985.

The formation of this congress represents a tremendous victory for the working class. Never before has it been so powerful and so poised to make a mark in society.

We are all living in urgent times, and it is urgent to make it clear to the South African government, employers and all sections of society where the working class, united under the banner of COSATU, will stand.

The reforms that have been proposed by the government and employers are not offering any solution. The rand is continuing to drop, there is high inflation and the cost of living is rising every day.

While all this is happening the people in the country are continuing to resist. Confrontation with the police has become a daily occurrence. Some of the townships have become completely ungovernable. The government has clearly demonstrated that it is not in control of this country, and P. W. Botha has failed to provide a direction. It is time that the working class told him to lay down his powers and let the legitimate leaders of the country take over the seat he now occupies.

We have seen in the past four years that organizations of the oppressed have grown stronger. And at the same time we have seen trade unions growing stronger as well. We have seen trade unions not only broaden their areas of struggle on the shop floor, we have seen them also contribute to community struggles.

The pace of these struggles has been determined by the people in the community. As trade unions we have always thought that our main area of activity was on the shop floor—the struggle against the bosses. Yet we have always recognized that industrial issues are political. Workers have long realized that when they are paid lower wages, it is a political issue. But what is difficult is how to make the link between economic and political issues.

We all agree that the struggle of workers on the shop floor cannot be separated from the wider struggle for liberation. The important question we have to ask ourselves is how is COSATU going to contribute to the struggle for our liberation. As unions we have sought to develop a consciousness among workers, not only of racial oppression but also of their exploitation as a working class.

As unions we have influenced the wider political struggle. Our struggles on the shop floor have widened the space for struggles in the community. Through interaction with community organizations, we have developed the principle of worker-controlled democratic organization. But our main political task as workers is to develop organization among workers as well as a strong worker leadership. We have to act decisively as unions, to ensure that we, as workers, lead the struggle. Workers' political strength depends upon building strong and militant organization in the workplace.

We also have to realize that organized workers are not representative of the working class as a whole but are its most effective weapon. Therefore, for workers it is important that organization on the shop floor be strengthened; in this way we will be able to contribute to the struggle of the working class as a whole and to the struggle of the oppressed people in this country.

It is also important to draw people into a program for the restructuring of society in order to make sure that the wealth of our society is democratically controlled and shared by all its people.

It is important to realize that the political struggle is not only to remove the government. We must also eliminate unemployment and improve education and health facilities. The wealth of society must be shared among all those that work in this country.

It is important that the politics of the working class eventually become the politics of all the oppressed people of this country.

Our most urgent task is to develop a unity among workers. We want COSATU to give firm political direction to workers. If workers are to lead the struggle for liberation, we have to win the confidence of other sectors of society. It is important for us to work in alliance with other classes in society. But if we are to enter into alliance with other progressive organizations, it must be on terms that are favorable to us as workers.

To make sure that we establish alliances that are progressive, we must be strong and united. And it is COSATU that is going to unite us under one banner. To do this, we have to give concrete expression to the basic principles on which COSATU was formed. All these principles must be put into practice in order to build a stronger unity and enable us to participate better in the struggle for liberation.

When we do plunge into political activity, we must make sure that the unions under COSATU have a strong shop floor base, to take on not only the employers but the state as well. Our rule in the political struggle will depend upon our organizational strength.

We must meet with progressive political organizations. We have to work in cooperation with them on realistic campaigns. We must not shy away and pretend that they do not exist. We have to pay particular attention to worker education and our role in the political struggle. We must encourage a healthy exchange between our Congress and other progressive organizations.

In the near future, we will be considering resolutions that will point the direction COSATU will take. We will be putting our heads together not only to make sure that we reach Pretoria but also to make a better life for us workers in this country. What we have to make clear is that a giant has risen, and it will confront all who stand in its way. COSATU is going to determine the direction of the working class in this country.

Township Resident

This statement was given by A.N.M., a 17-year-old black woman who lives in Uitenhage. Her affidavit was one of hundreds recorded by members of the Black Sash, an antiapartheid women's group that documents human rights abuses in South Africa and assists people charged with violating pass laws and other discriminatory legislation.

On Friday, January 11, 1985, all the schools in Uitenhage were boycotted by the students. I was at home and heard the students singing in the street. It was about 11 A.M. I left my house and walked towards the singing. The students were standing around the streets near my house. I was in Mabadla Street and joined the singing. Two hippos (armored riot-control vehicles) came up Mabadla Street behind the group of students who were walking in the direction of the school. Tear gas canisters were thrown from the hippos in the direction of the group of students. I ran into a nearby house, and the other students also scattered into the nearby houses. The hippos continued up the street. I then decided to go back home. I found my sister, N., ten years old, in the crowd, took her by the hand and started to return home.

We were in Mabadla Street when we saw one hippo come back up the street. There is a square in Mabadla Street where vendors sell vegetables. When I saw the hippo, I took my sister, and we ducked down behind one of the vendor's tables. When we were kneeling behind the table, a woman, S.V.G., whom I know as one of the vendors, came past the table carrying a loaf of bread. There were still shots coming from the hippo truck which I thought were tear gas canisters being shot. But then I saw S.V.G. fall. When I saw her face and neck spattered with blood and her face suddenly swell up, I knew that she must have been shot. There was terrible confusion. A car stopped. We drove to the Day Hospital at Kwanobuhle. They sent for an ambulance. The ambulance took S.V.G. to Livingstone Hospital. We went to S.V.G.'s house, and we heard later the same day that S.V.G. had died.

I went to a nearby house to ask for something clean to put on because my top was full of blood. As I emerged from this house, dressed in a clean top, I saw a hippo coming up Mabadla Street and ran to the corner house. I went inside and watched through the window. I saw students in the street running. I also saw M.M., who I knew to be mentally retarded. He did not run like the other students, but when they called loudly to him to run, he turned and jumped. He grabbed hold of a lamp pole. He had his shirt under his arm. Suddenly I saw his body covered with blood, and he collapsed. The hippo passed by with the policemen carrying on shooting from the top of the vehicle. The policemen were firing indiscriminately from the hippo. M.M.'s body was full of pellets. The owner of the house sent for blades which we used to remove some of the pellets. We managed to remove sixteen pellets. We could feel that there were still pellets in his stomach. I accompanied M.M. to a private doctor. This doctor found that there were still four pellets in the stomach which would have to be removed at a hospital. M.M.'s parents arrived at the surgery and took him home. They were afraid to go to hospital because the police were reported to be there. I heard later that M.M. died on Monday, January 14, 1985, at two P.M.

On Thursday, January 17, 1985, I went to M.M.'s house with other students. We had taken a financial contribution to the family. The house was surrounded by police vans. Policemen shouted that if any of the students ran they would be shot. Many policemen emerged from the vans and converged on the students. They were wielding batons, sticks and pickaxes. Many of us were hit—I was the first to be hit with a pick handle on my head. I fell unconscious to the ground. I remember being picked up by the left arm and thrown into the van. Other students were also thrown into the van until it was full. I must have fallen unconscious again as I found we were in the van in Church Street when I woke up. As we were taken from the van to the police station we were beaten.

Once inside, we were instructed to sing our freedom songs. As we were singing, we were being thoroughly beaten. I was called. They, that is the police, crowded me and beat me still more. I was then taken to a separate office, where I was questioned about the names in an exercise book that the police had found on me. They asked me for an explanation of why the students had gone to M.M.'s house. I explained about the money, but they said I was lying, and that we were attending an illegal gathering. I was continuously beaten during the questions.

The police then asked me to be an informer. It was more of a demand than a request. They offered to send me to school in Lesotho and offered me 200 rand. One of the policemen offered to marry me. I was told to bring the police information on Monday. I was then taken home in a Golf motor car with four security policemen in the car.

NOTES

1. Daniel F. Malan served as National Party leader and prime minister of South Africa from 1948 to 1954, J. G. Strijdom occupied the same posts from 1954 to 1958, and Hendrik F. Verwoerd, from 1958 to 1966.
2. Leader of the South-West Africa People's Organization, an armed guerrilla organization fighting South African rule in Namibia, also known as South-West Africa. Toivo ja Toivo was released unconditionally by South Africa on March 1, 1984, after serving twelve years in prison.

THE ECONOMY

THE HIGH COST OF REFORM

Michael K. Gavin

Michael K. Gavin is an economist with the Division of International Finance of the Board of Governors of the U.S. Federal Reserve System. (This chapter was begun before the author took up his duties at the Board of Governors. It reflects the views of the author, and should not be interpreted as representing the views of the Board or of any other members of its staff.)

> The country's political and economic standing in the outside world is lower than it has been for thirty years . . . South Africa cannot hope to attract foreign capital on realistic terms until it has developed a policy of racial co-existence that is acceptable to the outside world.
>
> (*Economist,* June 4, 1960)

> South Africa is being served notice that it cannot maintain its present system of apartheid and remain a paid-up member of the international financial community.
>
> (*Economist,* September 6, 1985)

Since the gold and diamond discoveries that triggered the transformation of South Africa from a society of subsistence farmers into a dynamic capitalist economy, international economic relations have been at the center of its economic development. South Africa has relied upon the world to provide capital to finance its investment, skilled labor to man the country's industrial plant and markets for its output. The world, in turn, has found in South Africa an exceedingly profitable outlet for investable resources, a market for the goods that South Africa does not produce and a supplier of a wide range of important raw materials that are, in some cases, almost unobtainable from alternative sources.

As the international community's disapproval of South Africa's domestic and foreign policies has increased, many observers have urged the world to recognize and exploit South Africa's economic vulnerabilities. The financial and political crisis created by the unwillingness of foreign banks to roll over outstanding credits to South Africa in mid-1985 highlighted South Africa's economic vulnerability and intensified debate over the role of international economic events in South African politics. Always pivotal in the economic development of South Africa, the behavior of South Africa's creditors and trading partners is now widely believed, or hoped, to be a key determinant of its future political development.

But these hopes have flared sporadically and with varying degrees of conviction for at least twenty-five years. And always the South Africans have weathered the world's censure, ridden out the economic crisis and rejected the path of reform. Despite its evident vulnerabilities, South Africa's rich, resilient economy has so far given it an impressive ability to manage and adapt to any adverse economic consequences of apartheid. Is the current crisis different? How are economic forces likely to affect South Africa's political development?

There are two means by which international economic events can impinge upon South Africa's domestic politics. First, there is the possibility of politically inspired economic pressure—that is, sanctions. Second, there is the possibility that domestic unrest will lead to a collapse of confidence in South Africa as a safe and profitable place to do business. The first depends upon the motivation and leverage of political leaders in the industrial countries, while the second depends upon the actions of international and South African investors and skilled white South African labor.

A realistic reading of the economic interdependence between South Africa and the world economy leads to the pessimistic conclusion that politically inspired sanctions are unlikely to provide more than a minor incentive for South Africa to reform its racial policies. A significant interruption of South Africa's foreign trade would require a declaration of economic war by most, perhaps all, of the industrial nations. Such an act would seriously compromise the West's considerable economic and strategic interests in southern Africa and might well promote the very instability that the West most fears, without enhancing the prospects for peaceful reform. While it is conceivable that the industrial countries would agree en masse to such a risky policy, it must be considered implausible for the near future. The paltry sanctions that have been imposed so far —over bitter domestic opposition—are, if anything, evidence of how difficult it would be to achieve a broader consensus on truly effective measures.

The plausibility and potential effects of a crisis of investor confidence, on the other hand, were vividly demonstrated by the massive flight of capital that took place during the summer and fall of 1985. The financial panic was triggered by the well-publicized political violence in the townships of South Africa, which generated fears for South Africa's stability and therefore its ability to repay its debts. This episode demonstrates that fears of instability can be seriously disruptive and may be an important source of pressure for reform.

Here again, however, there may be less than initially

meets the eye. The current crisis has stemmed primarily from the refusal of international banks to renew short-term credits to South African borrowers—a move that led to a panicked flight from the rand and that was met by a suspension of repayment on $14 billion of bank debt owed by private South African borrowers. In the ongoing negotiations between South Africa and the banks, the banks have demanded reform. But, since they are owed more than they can afford to lose, the banks are to some extent captive rather than captor, and their leverage over South Africa is limited. In the likely event that the banks are offered repayment, they are unlikely to refuse it, whether it comes with reform or without. The repayment process will be painful to South Africa, as it is for any debtor country, and the resulting economic costs and insecurity may increase the intensity of the current unrest, but it will provide no direct incentive for South Africa's leaders to alter the apartheid system.

This assessment depends upon a return to a "manageable" level of racial unrest, one that does not seriously threaten foreign investments and the safety of South Africa's white working and business class. Should civil unrest continue to escalate, however, there is the possibility not only of intensified capital flight, but also of "white flight," emigration of South Africa's skilled white workers. The scarcity of skilled labor in the South African economy has long been viewed as a source of hope for peaceful change, making the advancement of at least a small class of black laborers into the skilled work force an economic imperative. And it is possible to argue that an increased scarcity of skilled labor due to "white flight" would accelerate this natural process, thereby leading to orderly, evolutionary reform. The very presence of white emigration, however, indicates that those people with the most intimate familiarity with the South African political climate have decided—often at personal cost—that it is too late for evolutionary processes.

Despite South Africa's profound economic vulnerabilities, we are thus left with a rather pessimistic conclusion about the role of economic factors in forcing change in the apartheid system. External economic pressures can be expected to make life more difficult for both whites and blacks, but not difficult enough to compare with the costs to whites of relinquishing their privileged position. Instead, the economic deterioration is likely to increase the bitterness of the emerging civil conflict. Only if economic decline convinces white leaders they cannot prevail—a conviction that is unlikely to appear in the absence of severe political and military pressure—will it contribute significantly to political reform. And by then the time for peaceful change may well have passed.

South Africa's reliance on foreign trade and investment renders it acutely vulnerable to outside economic developments. But this vulnerability must be set against fundamental economic strengths that give the South African government impressive abilities to cope with economic pressures. For, from a macroeconomic perspective, South Africa's development can only be described as a spectacular success. And in regional terms South Africa is an economic behemoth.

In the fifty years from 1919 to 1969, South Africa's real national income grew an average of more than 5.5 percent per year, making it one of the fastest-developing countries in the world. Growth slowed dramatically in the 1970s, as it did around the world, and the recession that began in 1982 has resulted in even worse economic performance in the first half of the 1980s.

Yet despite these recent difficulties the South African economy remains the most powerful and advanced economy in sub-Saharan Africa. With 7.5 percent of sub-Saharan Africa's population, South Africa generates fully one-third of the region's gross product. Its 1983 per capita income of $2,490 was more than six times the average for the rest of sub-Saharan Africa and put South Africa, almost alone among the sub-Saharan African countries, into the World Bank's category for "upper-middle income developing economies."

While mining remains important, South Africa's economic development has generated a diverse economic base. As indicated by Table 1, manufacturing is the largest sector of the South African economy: in 1984, it generated almost 23 percent of South Africa's gross domestic product, while mining generated almost 14 percent. Table 1 also illustrates the sensitivity of the South African economy to movements in the price of gold. In 1980, for example, when the price of gold averaged more than $600 an ounce, the percentage contribution of mining was over one

Table 1

Contribution of Selected Sectors to South African GDP

	1970	1980	1984
Agriculture	8.3	6.9	5.2
Mining	10.3	22.2	13.9
Manufacturing	24.2	21.7	22.8
Trade, catering, accommodation	15.1	11.6	12.0
Finance, insurance, real estate	11.1	10.9	13.8
General government	9.6	9.2	12.5
Other	21.4	17.5	19.8

Source: South African Reserve Bank, *Quarterly Bulletin,* various issues.

and a half times that of 1984, when the price of gold fell to $360 an ounce.

The development of a reasonably broad economic base is in part the result of explicit "industrial policies," beginning as early as the 1920s (in response to the realization that gold and diamonds were a "wasting asset") and accelerated in the 1970's largely in response to the strategic economic challenges posed by embargoes on shipments of oil and arms to South Africa. Despite the aggressively capitalistic rhetoric of the South African leadership, the government's role in the economy is quite pervasive. In 1984, almost 60 percent of the fixed capital stock was in the hands of the public authorities and public corporations. Industries run largely or entirely by the public sector are responsible for the production of South Africa's iron and steel, electricity, arms and much of its energy. This may, as many South African businessmen and economists complain, involve some loss in microeconomic efficiency. It also, however, greatly increases the government's ability to override private interests in response to political imperatives.

Table 2

The Direction of South Africa's* Trade, 1984

	Exports, %	Imports, %
Industrialized countries	43.4	76.7
Developing countries	9.6	7.7
USSR, Eastern Europe, etc.	0.1	0.1
Special categories	46.9	14.9

*Includes Namibia, Lesotho, and Swaziland.
Source: International Monetary Fund, *Direction of Trade Statistics* (Washington, D.C.: International Monetary Fund, 1985).

South Africa owes much of its prosperity to international trade. The value of the country's exports of goods and services fluctuates at around 25 to 30 percent of GDP. As Table 2 indicates, most of South Africa's trade is with the industrialized countries.

Almost one-half of South Africa's exports go to the industrialized countries. Actually, that figure is a substantial understatement of the proportion of exports that go to industrialized countries; the exports listed as "special categories" are in large part gold sales to which it is difficult to assign a destination but which probably go primarily to industrialized countries. Developing countries account for less than 10 percent of South Africa's exports, although this figure, too, may be understated as a result of the unwillingness of many developing countries to report their trade with South Africa because of the sensitive political issues at stake. It should also be noted that these trade data are drawn from the combined territories of South Africa, Namibia, Lesotho and Swaziland, so that trade between these countries is excluded from the figures listed.

An even larger share of South Africa's imports comes from the industrialized countries. In 1983 over three-quarters of South Africa's imports came from developed countries and less than 8 percent from developing countries. Again, this latter figure is understated because of the developing countries' secretiveness about their trade with South Africa and South Africa's secretiveness about its trade in oil, most of which must come—via anonymous spot-market purchases—from developing countries.[1]

Historically, the United Kingdom has been South Africa's most important trading partner, but as Britain's role in the world economy has declined and her political ties to South Africa have withered, the United States has taken her place. In 1984, as shown in Table 3, the United

Table 3

South Africa's Major Trading Partners, 1984

	Exports, %	Imports, %
United States	8.5	16.2
United Kingdom	7.7	13.2
Japan	3.9	15.9
Germany	4.3	11.3
Switzerland	6.8	1.8
Other industrialized countries	12.2	18.3
Total industrialized countries	43.4	76.7

Source: International Monetary Fund, *Direction of Trade Statistics* (Washington, D.C. International Monetary Fund, 1985).

States was followed in importance (measured by the sum of imports and exports) by the U.K., Japan, Germany and Switzerland.

In sheer quantitative terms, South Africa is much more reliant on trade with the industrialized countries than they are upon trade with South Africa. In 1984, trade with South Africa comprised less than one percent of the industrialized countries' total trade. However, this somewhat simplistic consideration is modified considerably by an examination of the composition of South Africa's trade.

Table 4 shows that, in terms of the commodities involved, South Africa's international trade is much more specialized than the country's total production. Gold accounts for roughly half of South Africa's merchandise exports, its share fluctuating considerably due to the volatility of international gold prices. Manufactured goods are the next-largest export, followed by mining of minerals other than gold and agriculture. Almost all of

Table 4

The Composition of South Africa's International Trade, 1983

	Exports, million rand	Imports, million rand
Agriculture	820.4	530.3
Gold	9,929.5	—
Other mining and quarrying	2,845.1	197.0
Manufacturing	6,410.3	12,260.0
Other	614.8	3,216.7
Total	20,620.0	16,204.0

Source: Republic of South Africa, Central Statistical Services, *Bulletin of Statistics* (September 1984).

South Africa's imports are manufactured goods, especially transportation equipment and industrial machinery. The "other" category probably consists largely of oil imports although, again, such information is held in strict secrecy.

One important aspect of South Africa's foreign trade that is obscured by these aggregate statistics is the country's role as a provider of a wide range of strategic minerals that are of central importance to the western economies. South Africa is a major supplier of antimony, chromium, manganese, the platinum-group metals and vanadium, most of which are used as alloying agents in the production of high-strength metals of particular importance to the aerospace and defense industries. A 1980 study for the U.S. Congress on U.S. dependency on imports of various materials identified four critical minerals, supplies of which would be most vulnerable in a national emergency. Of these four, South Africa is a major producer of three: chromium, manganese and the platinum-group metals (see Table 5). The other major producer of these metals is the Soviet Union. South Africa is not a major supplier of the fourth mineral, cobalt, but other countries in the region, notably Zambia and Zaire, are.

South Africa's rapid economic development would have been impossible without foreign capital, which became an important factor in the economy after the discovery of diamonds in 1867 and gold in 1884. It has been estimated that by 1936 1.046 billion rand had been invested in what is now South Africa—43 percent of the total foreign investment in Africa.

This massive inflow of foreign investment permitted the rapid exploitation of South Africa's mineral deposits and financed the growth of industries related to gold and diamond mining, including coal mining, explosives manufacture and railway building. As South Africa's wealth and the size of her internal market began to increase, foreign investment financed the increasingly diversified economic infrastructure needed to satisfy consumer demands.

Table 5

Production of Selected Strategic Minerals, 1984
(percent of world total)

	South Africa	USSR
Antimony	16.7	17.4
Chromium	27.3	29.5
Manganese	10.5	45.3
Platinum-group metals	41.8	53.8
Vanadium	29.9	33.0

Source: American Metal Market, *Metal Statistics* (New York: Fairchild Publications, 1985).

South Africa's increasing wealth has led to an increased capacity to finance investment out of domestic savings. After a burst of foreign investment immediately following World War II, which was associated with the development of the Orange Free State gold fields, domestic savings have financed most of South Africa's investment. From 1950 to 1984, almost 95 percent of domestic investment was financed by domestic savings and just over 5 percent by foreign savings. However, foreign investment has remained very important on an episodic basis, helping in particular to finance the investment boom of the late 1960s and early 1970s. The country's historical reliance on foreign investment left it, at the end of 1984, with net foreign liabilities of 42 billion rand, roughly 40 percent of the country's GDP.

Another central element in South Africa's economic and political development has been the immigration of skilled labor from abroad. Shortages of skilled labor have long been recognized as a key constraint on rapid economic growth and have generated political conflict between the architects of apartheid and the white business class, whose need for skilled labor has been frustrated by both the restrictions on the mobility of the black labor force and the grossly inadequate educational system provided for blacks, which together have prevented the emergence of a significant number of skilled black workers.

Until recently the main official response to this situation has been to increase efforts to maintain immigration, and it is no overstatement to assert that it is immigration that has made apartheid an economically viable strategy in South Africa. In recent decades, immigration has slowed dramatically, and a continuation of the recent political unrest could well lead to emigration from South Africa of a significant proportion of the white population, many of whom hold British passports.

In large part because of the barriers to upward mobility imposed by the legal constraints on the employment of blacks and the substandard educational system available to blacks, the fruits of South Africa's considerable economic success are distributed in a notoriously unequal manner. The white minority, which makes up 17 percent of the population, receives almost two-thirds of the nation's income. This means an average per capita income for whites of over $10,000 per year, a figure bettered only by the ten or twelve richest nations in the world. Nonwhites, who comprise roughly 73 percent of the population, live on less than one-third of the country's income, for a per capita income that is roughly one-tenth that of the white population. These differences are compounded by the disparities of income between rural and urban blacks: one recent study estimated that the per capita income of rural blacks averages only one-fifth that of urban blacks, which puts the rural South African black population in a per capita income category with the poorest countries in the world, including Burma, Malawi and Uganda.

These demographic and income statistics reveal at least one important reality that influences all calculations about the likelihood of political change in South Africa—the economic cost to whites of any kind of reform. The disparities in the standard of living of South African whites and blacks are so great that, even without considering the general economic dislocations produced by any dramatic restructuring of society, meaningful reform efforts will be exceedingly costly in terms of white incomes. To raise the per capita income of blacks by $1, whites would have to sacrifice roughly $5.50. Thus, even in the most peaceful reform scenarios, white incomes can be expected to fall relatively closer to black incomes than vice versa. For economic sanctions or losses in investor confidence to change white economic calculations about reform, the burden they impose on whites must be nearly catastrophic in its proportions.

Economic sanctions have been applied against South Africa several times in the past, and, while they have obviously not toppled the apartheid system, it would be incorrect to assert that they have never affected South African politics. A precedent exists in the 1974 repeal of the Masters and Servants Act due to pressure from U.S. labor unions, which objected to imports produced with forced labor. And it is also true that international boycotts against South African athletic teams have enjoyed a limited success in forcing the integration of South African sports.

However, the more ambitious attempts to exercise leverage over South Africa have not been successful. The ostensible international embargo on oil exports to South Africa has been circumvented with only minor difficulty —first by shipments from Iran, then by secret purchases from the spot market. The major effect of the embargo has been to increase South Africa's self-sufficiency in petroleum products by encouraging the country's development of an oil-from-coal industry and its own large petroleum reserves. The international embargo on arms sales to South Africa has been more successful but has been offset by South Africa's development of an indigenous arms industry which now produces a wide variety of relatively sophisticated weaponry. These examples suggest that South Africa's economic strengths give it an impressive ability to overcome selective trade disruptions.

There can be no doubt, of course, that a sufficiently comprehensive interruption of South Africa's trade would result in major, even catastrophic damage to the country's economy. It is one thing for South Africa to develop an arms industry; it would be quite another for the country to develop the many industries needed to produce the industrial machinery it now imports, and economic development without such goods would be quite impossible. It is one thing for South Africa to lose the 2.5 percent premium that Krugerrands bring over uncoined gold; it would be quite another for Pretoria to do without any significant fraction of its gold exports.

However, previous attempts to interrupt South Africa's trade suggest that, to be successful, such action would have to cover a substantial portion of the country's trade and would have to be almost unanimously applied. As noted above, the developing countries' trade with South Africa is inadequate to generate significant economic leverage; action by the industrial nations would be required to enforce any effective program of sanctions. Furthermore, a sufficiently comprehensive interruption of South Africa's trade is unlikely to arise from a spontaneous eruption of disgust by private consumers of South African products. While private boycotts of South African goods have been attempted in the past, they have always been, and are likely to remain, ineffective. Too few consumers in the industrial countries care enough about apartheid to make a voluntary boycott work—a difficulty that is compounded by the nature of most of South Africa's exports. How is the consumer to know whether the chrome on his new automobile comes from South Africa or the Soviet Union? Consumers may, and do, avoid South African Krugerrands, but they have no way of identifying the origin of the gold in their earrings.

This means that a significant disruption of South Africa's trade would require action by the governments of the major industrial countries. This action must be based on essentially unanimous agreement about the goals the sanctions are intended to achieve, as well as about specific tactics that will necessarily be costly to each country involved and that will be perceived by the South Africans as an explicit and threatening act of aggression.

The objectives that industrial-country governments pursue in their policies toward South Africa are several, including a desire to play to the antiapartheid gallery both at home and abroad, to protect financial interests in South Africa and, most important, to maintain, as far as possible, some semblance of political stability in this strategically important part of the world. In addition, there is undoubtedly a genuine desire on the part of many governments to see apartheid eliminated, if only in hopes of reducing the racial and economic class tensions that endanger South Africa's political stability.

But orchestrating an effective program of common sanctions that involves the complex economies of all the major industrial states would be a monumental task. As mentioned earlier, South Africa has demonstrated an impressive ability to adjust to strategic economic challenges. Moreover, the incentives for individual nations or firms to cheat on any international program of sanctions would be quite large. Quite apart from the costs that going along with sanctions would entail, there would be an economic bonanza for countries or firms willing to fulfill South Africa's frustrated demand for industrial imports and the unsatisfied world demand for South African exports. In the absence of a military blockade, it would be very difficult to prevent such evasive behavior.

A further problem arises in attempting to ensure that the costs imposed on South Africa by any sanctions effort will promote the desired objective of political reform. It is reasonable to suppose that even partial sanctions would impose some economic costs on South Africa. Yet many of those costs could be shifted away from the white South Africans who now hold power. Foreign investors, in particular, would likely bear a large share of the burden. But while this may "serve them right" for investing in a morally repugnant system, it is unlikely to promote reform. Other economic burdens, such as increased unemployment, may be largely passed off to neighboring countries if South Africa chooses to expel some or all of the estimated 1.5 million migrant workers from Botswana, Lesotho, Malawi, Mozambique and Swaziland who now earn their livelihood in South Africa. And there can be little doubt that within South Africa itself a disproportionate share of the economic disruption caused by sanctions would be borne by South African blacks, not whites.

The political impact of the costs that are borne by whites may be quite perverse. It is reasonable to suppose that white businessmen will become increasingly sensitive to the costs of retaining the apartheid system. But, again, those businessmen may be expected to weigh the costs of sanctions against the likely costs of reform. And, since sanctions would by definition be externally imposed, they would undoubtedly feed the delusion that South Africa's troubles are caused by foreign agitators. Thus, the intensified misery and radicalization of the black population could well be matched by increased white intransigence—a recipe for civil war, not peaceful reform.

For the West, increased civil unrest would jeopardize the flow of critical minerals—not only those that South Africa supplies, but, given the risk that violence would spread throughout the region, those provided by neighboring countries as well. Western nations could certainly survive a short disruption of supplies by consuming strategic stockpiles, using substitute materials and curtailing nonessential uses. Nevertheless, even in an optimistic scenario such a disruption would be very costly, and it would ultimately place the West in a very vulnerable position vis-à-vis the Soviet Union as the only major alternative supplier.

The possible loss of chromium, manganese and cobalt would be one, but not the only, cost to the industrialized countries of imposing sanctions. The reduction in trade would hurt the industrialized countries as well as South Africa—after all, countries trade precisely because each needs the other's product. The lost trade might be small in a macroeconomic context, but some firms would be badly damaged, and the loss of profits and jobs in the industrialized countries would certainly be unwelcome. More damaging would be the retaliation invited by such an explicitly hostile foreign policy. South Africa could retaliate against sanctions by denying further access to the country's strategic minerals, nationalizing foreign investments, defaulting on its international debt and possibly lashing out at its vulnerable neighbors to the north.

It is hard to imagine any, much less all, of the nations with significant interests in South Africa taking such risks lightly. Thus, while it is possible that the desire to "do something about apartheid" will lead the Western nations to agree on effective trade sanctions against South Africa, such a development is highly unlikely. It would seriously endanger their considerable economic and political interests in the region and could well promote the very instability the West most fears—without enhancing the prospects for peaceful reform.

Another important tool that might be used to bring pressure against Pretoria is the reduction or prohibition of international credit to South Africa. And, in fact, the U.S. sanctions imposed against South Africa in 1985 included a ban on most bank loans to the South African government, though not on loans to the private sector. This ban was largely cosmetic, since it was imposed at a time when U.S. banks were already engaged in a desperate attempt to reduce their exposure in South Africa. And the likelihood of more effective government action by most or all of the industrialized countries to restrict credit to South Africa is as slim as it is for trade sanctions. Sanctions of this nature have all the drawbacks of trade restrictions, with the added consideration that credit restrictions would be even more difficult to enforce.

The prospect of an effective voluntary withdrawal of credit to South Africa must be considered, however, if only because of its growing popularity as a focus of antiapartheid activism. A substantial number of universities, municipalities and pension funds have divested themselves of holdings in South African companies and in foreign firms doing business in South Africa. And divestment has been urged on a wide cross-section of other institutions as a test of moral rectitude.

These institutions control a substantial proportion of wealth in the industrialized nations, and thus the divestment movement places a large proportion of the world's financial resources off limits for South Africa. But the short-term impact of these actions is likely to be minor: to the extent that such sales of shares in South African firms depress their market price, the principal effect will be to provide South African investors—or less scrupulous foreign investors—with an investment bargain. If, over time, these incentives reduce foreign direct investment in South Africa and make it harder for South Africa to find international financing for its domestic investment, the country's growth will be slower than it would otherwise have been. But this effect can easily be overstated. For every businessman willing to pass up a good investment for moral reasons, there are many who would be anxious to take advantage of a bargain and enjoy the associated high financial returns. Furthermore, as mentioned earlier, South Africa has for the past thirty-five years financed almost all of its investment internally; loss of access to the international capital market would make it harder to finance investment booms like that of the late 1960s, but would not have a large effect on long-term investment trends.

A reduction in foreign direct investment is of potentially greater importance. For example, when the Ford Motor Company builds a plant in South Africa, it provides not only financing for investment but also a transfer of advanced equipment, training and technological expertise that might otherwise be difficult for South Africa to obtain. However, there are other ways to obtain such training, and this is in any event a very long-term concern that is unlikely to have a major impact on contemporary politics.

While there is room for doubt about the likelihood and effectiveness of voluntary or government-sponsored sanctions against South Africa, there is no such doubt about the withdrawal of private capital from the country, a trend that was evident on a spectacular scale in 1985. During the summer of 1985 the well-publicized violence in many black South African townships made several foreign banks uneasy about the prospects for the country's future stability and prompt repayment of its foreign debt. This unease was compounded by the South African government's refusal to make expected political concessions to blacks.

When the Chase Manhattan Bank halted all lending to South Africa in late July, the uneasiness turned into a minor panic as it became apparent that outstanding bank credits would not be rolled over as expected and South

Africa's $2.5 billion current account surplus would be inadequate to service all the debt coming due in 1985. The result was a run on the rand, which led to an effective exchange rate depreciation of 30 percent between the end of June and late August, forcing the South African authorities to impose a moratorium on debt repayment and to reinstitute the controls on capital flow that had been lifted in February 1983. Less dramatic, but of potentially greater long-term significance, is the recent increase in multinational disinvestment from South Africa, which has been motivated by business, rather than moral, considerations.

Much excitement has been generated by this turn of events, which has been seen as a demonstration of South Africa's economic vulnerability and has encouraged hopes that the South African authorities will be forced to change their racial policies to placate foreign banks. The episode certainly demonstrates South Africa's vulnerability to private capital flight and to a general loss of business confidence. But a realistic reading of history and of the interdependence between South Africa and its creditors affords less room for optimism that the current crisis will generate effective pressures for reform.

History provides several episodes of capital flight from South Africa, all associated with political stress and apparent instability. Political disturbances, notably the Sharpeville incident in 1960, the 1975 invasion of Angola and the Soweto riots of 1976, have all been accompanied by frantic attempts by foreign and domestic investors to get their capital out of South Africa. But in each case, when the political disturbance was quelled, the capital flight ceased.

The events that followed the 1960 Sharpeville episode, when sixty-nine unarmed black demonstrators were killed by police, are particularly instructive for their parallels with today's situation. In the two months following the Sharpeville shootings, a run on the rand led to a $92 million loss in foreign exchange reserves, forcing the central bank to institute the very capital controls that it reinstituted in September 1985. Sales of South African shares by foreign investors led to a $840 million reduction in the value of industrial and mining shares listed on the Johannesburg Stock Exchange, and prominent industrial leaders sought a meeting with the government to propose immediate consultation with moderate black leaders. Editorial writers speculated that South Africa would have to modify its racial policies to attract foreign capital. On April 9, 1960, the *Economist* declared, "No one but a madman would buy South African shares now, though madmen sometimes make money."

Indeed they do. Within a few short years, foreign investors were happily financing the South African "great boom" of 1961–70, and those who had kept their nerve in 1960 reaped enormous profits. Similarly, even after the 1976–77 Soweto disturbances, foreign investors were willing in 1981 and 1982 to finance South Africa's large current account deficits. Such investor behavior vindicated a 1961 prediction by Prime Minister Hendrik Verwoerd, one of the chief architects of the apartheid system. "Foreign investors," he declared, "look at the stability of the government rather than the policy of the government. . . . The simple fact that the White man is determined to maintain himself here is not a factor against investment, but a factor in favor of investment."[2]

The precise modalities of the 1960 crisis differed from those of the current situation. For example, the Western nations were then operating on a system of fixed exchange rates, so capital flight manifested itself in a loss of international reserves rather than a plunge in the value of the rand. Perhaps more significant, international lending by commercial banks was much less important in 1960 than it is now, so the 1960 capital flight primarily took the form of massive sales of South African stock shares rather than an abrupt withdrawal of commercial bank credit. These differences make quantitative comparison of the two crises difficult, and, more important, they raise questions as to whether the current crisis will result in more effective pressure for reform.

That banks have much greater negotiating ability than individual investors can be seen by comparing their enormous ability (with the help, it must be admitted, of the International Monetary Fund) to influence debtor-country behavior with the pathetic record of the poorly organized creditor cartels of the 1930s. It does not follow, however, that the banks have the power to force the South Africans to alter their domestic policies. The South Africans have an enormous stake in the ongoing debt negotiations, and they will certainly want to come to terms with the banks. But the banks badly need to reach an agreement as well; they are, after all, owed $24 billion by South Africa, and they want it back.

In the meantime, while the banks are undoubtedly unhappy to have so much money tied up in a country that is in the throes of violent civil unrest, it is striking how little they have suffered as a result of South Africa's decision to suspend repayment. South Africa is still paying interest on all outstanding loans, and loans to the public sector ($10 billion of the $24 billion total that South Africa owes to foreign banks) are being repaid on schedule. So far, South Africa has been an uncomfortable, but not unprofitable, place for the banks to do business. If South Africa maintains a repayment schedule that provides the banks with some assurances that they will be repaid in a reasonable period of time, they are unlikely to press for racial reforms, even if they would sincerely like to see them adopted.

This pessimistic conclusion is at odds with some of the rhetoric emanating from the commercial banks and their representatives. For example, Fritz Leutwiler, the Swiss mediator between South Africa and the commercial banks, has warned that no rescheduling agreement is in prospect unless Pretoria issues "a positive statement at the highest level" about political reform.[3]

Such calls for reform are motivated in large part by two considerations: first, a belief that political stability, and therefore prospects for repayment, will be enhanced by reform; and second, a felt need to demonstrate to the banks' customers at home that they are not "propping up apartheid." But in reality the banks' options are rather limited. If, for instance, reform does not materialize and South Africa continues to use its large current account surplus (about $2.5 billion in 1985 and likely to grow as the rand's depreciation takes effect) to offer repayment, it is unlikely that any bank could refuse, since in doing so it would risk large amounts of its shareholders' wealth to make a political point.

Thus, it should never have been considered plausible that South Africa's commercial bank creditors would exert more than rhetorical pressure upon Pretoria to reform its domestic policies. And in fact, in February 1986, when South African censorship had made the political violence in the townships less visible to the outside world, the commercial banks came to a rescheduling agreement with South Africa that included a $500 million downpayment on its debt, and a renewal of outstanding short-term loans. In March, the banks agreed to extend this interim rescheduling agreement for an additional four months, through the end of June 1987.

If, in future years, South Africa must continue to repay its commercial bank loans, there will necessarily be adverse effects on the standard of living, and investment possibilities. However, the burden of such repayment should not be exaggerated. South Africa's debt service, including interest and repayment of principal, is on now on the order of 20 percent of goods and service exports. Interest alone costs Argentina 50 percent of its exports; in Brazil the ratio is 40 percent, and in Mexico it is 35 percent.

Thus, if the current unrest in South Africa quiets down, the financial crisis will be manageable with or without political reform. If the unrest worsens, then no degree of political reform is likely to lure capital into the country. Which is to say that international capital flows are an ineffective force for. promoting change in South Africa because they depend not on political reform but on political stability. If threatened with the prospect of capital flight and investor panic, the South African authorities will respond by trying to secure stability, and they clearly believe that this can best be achieved by censorship and repression. In short, capital flows should be considered an index of international confidence in white South Africa's ability to prevail in a potential or ongoing civil war with black South Africa—not a measure of international approval or disapproval of the apartheid system.

A loss of confidence in South Africa's stability would lead not only to capital flight but, if the political violence intensifies and begins seriously to threaten the security of white South Africans, to large-scale emigration of the whites who now compromise the skilled work force and experienced business class. This loss would have an enormous effect on the South African economy.

Traditionally, South Africa has relied upon immigration to alleviate shortages of skilled labor. With decreasing rates of immigration, the industrial color bars that prevented the employment of blacks as skilled workers have become economically untenable as the limited supply of skilled workers has placed increasingly severe constraints on economic growth. Thus, the labor market reforms proposed in recent official studies such as the Reikert and Wiehahn commission reports may be viewed, at least in part, as a capitulation to economic reality rather than to political pressure.

Shortages of skilled labor have thus been a major force for political reform in South Africa, and it is pleasant to contemplate the possible consequences of the forces that make black advancement economically rational, arguably even imperative. The image is a seductive one, because in it the integration of blacks into a more privileged stratum of South African economic life provides not a threat but a benefit to white South Africa. One can even imagine that, as whites are forced by economic necessity to work with blacks on an increasingly equal footing, the entire ideological and political infrastructure supporting apartheid will wither away. The South African economist D. J. J. Botha gave in to this temptation in a 1978 article in which he observed, "The whole process of the slow but systematic dismantling of the underlying structure of politically inspired restrictive legislation is extremely interesting to the economist, and points fascinatingly to the superiority of economic forces over ideology as factors which in the final analysis shape the destiny of the country."[4] The question remains whether intensified shortages of skilled labor occasioned by "white flight" will accelerate this process, leading to the possibility of peaceful reform.

Unfortunately, this hopeful image is likely to prove a mirage. Although the recent labor market reforms have marked a milestone in the history of apartheid, their economic impact is marginal when viewed alongside the extent of black poverty and deprivation. And, while it is conceivable that whites will approve more sweeping changes, the staggering cost of meaningful reforms makes them unlikely as a voluntary initiative. The costs of raising black educational opportunities to white levels, a minimal prerequisite for moving blacks toward skilled employment, alone would be on the order of 10 percent of South Africa's national income.

Perhaps the most decisive argument against the optimistic kind of economic determinism implied by this scenario is that it is a plan for evolutionary reform. Even if dramatic efforts were made to bring blacks into the economic mainstream, the process would be time-consuming. It would require not only opening up new professional opportunities for blacks but also providing education and training to permit them to take advantage of these opportunities. South Africa may or may not have the time to pursue such long-term strategies. But, as noted earlier, rather than serving as a spur to peaceful change, "white flight" will be a signal that those with the most intimate familiarity with the political system and the largest stake in the South African economy have given up on the hope of a peaceful settlement.

Is South Africa's current economic crisis different from those that preceded it? If so, it is not because the governments of the world are ready to take definitive action against apartheid. Their ability to hurt South Africa economically is considerable, but they do not have the means to translate that pain into the impetus for political reform. The industrialized countries can live with apartheid, and they could live with black rule, but a protracted and incapacitating civil war in South Africa would pose a serious threat to their economic and security interests. They cannot be expected to take actions that might increase the probability of such a war.

If the current economic crisis is different, it is not because South Africa's international creditors will suddenly demand reform as a condition for doing business. Some will, but if the violence and unrest in the black townships are quelled, investors will return to the country, just as they did after Sharpeville and Soweto.

If the current economic crisis is different, it will be because this time the civil unrest does not subside but intensifies and begins to pose a serious threat to the safety of foreign investments and the security of the white population. The resulting flight of capital and labor could undermine the South African economy and the ability of the white political leadership to prevail in a civil war. The tragic irony is that this is likely to occur only after—and, indeed, because—the time for peaceful reform has passed.

NOTES

1. South Africa's secretiveness about oil imports derives, of course, from the embargo on shipments to South Africa imposed by most of the major oil producers. In South Africa, in fact, it is a crime punishable by seven years' imprisonment to reveal information about the country's oil imports.
2. Quoted in Freda Troup, *South Africa: An Historical Introduction* (London: Penguin, 1975).
3. *Financial Times,* November 25, 1985, p. 1.
4. Botha, D. J. J., "An Economic Boycott of South Africa?" *South African Journal of Economics* Vol. 46, No. 3, (1978).

SOUTH AFRICA AND THE WORLD

WHY CONSTRUCTIVE ENGAGEMENT FAILED

Sanford J. Ungar and Peter Vale

Sanford J. Ungar, former managing editor of Foreign Policy, *was until recently a Senior Associate of the Carnegie Endowment for International Peace.* He is the author of Africa: The People and Politics of an Emerging Continent. *Peter Vale is Research Professor and Director of the Institute of Social and Economic Research at Rhodes University in Grahamstown, South Africa.*

R onald Reagan's imposition of limited economic sanctions against the South African regime in September 1985 was a tacit admission that his policy of "constructive engagement"—encouraging change in the apartheid system through a quiet dialogue with that country's white minority leaders—had failed. Having been offered many carrots by the United States over a period of four and a half years as incentives to institute meaningful reforms, the South African authorities had simply made a carrot stew and eaten it. Under the combined pressures of the seemingly cataclysmic events in South Africa since September 1984 and the dramatic surge of antiapartheid protest and political activism in the United States, the Reagan administration was finally embarrassed into brandishing some small sticks as an element of American policy.

The Reagan sanctions, however limited, are an important symbol: a demonstration to the ruling white South African nationalists that even an American president whom they had come to regard as their virtual savior could turn against them. Only a few weeks after inexplicably hailing South Africa for an American-style solution to racial segregation,[1] Mr. Reagan, beating Congress to the punch, signed an executive order banning the export of computers to all official South African agencies that enforce apartheid; prohibiting most transfers of nuclear technology, preventing loans to the South African government unless they would improve social conditions for all races, ending the importation of South African Krugerrands gold coins into the United States; and limiting export assistance to American companies operating in South Africa that do not adhere to fair employment guidelines. By any measure, this was a significant development, and Pretoria's reaction of shock, anger and defiance underlined its impact.

But the sanctions, applied at once with fanfare and apologies, do not represent a fundamental change in American policy toward South Africa. Nor do they portend or promote a meaningful evolution in the South African political and social system. On the contrary, they continue the recent American practice of attempting to reform the South African system by working entirely within it and honoring its rules. "Active constructive engagement" (the new, impromptu name the President seems to have given his policy during a press conference) is still a policy that engages the attention and the interests of only a small, privileged stratum of South Africans. It relies almost entirely on white-led change, as designed and defined by a regime that is becoming more embattled by the day. And it ignores the needs, the politics and the passions of the black majority in South Africa. The policy will continue to fail.

Constructive engagement has not merely caused the United States to lose valuable time when it might have influenced South Africa to begin negotiating a settlement of its unique and extraordinary racial problems. Many would argue that constructive engagement was a necessary step in the evolution of American attitudes toward South Africa, but the cost has been great. American policy has actually exacerbated the situation inside South Africa by encouraging and indulging the white regime's divide-and-rule tactics—leading that regime, its internal and external victims and much of the international community to believe that, whatever the rhetoric emanating from Washington, American prestige is on the side of the Pretoria government.

Indeed, from the time constructive engagement took effect, American trade with and investment in South Africa increased, and the Reagan Administration expanded the scope of U.S. cooperation with the South African government. It lifted previous restrictions on the export of military equipment and equipment with potential military uses; permitted (until President Reagan's change of heart) the sale of American computers to the police, military and other agencies of the South African government that administer apartheid; and approved the sale of shock batons to the police. The Administration also allowed the return of South African military attachés to the United States and otherwise expanded diplomatic, military and intelligence relationships between the two countries—including the establishment of several new South African honorary consulates around the United States, the provision of American training for the South African coast guard, and the resumption of official nuclear advisory contacts.[2]

In addition, the Reagan Administration frequently stood alone on South Africa's side in the U.N. Security Council—vetoing resolutions critical of South Africa on occasions when Britain and France abstained, and, in some cases, registering the only abstention when Western allies voted to condemn South African actions.

No specific conditions were imposed on South Africa in exchange for these American favors. On the contrary, they were granted at a time when many of the restrictions on black South Africans were being tightened and tensions inside South Africa were growing. One important consequence was that, while America's official gaze was averted, a whole stratum of black South African leaders who had appeared willing to negotiate over the country's future seems to have been pushed aside by groups that advocate violent solutions. The arguments in favor of American-style, if not American-sponsored, conciliation and negotiation in South Africa may now have lost their force, as the South African drama has taken new and significant turns toward a tragic resolution.

Viewed in the context of the events since September 1984, South Africa's problem today is a manifestly new one. Unless steps are taken to prevent further deterioration, that country is liable to drift into uncontrollable violence fueled from the extreme right and extreme left. What is needed from the United States is not a withering debate over disinvestment or a domestic public relations campaign on behalf of constructive engagement, but an entirely new and more imaginative approach to South Africa. A policy must be crafted that not only recognizes and works with the current grim realities there, but also tries to ease the transition to an altogether different, albeit unknown, future in which blacks will take part in the government of their country. There is no longer any question that this change will occur in South Africa; the question is how, according to whose timetable and with what sort of outside involvement.

Only by establishing much more direct communication

with the South African majority and by granting it far greater and more practical assistance can the United States hope to influence the course of events there. In effect, a new, parallel set of diplomatic relationships is necessary. And only by taking further steps that risk hurting the pride of South Africa's current rulers can American leaders hope to win enough credibility among South African blacks to be listened to in the debate over the country's future—a debate that will have profound consequences in all of Africa, the United States and much of the rest of the world.

From the start, constructive engagement meant quite different things to the four constituencies that would be most affected by it: the Reagan Administration itself, and by extension the American public; the South African government and the white population it represents; the South African black majority; and other countries in southern Africa.

The policy of constructive engagement was spelled out in 1980 by Chester A. Crocker, shortly before he became assistant secretary of state for African affairs. One of its first principles was that the previous U.S. policy of putting overt, public pressure for change on the South African regime had seemed to promise much more to black South Africans than it could deliver. "Americans need to do their homework," wrote Mr. Crocker in a landmark article:

A tone of empathy is required not only for the suffering and injustice caused to blacks in a racist system, but also for the awesome political dilemma in which Afrikaners and other whites find themselves. . . . American powder should be kept dry for genuine opportunities to exert influence. As in other foreign policy agendas for the 1980s, the motto should be: underpromise and overdeliver—for a change.[3]

Ironically, the Crocker approach made its own very ambitious promises, this time to the American public and the international community. Among other things, it offered the prospect of increased American prestige in southern Africa (with the implication that Soviet influence there would correspondingly be neutralized); a solution to the diplomatic and military conflict over Namibia (or South-West Africa), the former German colony that South Africa has continued to rule in defiance of the United Nations, and a withdrawal of Cuban troops and advisers from Angola. The latter—the prospect of an apparent setback for the Cubans—carried particular domestic political appeal in the United States, and it alone seemed to justify the sudden focus of high-level attention on Africa.

Finally, and most fundamentally, constructive engagement promised that if the United States could, as Crocker put it, "steer between the twin dangers of abetting violence in the Republic and aligning ourselves with the cause of white rule," then it could contribute to the achievement of change in South Africa. The Reagan Administration seemed to believe that P. W. Botha, who had become prime minister in 1978 and elevated himself to state president in 1984 under a new constitutional scheme, was significantly different from other, more orthodox postwar South African leaders. Botha's program of limited reforms, Crocker felt, should be encouraged and applauded by the United States, if only to safeguard American interests in South Africa and the region.

In the early days of constructive engagement, Botha

appeared to be impervious to, or at least capable of out-smarting, the increasingly assertive South African right wing, composed mostly of disaffected members of the ruling National Party. What is more, the domestic situation in South Africa seemed to be secure. The nationwide upheavals associated with the Soweto riots of 1976 had subsided. Despite localized incidents of black unrest and sporadic attacks inside the country by members of the exiled African National Congress, there was no obvious political force that might be able to dislodge, or even unnerve, the Botha government. When ANC attacks got out of hand, the South African government seemed capable of neutralizing the organization with commando raids into neighboring black-ruled countries.

Reinforcing all this was the widespread impression that the South African business community—led primarily by relatively liberal English-speaking men with extensive ties to the outside world—was not only poised to play a more active role in setting the pace of reform and determining the country's future, but was also being encouraged to do so by the Afrikaner-dominated political establishment. After the uprisings of 1976, business leaders had established new foundations that would attempt to improve the lives of black people in ways that the government itself was not yet prepared to attempt. At a widely publicized meeting in Johannesburg in 1979, Botha had explicitly asked the captains of South African business and industry to help him lead the country along a new political path, and they had, for the most part, responded enthusiastically.

The Reagan Administration seemed to believe that with its domestic situation under control and improving all the time, South Africa, with American backing, could also play the role of a regional power promoting peace. Once

Namibia had achieved independence under U.N. supervision (in direct exchange for the withdrawal of the Cubans from Angola, a linkage that Washington introduced into the negotiations), other regional tensions would be reduced and, the State Department hoped, recalcitrant South African whites would see the advantages of peaceful coexistence with neighboring black-ruled states.

The Botha government had different expectations of constructive engagement. Indeed, for Pretoria, Ronald Reagan's victory in 1980 stirred ambitious hopes. It seemed to signal a return to the days when the South African white regime could get away with portraying itself as a protector of the Western way of life, a bastion of freedom, decency and economic development at the tip of a continent afflicted by tyranny, chaos and abject poverty—above all, a bulwark against communism.

For the four previous years, that pose had been weakened, if not entirely rejected, by Washington. Jimmy Carter, with his emphasis on human rights and his public criticisms of apartheid (made, for example, during a visit to Nigeria) had come to be regarded as public enemy number one by many South African whites, who believed that he was trying to humiliate, or perhaps even destroy them. During a press conference at the end of a dramatic confrontation with then Prime Minister John Vorster in Vienna in 1977, Vice President Walter Mondale had appeared to advocate a one-man/one-vote system for South Africa. Two of Carter's other lieutenants who applied pressure on the country, U.N. Ambassadors Andrew Young and Donald McHenry, were black. Some white South Africans held Young and McHenry personally responsible for forcing a supposedly unwitting and, at the time, somewhat disorganized National Party government into a fateful concession—an agreement that Namibia should move toward independence under the terms of U.N. Security Council Resolution 435.

Anti-Americanism became a powerful force in South African white politics during the Carter Administration. In an election held some months after his showdown with Mondale, Vorster was able to add fifteen seats to his majority in the white parliament simply by focusing the electorate's attention on alleged U.S. meddling in the country's affairs. Indeed, Carter's promotion of a climate of distrust between Washington and Pretoria, his refusal to acknowledge and endorse South Africa's dominant role in the region, may have contributed to the growing determination of the South African military to demonstrate the country's hegemony by destabilizing the governments and economies of neighboring states.

For the National Party government, Reagan's election raised hopes for more than just a return to a "normal" relationship between the United States and South Africa. There was the prospect of a valuable endorsement of the legitimacy of the white regime and the promotion of South African leadership in the region, perhaps through the "constellation of states" concept that Vorster had introduced and Botha had promoted. When President Reagan himself, in a television interview early in his term, extolled South Africa as "a country that has stood beside us in every war we've ever fought, a country that strategically is essential to the free world in its production of minerals,"[4] some South African politicians began to fantasize that their wildest dreams might come true.

Pretoria was encouraged that the Reagan Administration viewed the problems of southern Africa in the context of East-West relations, a perspective that South Africa felt had been naïvely missing from Carter's policy. South

Africa's suspicion of the Soviet Union bordered on paranoia, and the new American government's tough line toward Moscow was greeted in South Africa as "political realism." Indeed, white South Africans hoped they would finally be regarded as an integral part of Western defense requirements.

In a "scope paper" to brief then–Secretary of State Alexander Haig for a meeting with South African Foreign Minister Roelof F. "Pik" Botha in 1981 (and later made public by TransAfrica, the Black American foreign policy lobbying organization), Crocker gave every indication that the Reagan administration might be prepared to trust South Africa with just such responsibilities. He wrote:

> The political relationship between the United States and South Africa has now arrived at a crossroads of perhaps historic significance; the possibility may exist for a more positive and reciprocal relationship between the two countries based upon shared strategic concerns in southern Africa, our recognition that the government of P. W. Botha represents a unique opportunity for domestic change, and willingness of the Reagan administration to deal realistically with South Africa.[5]

If the South Africans cooperated on the Namibian issue, the Crocker memo went on to argue, the United States could "work to end South Africa's polecat status in the world and seek to restore its place as a legitimate and important regional actor with whom we can cooperate pragmatically." The United States was prepared to begin this process of new, "realistic" dealings with South Africa by taking "concrete steps such as the normalization of our military attaché relationship." In other words, the State Department leadership was so enthusiastic and hopeful about this course that it was willing to make symbolic gestures to Pretoria without any advance indication that reciprocal measures would be forthcoming.

Aware of this attitude, the Botha government expected still more concessions out of constructive engagement— perhaps even some form of American recognition of the South African-designed "independent homelands" of Transkei, Bophuthatswana, Venda and Ciskei, which had been scorned and shunned by the international community but remained an important part of the grand fabric of apartheid. At one meeting with Crocker in Pretoria, Foreign Minister Pik Botha attempted to promote direct communication between the United States and the homelands by passing along messages from the leaders of two of these pseudo-states. The thought was that if America conferred some legitimacy on the homelands, then other Western nations might follow suit and, before long, the established, genuinely independent states of the region, such as Botswana, Lesotho and Swaziland, would be forced out of weakness to deal with the homelands directly and perhaps even to join them in Botha's "constellation."

As far as Namibia was concerned, given the rich enticements that were being offered, South Africa seemed willing to play along with Crocker's patient, if overly optimistic, efforts to secure a settlement. Pretoria was, of course, deeply suspicious of the United Nations and skeptical of any transition to independence in Namibia that would operate in favor of the South-West Africa People's Organization, which had been designated by the United Nations as the sole legitimate representative of the territory's inhabitants. SWAPO, although it included in its membership many old-line nationalists whose views were consistent with those of European social democrats, had long been aided by the Soviet Union and other communist countries and, as an organization, officially followed a Marxist political line. Once the connection of a Namibian settlement with the departure of the Cubans from Angola had been introduced by Washington, however, it was much easier for South Africa to cooperate—or at least to give the impression of cooperating—with the Reagan administration's efforts, which most South African political analysts thought were doomed to fail anyway.

Whether the Botha government ever could have delivered on a Namibia deal without provoking a severe crisis in the ranks of white South Africans is another question; the South African Defense Force, whose influence over the country's regional policies is profound, was, and apparently remains, hostile to any negotiations to "give away" the territory.

When it came to the issue of internal reform, P. W. Botha found it relatively easy to satisfy the Reagan Administration with his own limited agenda. Botha, as a lifelong party organizer and long-standing member of the white parliament from southern Cape province, where the population is evenly divided between whites and so-called Coloureds, had very little direct experience with other blacks. Thus, when he promoted a new constitutional scheme in 1983 establishing separate chambers of parliament for the so-called Coloureds and Asians, he was still groping to construct an alliance of minority groups that would exclude, and defend itself against, the black South African majority. When the United States appeared willing to accept the new constitution as a step in the right direction, Botha and his reformist allies were encouraged to think that they had American support on this important front.[6] It was the impression that the United States was identifying itself with the South African government's latest scheme for preserving and prolonging apartheid that was critical to the view of constructive engagement held by most black South Africans.

A major complicating factor for any outsiders who attempt to deal with the South African issue is that black South Africans have a view of the world quite different from their white countrymen. But they have no formal diplomatic representation—the few overseas offices of the ANC and the Pan Africanist Congress (PAC) have no meaningful diplomatic status, except at the United Nations—and not even any reliable informal ways of making their views known to the international community. They are as disenfranchised in the outside world as they are at home.

For years, contacts between Americans and black South Africans had grown stronger, in part through greater journalistic attention to South Africa in the United States, and in part through the growing inclination of American civil-rights and other organizations to become concerned about the South African problem. An assumption gained currency in South Africa during the presidency of John F. Kennedy that the United States sympathized with the plight of black South Africans and tended to take their side during incidents of repression and violence. Among other gestures, Kennedy's State Department for the first time required the American embassy in South Africa to invite blacks to official functions; the President's brother, Robert, was particularly involved with South Africa, and his visit there in 1964 is still remembered as an important gesture of solidarity with those who were fighting apartheid.

The Carter Administration sought to rekindle this spirit in American relations with South Africa, especially during its first two years in office. After the death of Black Consciousness leader Steve Biko at the hands of the South African police in 1977, the Carter Administration led the international chorus of outrage, and for a time it seemed as if American protests had helped to end deaths in detention in South Africa. Carter's rhetoric on the South African issue subsided as the practitioners of realpolitik gained the upper hand in his Administration, and he repeatedly disappointed those who were waiting for the United States to vote in the United Nations for international economic sanctions against South Africa. Yet the Carter years are nonetheless regarded by some South African blacks as a time when America was ready to help.

In the heady early days of constructive engagement, however, the Reagan Administration seemed obsessed with a need to demonstrate classic American qualities of evenhandedness. In one speech in August 1981 to the annual convention of the American Legion in Honolulu, Mr. Crocker stressed that "it is not our task to choose between black and white" in South Africa, where the United States sought "to build a more constructive relationship . . . based on shared interests, persuasion, and improved communication." While reiterating that the Reagan Administration disapproved of "apartheid policies that are abhorrent to our own multiracial democracy," Crocker said that "we must avoid action that aggravates the awesome challenges facing South Africans of all races. The Reagan Administration has no intention of destabilizing South Africa in order to curry favor elsewhere."[7]

To some black South African leaders, not to choose sides between the oppressors and the oppressed was tantamount to buttressing the oppressors. Already, in March 1981, Bishop Desmond Tutu, then secretary-general of the South African Council of Churches, had warned that "a United States decision to align itself with the South African government would be an unmitigated disaster for both South Africa and the United States." Tutu cautioned that the appearance of a reconciliation between Pretoria and the most influential government in the West would negate years of attempts by black South Africans to achieve a peaceful realization of their political ambitions.[8]

Four months later, a well-known black South African academic, N. Chabani Manganyi of the University of the Witwatersrand, told a Johannesburg conference that "blacks, both in South Africa and elsewhere in Africa, interpreted the policy of constructive engagement as an act of choice—or moral choice. They see the choice as a very simple matter in that it is a choice between South Africa and its domestic policies and the rest of the world." Manganyi called upon the Reagan Administration to fulfill its moral obligation to the people of South Africa and the international community by applying pressure for change; he said that whereas the Carter Administration had given blacks hope, "it could well be that President Reagan is preparing us for despair."[9]

So preoccupied was the Reagan Administration with sending signals to South Africa's white minority, however, that it is not clear its representatives paid heed to such warnings. Crocker exacerbated the situation by failing to include formal, public meetings with black South Africans on the itineraries of his many trips to South Africa, which received prominent coverage in the South African press. One black South African newspaper claimed that between January 1982 and December 1984, Crocker had met formally with only fifteen South African blacks, and that all of those meetings took place in the United States.[10] As a result, it became all the more difficult for him and other representatives of the American government to encounter blacks and solicit their views informally; increasing numbers of them (and even of white liberals) refused to attend functions given by U.S. diplomats in South Africa.

Especially offensive to some black South Africans was the fact that the United States expressed no opposition to the Pretoria government's latest divide-and-rule tactic, the new constitution creating separate chambers of parliament for so-called Coloureds and Asians—nor to the conduct of a whites-only referendum in November 1983 for approval of the constitution. In a speech to the National Conference of Editorial Writers in San Francisco in June 1983, U.S. Under Secretary of State Lawrence Eagleburger stated:

> I do not see it as our business to enter into this debate or to endorse the constitutional proposals now under consideration. Nor do we offer tactical advice to any of the interested parties. Yet the indisputable fact which we must recognize is that the South African government has taken the first step toward extending political rights beyond the white minority.[11]

In the view of black South Africans, who were almost universally opposed to the new constitution (even the leaders of six of the homelands urged a negative vote in the referendum), the United States could hardly have devised a clearer endorsement of the proposals.

In August 1983 more than 570 organizations, with members from all races, joined in a movement that pledged to work actively against the new constitution. The result was the United Democratic Front (UDF), which eventually orchestrated a massive boycott of the September 1984 elections for "Coloured" and Indian members of parliament. Only 30.9 percent of "Coloureds" and 20.3 percent of Indians who had taken the step of registering actually cast their votes; some of South Africa's new non-white parliamentarians went to Cape Town on the basis of the votes of only a few hundred people.[12] Most blacks saw the new institutions as a farce.

The identification of Washington with some of the most detested devices of the white regime may have helped to discredit black South African leaders who were not entirely ill-disposed to the United States, as well as American liberal politicians who were willing to support only moderate tactics in the struggle against apartheid. Thus, the radical Azanian People's Organization (AZAPO), a Black Consciousness group, demonstrated against Senator Edward M. Kennedy (D-Mass.) and succeeded in ruining his visit to South Africa early in 1985. Meanwhile, black spokesmen such as Dr. Nthatho Motlana, who had been an early activist in the ANC and, as chairman of the "Committee of Ten," had the support of his community in confronting the authorities during the Soweto riots of 1976, now appeared increasingly irrelevant to the more militant youths in the townships who called each other "comrade."[13]

So far had things moved by the time P. W. Botha declared a state of emergency in certain parts of the country in July 1985 that it was not clear that the countrywide violence could be halted even if the ANC were brought into the dialogue. It seemed obvious that the ANC leaders sitting in other African capitals were as surprised as anyone else by the turn of events inside South Africa, and perhaps equally unable to control what happened. Whereas the ANC banner had often been displayed at political funerals over the years, on at least one occasion, in Cradock, eastern Cape province, it was now accompanied by the Soviet flag.

American officials who spoke on behalf of constructive engagement liked to stress as often as possible that it was intended not merely as a policy toward South Africa, but as an effort to deal with the entire southern African region and its problems—thus Washington's promotion of direct talks between South Africa and Angola and its pleasure over the signing of the Nkomati accord between South Africa and Mozambique.

Most governments in the region, however, saw few benefits from constructive engagement. On the contrary, they saw evidence of a dangerous new South African military ascendancy, as the South African Defense Force seemed newly emboldened to strike across frontiers—into Mozambique, Lesotho, Botswana and, above all, Angola —in pursuit of ANC or SWAPO guerrillas and activists. The South Africans certainly supplied and trained the Mozambique National Resistance (MNR or Renamo), whose destructive war against the hard-pressed government of Samora Machel drove him to sign the Nkomati Accord. (The accord called for Mozambique to expel ANC guerrillas in exchange for a suspension of South African aid to the MNR; documents recently discovered in Pretoria revealed that while Mozambique kept its part of the bargain, South Africa did not.) South Africa also kept up the pressure on the Marxist government in Angola by continuing to supply the rebel forces of the National Union for the Total Independence of Angola (UNITA) led by Jonas Savimbi. What is more, there have been few moments during the past ten years when there were not substantial numbers of South African troops inside Angola itself; last spring, South African commandos were captured in the Cabinda enclave (a part of Angola that is separated from the rest by a thin piece of Zaire) as they were preparing to sabotage an American-owned oil drilling installation.

At the same time, South Africa also found economic means of destabilizing its neighbors and demonstrating its political hegemony over weaker states. The United States tried to put distance between itself and the South Africans on the issue of destabilization, frequently condemning its cross-border incursions and finally, after the raids in Cabinda and Botswana, withdrawing the American ambassador to Pretoria, Herman Nickel, for several months. Yet it seems clear that South Africa felt comfortable taking these steps against its neighbors without fear of serious recriminations from Washington.

Indeed, the U.S. Congress has been pushing the Administration to resume American aid to UNITA; while intended as a means of demonstrating toughness toward Cuba and the Soviet Union, this action would have the primary effect of advancing South Africa's interests in the region. Savimbi is clearly Pretoria's client, and is regarded as such throughout Africa; in fact, there is no way to aid him without going through South Africa.

For a time it appeared that the Reagan Administration would be willing to complement its new closeness with Pretoria with substantial aid programs for nearby black-ruled states. But those programs rarely materialized, and when they did, as in the case of Mozambique, opposition from conservatives on Capitol Hill made them almost impossible to carry out. In the case of Zimbabwe, where the United States had made an international commitment of aid at the time of independence in 1980, the Reagan Administration decided to punish Prime Minister Robert Mugabe for his foreign policy positions—including his sponsorship of a U.N. resolution condemning the U.S. invasion of Grenada in 1983—by cutting back substantially.

Constructive engagement, then, has failed on every front and with all of its constituencies.

The American public has seen little to indicate new U.S. diplomatic or strategic strength in southern Africa; on the contrary, the region is in as much turmoil as ever, and the Soviets have suffered few notable setbacks. The Cubans are still in Angola, and Namibia is no closer to independence; indeed, the South Africans instituted a new internal regime there, in direct defiance of American wishes.

Within South Africa itself, the United States has given a great deal and seen little progress as a result. The only concrete achievements of constructive engagement, apart from the shattered Angolan–South African truce and the now discredited Nkomati accord, were a brief period of leniency by the Pretoria government toward black trade unions and the granting of passports to black spokesmen invited to the United States, such as Tutu and Motlana.

But the Reagan Administration can hardly claim that constructive engagement has brought about genuine improvements in the lives of South Africans. On the contrary, the piecemeal reforms that have been enacted in the past five years have been the object of resentment. The introduction of the new tricameral parliamentary system has coincided with the most devastating internal violence the country has experienced since the formation of the unified South African state in 1910. Since September 1984, unrest has flared in every part of the country, and the imposition of the state of emergency has done little to quell it. In addition to hundreds of known deaths and thousands of detentions, more than one hundred South Africans have mysteriously vanished, many of them suspected victims of clandestine elements within the state security apparatus. The South African economy is in a shambles, and the country has been forced to postpone payment of many of its international debts. In some rural areas, such as the strife-torn eastern Cape, black unemployment is estimated to be as high as 60 percent.

The South African government, having expected so much, is itself disappointed with constructive engagement. It has reverted to old-style denunciations of American pressure as counterproductive, and it is furious over even the limited sanctions—worried that other nations may do the same or more and weaken the South African economy further. Far from strengthening its network of homelands, South Africa now finds itself having to think about dismantling them altogether or using them to create a new "federation." Its economic and military dominance of southern Africa is apparently intact, but it is not clear how long that will last if domestic turmoil continues. South Africa's formidable military machine is now required almost full time to help suppress internal unrest, despite an announced increase of 25 percent in recruitments into the police force.

Black South Africans are, if anything, becoming more disillusioned with the United States. Their impression is that, although some sanctions have been instituted by executive order and American officials continue to condemn apartheid and demand further reforms, Washington is still collaborating substantially with the apartheid system rather than calculating further measures against the white government. It was particularly telling that when a clinic run by Winnie Mandela, wife of Nelson Mandela, the imprisoned leader of the ANC, was firebombed during the recent violence, she refused an offer of official American assistance to rebuild it.

According to the limited opinion polls that are available, Nelson Mandela remains the most popular black leader in South Africa; having been ignored by the United States all these years, it is difficult to imagine that he would be sympathetic to American concerns in South Africa's crisis. Some analysts believe that Mandela himself may soon be overtaken by the quickening pace of radicalization in South Africa; it may be that those who inherit his mantle will be overtly hostile to the United States. With President Reagan appearing at times to justify the excesses committed by the South African government under the terms of the state of emergency and at other times seeming to exaggerate the degree of reform that has already taken place, the United States is viewed increasingly by black South Africans as part of the problem rather than part of the solution.

Similarly, other southern African states are blaming constructive engagement for much of their own distress. In some cases, overestimating the degree of actual American influence on the South African government, they have developed unrealistic expectations of what the United States can do to improve their situations, and they are bound to be disappointed.

It is time for a new American policy toward South Africa that will help restore the reputation of the United States as a defender of human rights and racial justice in that country and serve the broader interests of all South Africans and Americans.

There are, of course, important limitations on America's ability to affect the situation in South Africa. The U.S. military is not about to intervene on any side in any current or future crisis; it is foolish for whites or blacks in South Africa to believe otherwise (as some of them do). Nor can American leaders wave political or economic wands that will transform South Africa overnight. Indeed, American sanctions or moves toward disinvestment from the South African economy are sometimes more important on both sides as symbols than as practical measures; when sanctions are invoked, they should be carefully calibrated and thoughtfully applied. Given the level of suffering that already exists in the country, it is in no one's interest to destroy the South African economy or to induce further chaos in the country. And despite the frequent declarations from many quarters about the willingness of black South Africans to endure sacrifices in exchange for eventual freedom, it is not for the United States to condemn them to more abject poverty and deprivation. Disinvestment efforts within the United States should be directed only against particular firms that are known to have conducted themselves in an antisocial, regressive manner within South Africa. As for the continued presence of American business in South Africa, individual companies, evaluating their risks on the basis of hard-nosed, pragmatic criteria, are making their own rational decisions on whether to stay or not.

But there are some official steps that the United States can take in an effort to move South Africa toward meaningful change and full participation by all of its people in the affairs of the country. If Americans still want to try to assure that the South African transition occurs relatively peacefully and with a minimum of vindictiveness on the part of blacks, then there is little time left to act.

The first step, uncomfortable as it may seem to many Americans, is to restore a forthright atmosphere of public and private confrontation to relations between Washington and Pretoria—precisely the sort of independent attitude that Mr. Crocker has eschewed. Internal and external pressure is the only thing that has ever produced meaningful change in South Africa. American officials need to become far more direct and persistent in their condemnations of apartheid. Speeches at the National Press Club in Washington alone cannot do the job. U.S. representatives in South Africa must be willing to denounce and even defy the system whenever possible, making clear their official and personal support for organizations like the UDF and Black Sash, the women's group that represents the victims of arbitrary "pass arrests" and other government actions. Some things may have to be said or done many times before they are believed or credited by disillusioned blacks.

All of this would have the immediate effect of helping develop a healthier, more vigorous multiracial opposition within South Africa, which would be far more difficult for the regime to crush if it clearly enjoyed outside support. If an American decision to confront apartheid more boldly also stiffened the resolve of other Western nations and ultimately led to a growing international vote of no confidence in the leadership of P. W. Botha, that too would be a desirable turn of events. It is now obvious that as long as he remains in power, the National Party will not be able to form or endorse the alliances with other political factions that are necessary to head off full-scale civil war.

The current South African government, under the short-sighted impression that it has profited from a five-year interlude of conciliation with the United States, would be bitterly resentful of such a reversion to prior strategy by Washington. It would undoubtedly attempt once again to profit politically from American hostility and would proclaim, as it must, that this is the surest way for the United States to lose, rather than gain, influence in South Africa. But the truth is that South Africa has few other places to turn. It is dependent on the United States, in spirit as well as in fact; fellow "pariah states" such as Israel and Taiwan—its other current friends—simply cannot do for South Africa what America can do. And if constructive confrontation hastened the start of negotiations over real power in South Africa, which constructive engagement has failed to do, that would be a step forward.

Once having restored a proper sense of balance and confrontation to U.S.–South African relations, it would be important for the American government and private business interests to devise additional measures that might hurt the pride and prestige of the white South African government without inflicting undue economic damage on black South Africans. Some of the measures should be selectively instituted for predetermined periods, in response to particular events in South Africa, with the American government making it clear that they may be lifted if circumstances improve. Alternatively, if the situation continues to deteriorate, the pressures could be intensified.

The landing rights enjoyed by the state-owned South African Airways in the United States can be reduced or terminated. The availability of almost daily direct service between Johannesburg and New York, with only a stop in the Cape Verde Islands, is a great advantage to South African businessmen and officials, and, since Pan American abandoned its service for economic reasons last year, the South African state airline has had a monopoly on the route's substantial profits. Far from considering this step, which has frequently been proposed in the past, the Reagan Administration actually expanded South African Airways' landing rights in the United States in 1982, permitting direct service between Johannesburg and Houston (later suspended). The cancellation of direct air service is a sanction the United States has frequently taken to demonstrate disapproval of actions by other governments—including the Soviet Union, Cuba, Poland and Nicaragua. Because of the importance to South Africans of their links to the outside world, this would probably be more likely to have an effect in South Africa than it did in those other countries.

The United States can take steps to reduce South Africa's privileged diplomatic status here. South African military attachés can be expelled, for example, especially in the wake of external raids and other objectionable actions by the South African Defense Force. The visa-application process for South Africans who wish to travel to the United States can be made as complicated and cumbersome as it is already for Americans who seek to visit South Africa. And if Pretoria proceeds with its policy of making it more difficult for American journalists to travel to South Africa, and to have the necessary access when they do get there, then the number of official South African information officers permitted in the United States can be reduced.

The United States has recently sought South African permission to open a new consulate in Port Elizabeth to establish an official American presence in the troubled eastern Cape. The Reagan Administration must take care not to grant unnecessary concessions in exchange; South Africa already has four full-fledged and four honorary consulates in the United States.

The flow of new American technology to South Africa can be further restricted, especially as it relates to the repressive domestic tactics of the South African government and its raids against neighboring countries. President Reagan's restriction on the shipment of computers to South Africa had little immediate effect because most of the material to which it applied was already in South African hands or could easily be obtained from other countries. Rigorous steps can be taken, however, including the use of U.S. Customs Service agents and other law enforcement personnel, to be sure that other American technological advances do not reach the South African police or military, directly or through third countries. It would also be possible to improve American compliance with the international arms embargo against South Africa and to take further steps to prevent nuclear material from reaching the country. It is widely known that some American companies operating in South Africa are involved in strategic industries, and therefore in the regime's domestic and international war effort; this could be prevented with new federal rules governing American corporate behavior in South Africa.

The U.S. government can severely restrict, or even suspend entirely, its intelligence cooperation with the South African government. There is reason to believe that these ties have helped the South Africans far more than the United States, and they carry the implication that the United States is complicit in some of the worst abuses committed by South Africa against neighboring countries. One of the most troubling aspects of this problem is that some operatives of U.S. intelligence agencies and some State Department employees who have served in South Africa are outspokenly sympathetic to the apartheid policies of the white regime and have occasionally used their positions to thwart official American actions and directives.

The United States can seek to internationalize discussion of the South African issue by putting it on the agenda of the annual Western economic summits. This would be a way of coordinating economic pressures on South Africa, and also of trying to persuade recalcitrant nations, such as Japan, which has richly profited from its pragmatic relationship with South Africa (the Japanese have status as "honorary whites"), to go along with the measures.

Even more important, perhaps, are positive, lasting steps that the United States can take to demonstrate its sympathy for the black majority in South Africa and to show that it does not believe all change there must be white-led.

The United States must open a dialogue with the African National Congress and other black organizations that have widespread support among black South Africans, just as Secretary of State George Shultz has suggested the white South Africans themselves should do. Not to know what the ANC, the oldest black nationalist organization in South Africa, is thinking and doing is not only bad diplomacy but also foolish politics. If South African businessmen and white opposition politicians have recently held such discussions, certainly American officials will be taking no great risk by doing so. As it is, there is a feeling among some black South Africans that the attitude of the ANC may now be too moderate, in view of the pace of events within South Africa, and thus the United States may have to open relations with much more radical organizations. This contact with black South African leaders should take place at the ambassadorial level, both inside and outside South Africa, as a means of stressing the American rejection of the notion that the white government is the only meaningful political institution in the country.

The United States should send a black ambassador—a man or woman of international stature—to South Africa as

soon as possible, to demonstrate important points of princi-
ple to South Africans of all racial groups. Above all, this
would be an opportunity to emphasize the valuable role
that black people play in a multiracial society and a system
which South Africans often compare to their own. Some
might complain that such an appointment smacks of toke-
nism, but if the ambassador behaved in an appropriate
manner, his presence would be of more than symbolic
value. For example, this new ambassador should attend
the funerals of blacks killed by the police, political trials
and church services in black communities. He should provide facilities for the meetings of groups that are trying to
organize peaceful protests against the apartheid system
and, in other respects, make it clear that he is the ambassador of all Americans to all South Africans, not just of
white America to white South Africa. He should not take
it upon himself to play American politics in South Africa
—as the current U.S. ambassador did when he denounced
Senator Kennedy while introducing him at a meeting of
the American Chamber of Commerce of Johannesburg—
but rather should take it as one of his jobs to convey to
South Africans the depth of American feeling against
apartheid and the so far inadequate steps to dismantle it.

Massive aid programs, funded by the American govern-
ment, foundations and business, should be instituted to help
black South Africans attain better educations in a broad
range of fields, from engineering to international relations.
The money for such programs should be distributed to all
South African educational institutions, regardless of their
nature, but special attention should be paid to encouraging the further integration of the mostly white elite universities. The committees that decide how this money is to be
spent should have a majority of black South Africans.
American-sponsored educational programs already avail-

able have barely scratched the surface; what is needed now is an effort to help black South Africans learn how to help run their country, an eventuality that seems not to have occurred to the ruling whites.

The United States should offer publicly to send forensic pathologists and other experts from the Federal Bureau of Investigation into South Africa to help find South Africans who have mysteriously disappeared and to help determine the cause of death of those who have been found. This has proved to be an effective technique in Central American countries such as El Salvador, where the police do not always care to solve crimes. The South African police are - accused of acting to frustrate, rather than advance, the solution of some crimes against black people, and such outside help might well be appropriate. If the South Africans at first refuse such aid, the United States should offer it again and again, until its refusal becomes an embarrassment and a liability to the white government.

The United States government, in conjunction with professional groups such as the American Bar Association, should also send legal aid to black South Africans. Although the legal systems differ in certain important respects, the American experience with public defenders and government-funded legal services is an excellent example for the South Africans. American law schools and private foundations, for example, could help train black South Africans as paralegal workers, who in turn could establish elementary legal clinics in remote areas of the country, where the civil and human rights of blacks are the most egregiously and routinely violated; these paralegal workers could in turn report to lawyers, who make sure that the abuses are brought to the attention of the courts and the press. The American legal community could also assist the South Africans in the creation of a lawyers' organization in which blacks play a prominent role. (Such an association of doctors and dentists was recently established in South Africa, but unfortunately it is still not officially recognized by the American Medical Association.)

The United States should not only support the efforts of the black-led labor unions in South Africa, but where possible, should also send expert American union organizers to help them strengthen their institutions. Until and unless other structures are established, South Africa's black unions represent one of the few ways that the disenfranchised majority can become involved in political action, and American labor organizations have relevant experience to offer in this domain.

The American government should carefully monitor the performance of U.S. companies operating in South Africa, with a view toward creating and publicizing a list of those who treat their black workers badly. Indeed, American companies should be pressed by their government into playing a far more progressive role in South Africa—for example, by ignoring the Group Areas Act and establishing mixed housing areas where black and white South Africans can create de facto integrated neighborhoods. U.S. businesses operating in South Africa should also make every effort to visit any of their employees who are detained on political grounds and should establish a fund to be used for their legal defense.

The United States should help black South Africans increase and improve their means of communication with each other and the rest of the South African people. The exchange of South African and American journalists should be promoted, along with technical assistance in establishing black publications at the grass roots and black-oriented radio stations. Americans can help South

Africans understand that a free press can often be one of the most important safety valves available to a society where there is political discontent. Severe consequences should be invoked, such as restrictions on South African diplomatic personnel in the United States, if black publications are closed and banned in South Africa, as they often have been in the past.

In sum, courageous efforts must be made to convince black South Africans that Americans identify with their plight and are willing to help. There have been times in U.S.–South African relations—before constructive engagement—when officials from the American embassy were the first to be called by black activists in moments of crisis, and there were even U.S. officials in South Africa who occasionally sheltered political fugitives or helped them escape from the country. This was a role more consistent with American principles than the current one of keeping a distance from anyone charged by the government.

Recent developments indicate that P. W. Botha, far from responding creatively to the American confidence in him, is resorting once again to repression rather than reform. Concerned about minor electoral losses on the right, he is ignoring the rumbling volcano of discontent on the other side, from blacks and whites alike. His curbs on domestic and foreign press coverage of unrest in South Africa are a sign that the last vestiges of decency—South Africa's last claims to be part of the Western democratic tradition—may soon be destroyed in the defense of apartheid.

The United States must clearly and unequivocally disassociate itself from such measures. And it must resist the ever-present temptation to use southern Africa as a place to score points in the East-West struggle. Only after America rediscovers its voice—and its principles—in South Africa can it hope to play a truly constructive role in the region once again.

NOTES

1. In a telephone interview from his California ranch with WSB Radio in Atlanta on August 24, 1985, the President said that South Africa had "eliminated the segregation that we once had in our own country—the type of thing where hotels and restaurants and places of entertainment and so forth were segregated—that has all been eliminated. They recognize now interracial marriages and all." *Weekly Compilation of Presidential Documents,* Vol. 21, No. 35 (Sept. 2, 1985), Washington: G.P.O., p. 1004.
2. See Congressman John Conyers (D-Mich.), "Getting Tough with Pretoria," *The New York Times,* Jan. 23, 1985, p. A23.
3. Chester A. Crocker, "South Africa: Strategy for Change," *Foreign Affairs,* Winter 1980/81, pp. 323–351.
4. "U.S. Attitude Toward South Africa," Document 32, *The United States and South Africa: U.S. Public Statements and Related Documents, 1977–85,* Department of State, Washington: G.P.O., 1985, p. 58.
5. *TransAfrica News Report,* Washington, D.C., Vol. 1, No. 10 (Special Edition), August 1981.
6. The State Department has repeatedly sought to deny that it gave any encouragement to P. W. Botha's "new dispensation" for Asians and "Coloureds," but statements issued by U.S. Ambassador Herman Nickel in South Africa and by official spokesmen in Washington had that effect. Some of the statements were later withdrawn or amended, but the impression had already taken hold; many of the white liberals who campaigned for a negative vote in the whites-only referendum on the new constitution complained that Nickel seemed

to be taking the South African government's side. See, for example, the Johannesburg newspapers *Rand Daily Mail,* August 28, 1983, p. 13; *The Star,* October 3, 1983, p. 7; *The Sunday Express,* November 6, 1983, p. 10; and *Vaderland,* November 18, 1983, p. 12.

7. "Regional Security for Southern Africa," Document 50, *The United States and South Africa: U.S. Public Statements and Related Documents, 1977–85,* pp. 79–84.

8. *Sunday Times* (Johannesburg), March 12, 1981, p. 2.

9. N. Chabani Manganyi, "The Washington-Pretoria Connection: Is There a Black Perspective?" in *The United States and South Africa: Continuity or Change?* (Johannesburg: South African Institute of International Affairs, 1981), pp. 50, 53.

10. *City Press* (Johannesburg), May 19, 1985, p. 2.

11. "Southern Africa: America's Responsibility for Peace and Change," Document 115. *The United States and South Africa: U.S. Public Statements and Related Documents, 1977–85,* pp. 189–196.

12. Another way of stating the turnout in the elections for the new chambers of Parliament is that 18.2 percent of the Coloureds eligible to vote did so, and that among Asians the comparable figure was 16.2 percent.

13. See, for example, Alan Cowell, "Generation Gap Adds Tension Among South African Blacks," *The New York Times,* September 18, 1985, p. 1. "Comrade" is a term used in southern Africa over the years among those committed to the overthrow of white minority regimes. For other comments by black South Africans about American policy see Stephen Weissman, "Dateline South Africa: The Opposition Speaks," *Foreign Policy,* Spring 1985, pp. 151–170.

DESTABILIZATION AND DEPENDENCE

David Martin and Phyllis Johnson

David Martin and Phyllis Johnson, former correspondents for The Observer *(London) and the Canadian Broadcasting Corporation, respectively, are directors of the Harare-based Zimbabwe Publishing House, which they established in 1981. They are the authors of* The Struggle for Zimbabwe: The Chimurenga War, The Chitepo Assassination *and contributors and editors of* Destructive Engagement: Southern Africa at War.

Many explanations have been offered for the sudden, schizophrenic changes in South Africa's behavior toward its neighbors during the diplomatic and military maneuvers of the past few years. The factors most often cited include South Africa's economic weaknesses, the high cost of its war in Namibia, pressure from its allies and certainly the pressure of internal dissent. These are all valid considerations. But there is another aspect: the South African leadership has orchestrated wars against its neighbors with political and economic objectives in mind. The cynical view in Pretoria is that, in the words of the of the *Economist,* "detente failed because the black states were not well enough motivated to talk to 'racist' South Africa openly. Destabilization helped to provide that motivation."

There is no single term adequate to describe this heavy blend of military/economic destabilization and political dialogue that has evolved as South Africa's regional strat-

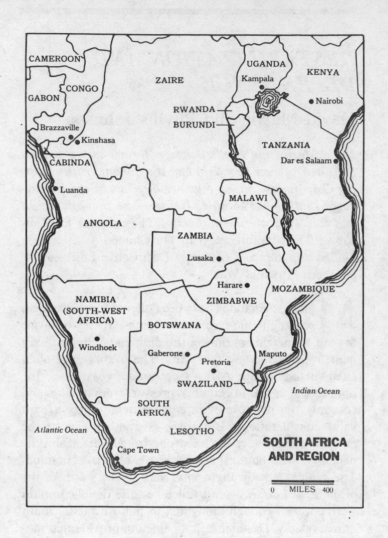

CAMEROON
CONGO
GABON
Brazzaville
Kinshasa
CABINDA
Luanda
ANGOLA
NAMIBIA
(SOUTH-WEST
AFRICA)
Windhoek
Atlantic Ocean
SOUTH
AFRICA
Cape Town
LESOTHO
ZAIRE
UGANDA
Kampala
RWANDA
BURUNDI
ZAMBIA
Lusaka
BOTSWANA
Gaberone
Pretoria
Harare
ZIMBABWE
SWAZILAND
KENYA
Nairobi
TANZANIA
Dar es Salaam
MALAWI
MOZAMBIQUE
Maputo
Indian Ocean

SOUTH AFRICA
AND REGION

0   MILES   400

egy after several shifts in emphasis over the past decade. The aims of this regional policy seem clear enough in the short term: to prevent neighboring states from hosting antiapartheid guerrillas and to tighten economic interdependence in the region in the hope of avoiding sanctions and broadening markets for South African goods. "Don't speak of destabilization," officials in Pretoria scoff. "Call it our forward policy, our foreign policy."

Attempts by former South African Prime Minister John Vorster to begin a "dialogue" between South Africa and its neighbors culminated in his crossing the Victoria Falls Bridge from Rhodesia into Zambia in August 1975, at the same time as his troops occupied a 30-mile strip of southern Angola. This "detente" collapsed a few weeks later when the South Africans moved north in a full-scale invasion of Angola, and the flames of future destabilization were ignited. Vorster's successor, Prime Minister P. W. Botha, announced his plan for a "constellation of states" in 1978. But this was disrupted by Robert Mugabe's victory in the Zimbabwe elections and the formation of the Southern African Development Coordination Conference (SADCC), a group of nine nations committed to regional development as a means of reducing their economic dependence on South Africa.

A parallel strategy grew out of the array of new circumstances that presented themselves, not the least of which was the outcome of elections in the United States and Ronald Reagan's move to the White House in 1981. The policy of "constructive engagement" developed by the State Department's Africa desk was also evolving under the Assistant Secretary of State for African Affairs, Chester A. Crocker, with a wide variety of options for "identifying regional strategy." These options included the possibility that South Africa might bludgeon its neighbors to the bargaining table.

Since two of the key states in the region—Mozambique and Angola—have close relations with the Soviet Union, that was not necessarily an uncomfortable option. Secretary of State George P. Shultz spoke of encouraging "positive change" in the apartheid policies of South Africa while building "an overall framework for regional security." Through 1982 and 1983 his negotiators made cautious contacts in the region, presenting themselves as the "honest brokers" who could deal with both sides. And they persuaded South African officials to cool their rhetoric regarding the need for a "total national strategy" against a "total onslaught."[1]

Meanwhile, South Africa had escalated its military pressure, covertly in Mozambique on its northeastern border, overtly in Angola on the west coast, and in varying degrees toward the states in the middle. This military action cloaked economic goals, concentrated as it was on the two states with outlets to the sea, thus determining the degree of economic dependence of the landlocked states in between. There are, of course, risks involved in such action. In December 1983, the South African Defence Force (SADF), pushing further into Southern Angola, ran headlong into Angolan government forces equipped with new Soviet weaponry which blunted the offensive (code-named Operation Askari) and curtailed South Africa's ability to intervene further.

By this time, the price of gold, which accounted for almost half of South Africa's export revenues, had dropped to roughly half its 1980 level, and the rand had begun to plummet on international money markets. The South African administration needed breathing space, time to reassess strategy and reequip, to rebuild some international credibility and await an economic upturn or outside assistance.

By early 1984, there were signed agreements between the South African government and three of its neighbors. On March 16, amid much pomp and ceremony beside a river on their common border, the leaders of Mozambique and South Africa, Samora Machel and P. W. Botha, signed an "Agreement on Non-Aggression and Good-Neighborliness," known as the Nkomati Accord. Swaziland then revealed the signing two years earlier of an agreement with South Africa on security matters. One month before Nkomati, South Africa and Angola had signed, in Lusaka, Zambia, an "understanding" which led to a phased but long-uncompleted withdrawal of South African troops from southern Angola.

After these and other maneuvers, the U.S. negotiators said publicly that they believed they were closer than ever before to achieving a package involving the final withdrawal of South African troops from Angola, the implementation of U.N. Resolution 435 leading to the independence of Namibia, and the phased withdrawal of Cuban troops from Angola. In reality, they had created breathing space until after the U.S. presidential election and before the next round of economic and military destabilization.

Ronald Reagan began his second term in early 1985, and by the end of the year the political climate in southern Africa had changed again. The South African military had reoccupied part of southern Angola after a preemptive strike in open support of antigovernment rebels. The South African foreign minister had publicly admitted that his government had violated the Nkomati Accord by continuing to supply the Mozambique National Resistance and that his deputy had clandestinely visited the main MNR base in central Mozambique three times since the accord was signed. South African commandos had raided the capitals of Botswana and Lesotho, and SADF patrols had threatened Swazi villagers. There had been threats to invade Zimbabwe and a military buildup on the border. Then, in early 1986, a South African blockade of Lesotho turned into southern Africa's first military coup d'etat.

As dialogue once again dissolved into destabilization, the most difficult pressure for South Africa to contain— militarily, economically, and psychologically—was on the home front, with the swelling of internal dissent and increased guerrilla attacks on economic and military targets inside the country. With most access routes through South Africa's immediate neighbors—known as the "front-line states"—sealed off, this showed a strong presence within the country of armed members of the African National Congress, including, no doubt, many young people who fled South Africa after the Soweto clashes almost ten years before and who have now returned as combatants.

Since no country bordering South Africa now allows, officially or unofficially, passage to armed guerrillas seeking to end the system of apartheid, can President Botha continue to insist that the country's enemy is external? Or must the South African government finally address itself to the source of the real threat to apartheid? Is it only a coincidence that South Africa has suffered its worst sustained outbreak of violence and demonstrations in the period since Nkomati? Or has the message "This is first and foremost your struggle" been received loud and clear in South Africa's black townships? And was not the Nkomati Accord a signal, quickly understood by the National Liberation Movement, to reexamine its strategies that relied heavily on neighboring countries, which could not hope to withstand South Africa's military might? Only time can answer these questions. But the curious irony of

Pretoria's regional behavior may well be that the Nkomati Accord made a major contribution to the acceleration of the struggle within South Africa itself.

Under the Nkomati Accord, Mozambique and South Africa undertook to respect each other's territorial integrity, refrain from interfering in each other's internal affairs, recognize the right of self-determination as well as the principle of "equal rights of all peoples," refrain from the threat of force against each other, prevent their territories from being used for acts of aggression against each other and promote good-neighborliness. Each side agreed to eliminate from its territory all bases, radio stations and other facilities that were being used by forces hostile to each other, and the two governments agreed to set up a joint security commission to monitor the accord.

Many friends of the Mozambican regime were stunned by the agreement, and the African National Congress, which had been using Mozambique as a rear base in its guerrilla war against the apartheid system, reacted angrily. A statement from the ANC national executive committee accused Pretoria of using "so-called nonaggression pacts" to reduce independent states in the region to the status of the Bantustans, or black "homeland" areas within South Africa. ANC President Oliver Tambo, however, urged understanding of Mozambique's position: "It must be accepted that the South African regime had decided to destroy Mozambique, to kill it as a state, and the leadership was forced to choose between life and death. So if it meant hugging the hyena, they had to do it."

At the time of Nkomati, Mozambique had been at war for almost twenty years. Its liberation war against Portuguese colonial rule lasted a decade, until the peace agreement of 1974, which led to independence the following year. By that time, Rhodesian troops were operating inside Mozambique against Zimbabwean guerrillas. The Rhodesian war had a devastating impact on the new nation's fragile economy and infrastructure. Then, after 1980, the Mozambique National Resistance began escalating its efforts, massively backed by South Africa, and war-weary Mozambique was plunged into a third consecutive conflict.

After the Nkomati Accord, President Machel observed that the struggle against the MNR had left his country with "severe wounds." No one knew the number of people murdered, maimed or mutilated by the *bandidos armados* (armed bandits), as they are known in Mozambique. By the end of 1983, South Africa had taken the war into all ten provinces and the MNR numbered about 15,000. Psychologically most important in understanding Mozambique's decision to sign the agreement was the fact that, as a result of MNR attacks against supply routes, thousands of people had died or were dying from the effects of drought.

In the Portuguese colonial era, Mozambique had been developed as a service country for South Africa and the landlocked African hinterland, and its transportation network provided the bulk of its foreign currency earnings. Sanctions against Rhodesia, which Mozambique imposed in 1976, a few months after its own independence, cost about one-third of Mozambique's foreign currency earnings. South Africa applied further economic pressure by reducing the flow of goods through the port of Maputo, limiting the influx of Mozambican labor to its mines and terminating a preferential agreement on gold prices. Bare shops and shelves, unending queues for the little that was available, rationing, arrested development, a total absence of foreign investment and, finally, the need to reschedule the national debt were all symptomatic of the horrendous price Mozambique was paying.

After Zimbabwe's independence in 1980, the government of Robert Mugabe began a concerted policy of returning to the country's traditional transportation routes, and movement through Mozambique increased to 53.9 percent of Zimbabwe's total traffic in 1983. This represented a prospective change in the regional dependence on South African ports and rail routes, used especially by Zimbabwe, Zambia and Zaire. This process of economic recovery and the growing signs of regional economic independence were the most important reasons for South Africa's decision to unleash the MNR against Mozambique, ensuring continued dependence upon South Africa's routes. In 1984, Zimbabwean rail traffic through Mozambique was reduced to 33.1 percent, of which more than half had to transit South Africa to reach Maputo. After the sabotage of the important Chicualacuala rail line to Maputo in August 1984, the figure in 1985 dropped below 10 percent.

On their side, the South Africans became deeply involved in supporting the MNR, which they had inherited from Rhodesia in March 1980 after Mugabe won the Zimbabwe elections. Immediately following that vote, South African military aircraft evacuated MNR personnel from Zimbabwe, moving them to Phalaborwa in the eastern Transvaal. It was a ragtag band of semitrained young men that had been set up by Rhodesian intelligence to monitor the movements of Mugabe's guerrillas in Mozambique. But the South Africans had other plans for them and began an intensive program of military training.

This adopted force was soon unleashed against Mozambique. By sea and air, trained MNR personnel and their equipment were carried into Mozambique, a sophisticated radio network was set up, SADF instructors were based inside Mozambique at MNR camps consisting of up to 800 huts and the MNR's clandestine "Voz de Africa Livre" (Voice of Free Africa) radio station broadcast its message from studios of the South African Broadcasting Corporation near Johannesburg. All the indications were that Pretoria was determined to overthrow the Mozambique government and that it was not too far from success. Why, then, did Pretoria sign the Nkomati Accord?

Although South Africa is militarily and economically the region's superpower, it confronted mounting difficulties in 1983 and early 1984. The Mozambican resistance did not have a viable leadership or a set of alternative policies and, in southern Angola, South African forces had suffered casualties in men and equipment in Operation Askari. Most important, the South African economy was under pressure. Gold prices, which in early 1980 peaked at $850 an ounce, fell to $340 an ounce in New York by mid-1984. Gold accounted for 49 percent of export revenue in 1983; for every dollar the price dropped, South Africa lost almost $20 million. Nor was the south spared the drought which affected much of the African continent. In 1981, South Africa's maize crop had been fourteen million tons, leaving an export surplus after domestic consumption of about seven million tons, but the crop prediction for 1984 was put as low as 3.5 million tons.

The strain of the gold slump and the drought had to be borne by the currency; the rand plummeted from a value of 85 U.S. cents in March 1984 to just under 50 cents at year's end. Three years earlier the rand had been worth $1.30. In addition, and in contrast to most of its main trading partners, South Africa faced a continued inflation rate of around 12 percent. Finally, defense spending accounted for 21.5 percent of the total South African budget in 1984. The war in Namibia and Angola, and assistance in topping up the budget of Namibia, cost South Africa over $1 billion. No figures are available for the cost of destabilization actions in Lesotho, Mozambique and Zimbabwe in that period, but the bill was obviously considerable. Clearly, by early 1984, the costs of confrontation, when viewed against the backdrop of a weakened economy (which would cause South Africa to renege on short-term foreign debts the following year), presented a telling argument for a parallel policy of diplomacy. In addition, Samora Machel and his government had indicated a willingness to improve relations with the United States, which now moved in to handle the bargaining.

The South African decision to pursue a policy diversion occurred in the last quarter of 1983, according to U.S. State Department officials closely involved in the "constructive engagement" process. These officials say the U.S. role consisted of "assisting communication" and "building confidence." When Assistant Secretary of State Crocker visited Mozambique in January 1983, the American perspective, presented in regional and global terms, was that Mozambique's support for the African National Congress threatened Washington's major ally in the region, South Africa, and that Washington's support for Pretoria was threatening U.S. relations with independent African states, some of whom might seek military aid from the Eastern Bloc. In addition, instability in the region was adversely affecting investment, but the American government accepted that there was a connection between regional instability and apartheid and saw the need for Pretoria to begin a process of reform.

The first round of the decisive series of public talks occurred in Mbabane, Swaziland, in December 1983 as a result of the efforts, the Mozambicans say, of Chester Crocker's deputy, Frank Wisner. After a second meeting in Pretoria, three South African government ministers traveled to Maputo, carrying their draft of a proposed agreement demanding the total removal of the ANC from Mozambique. This draft was very different from the one which was finally signed at Nkomati. "It went so far that it would have meant we could not even have Miriam Makeba in Mozambique to give a concert," a senior official said. The essence of the Nkomati Accord was that Mozambique undertook to prevent the ANC from using and traversing its territory for attacks on South Africa, and South Africa undertook to end its covert support for the MNR. It is noteworthy that the South African government, which had previously denied involvement with the MNR, tacitly admitted such involvement by signing the accord and later confirmed this in Parliament.

There were indications within a few months of its signing that the accord was in danger of foundering, amid suspicions that "elements" in South Africa were still supporting the MNR. By late 1984, some Mozambican and U.S. officials were suggesting that these "elements" included members of the Portuguese government and the Portuguese community in South Africa, which numbers almost one million people, including many who had fled from Angola and Mozambique. By the end of 1985 there was confirmation that the MNR's supporters also included senior members of the SADF.

Several attempts to arrange a "cessation of armed activity" were made, including a secret meeting in Europe between a Mozambican government official and the MNR secretary-general, Evo Fernandes, who is a Portuguese citizen. Fernandes rejected the government's offer of amnesty and reintegration of forces, and continued to press for power-sharing. Two more meetings in Pretoria resulted in the Pretoria Declaration "on a cessation of armed activity and conflict." Mozambican government officials, who for the first and only time appeared publicly with the MNR on October 3, 1984, had obtained two important concessions: (1) recognition by the MNR of President Machel and therefore his government; and (2) agreement in principle on an unconditional cease-fire. The declaration proposed that the South African government should consider playing a role in its implementation. A few days later the next round of talks was broken off by Fernandes just as agreement appeared imminent.

The security situation continued to deteriorate in Maputo province and in northern provinces bordering on Malawi; and there is no doubt that Malawi was, and is, being used as a rear base. In the central provinces of Mozambique, where the Zimbabwean army has been guarding its vital transportation routes for three years, the main roads are transversed with relative impunity, and the oil pipeline and railway to Beira are rarely disrupted.

In June 1985 the leaders of Mozambique, Tanzania and Zimbabwe met to assess the situation, with Zimbabwe pledging further military involvement and Tanzania offering training facilities and deployment assistance to the Mozambican army. On August 28 a massive air and ground attack was made on the operational headquarters of the MNR, a base called "Casa Banana" at the foot of Gorongosa Mountain in the central Mozambican province of Sofala. The base, from which the MNR forces fled, was well stocked with supplies, including power generators, office equipment, radios, vehicles and a computerized system for transmitting coded messages. There was also a wealth of documentation—including minutes of meetings between the MNR and senior South African military officials—that incriminated the South African government and led to Foreign Minister Roelof F. ("Pik") Botha's embarrassing admission that the MNR had continued to receive supplies in breach of the Nkomati Accord ("mostly humanitarian aid," he claimed rather unconvincingly) and that the SADF had maintained radio contact with MNR bases and built an airstrip inside Mozambique.

The scrum of defensive South African statements that followed revealed serious tensions between the military and the Ministry of Foreign Affairs but did little to clarify the personal position of Prime Minister P. W. Botha or the policy of his government. The then–defense force chief, General Constand Viljoen, proclaimed his loyalty to his government and country and insisted that the SADF had accepted the official "change of strategy" toward the MNR. But he admitted that many of the facts contained in the Gorongosa documents were correct (though, he protested, sometimes slanted). Prime Minister Botha, a former minister of defense who had blamed politicians for the embarrassing military withdrawal from Angola in 1975, said publicly that he trusted Viljoen "unquestioningly."

Among the Gorongosa documents was a message from Viljoen to MNR leader Alfonso Dhlakama, promising support and explaining the problems that "we, South African military men, have with our politicians." The message guaranteed the movement of MNR personnel in and through South Africa should the need arise, and said Viljoen and his colleagues would resign if ordered to fight against the MNR. A diary records that Viljoen assured the MNR in a meeting on September 6, 1984, that he would facilitate MNR contacts with foreign countries, especially in Africa. He advised MNR commanders not to accept the

Mozambican government's offer of amnesty and not to be deceived by Foreign Minister Botha because "he is treacherous." The diary also records that microphones were to be installed to bug Pik Botha's meetings with Mozambican officials and Western ambassadors.

Opposition political parties in South Africa denounced the whole affair as a scandal. The right-wing Conservative Party blamed the two Bothas and Malan and said the episode was worse than the "Muldergate" information scandal of 1978 that ended John Vorster's term in office. In an article published September 25, 1985, the Johannesburg *Star,* saying such events would normally bring down a democratic government, condemned the "dishonesty, double standards and brutality . . . [that] has destroyed the nation's reputation and threatens its existence." The newspaper blamed the failure of Nkomati on arrogance, "in the belief that our security forces can do anything they like, without telling anyone outside a government clique. . . . Who can believe that the breach of the Nkomati Accord will be the last in a long list of politically dishonest moves which our once proud country has made in Angola, the Seychelles, Lesotho, Maputo, Botswana, Cabinda. And again in Angola and again in Mozambique. And again and again and again at home. When will it end?"

When first revealing the contents of the documents at a news conference in Maputo on September 30, 1985, the Mozambican security minister, Colonel Sergio Vieira, said there had been a "gentleman's agreement" that neither South Africa nor Mozambique would use the period between the Mbabane meeting and the signing of the Nkomati Accord three months later to infiltrate men and equipment or carry out reprisals. Yet the array of information contained in the Gorongosa documents presents detailed evidence of South Africa's pre- and post-Nkomati planning to breach or ignore the accord. Two distinct planning phases are apparent: reorganization, advance training, infiltration and supply in preparation for Nkomati; and massive response to appeals for assistance some months later. The documents describe the training of MNR instructors and recruits in South Africa and Namibia as well as inside Mozambique, their infiltration routes, and the dates and methods of entry by air and by sea of a six-months supply of weapons and ammunition throughout January, February and March 1984. Minutes of meetings contain instructions from the head of the South African Department of Military Intelligence, General Pieter van der Westhuizen, to target the rural economy, regional communications routes, and foreign-aid workers.

This was more than a violation of the gentleman's agreement, or dishonoring one's word, Colonel Vieira said: "These facts reveal a premeditated and organized act not to fulfill the accord." When the Mozambican government had produced evidence of violations of the accord at successive meetings in early 1984 and had inquired as to the whereabouts of the armed bandits and their weapons caches, South African officials had claimed they had severed all links and had parted from the MNR on "not-so-good terms."

The South African military had campaigned for the installation of radar on the border to prevent violations of Mozambique airspace, but Vieira said, "It is now clear that the same institution that installed the radar violated the accord, sending aircraft and constructing landing strips. . . . When [we] . . . denounced the sea violations, the South African side denied them and . . . publicly stated that they were ready to patrol Mozambican waters to prevent sea landings. It is now clear . . . that the same institution that pretended to patrol our territorial waters sent submarines and assault ships to supply and transport the bandits." The work of the joint security commission was suspended in October 1985, but contacts on security matters are expected to continue.

Statistics showing the damage to infrastructure in Mozambique give bleak testimony to the social and financial impact MNR attacks have had on the national economy and the fabric of rural society and reveal that the situation in some provinces actually deteriorated after the Nkomati Accord was signed in March 1984. This applies to agriculture, health, transportation, mining, the rural-store network and other areas but is illustrated perhaps most starkly by figures showing the closure of schools and displacement of pupils and teachers—a problem with immeasurable consequences for the nation's future. For example, in Tete province in November 1983, sixteen schools had been closed, 2,239 pupils displaced and thirty-nine teachers displaced by MNR attacks. By April 15, 1985, there were 164 schools closed, 22,092 pupils displaced and 434 teachers displaced.

South African business, moreover, has directly profited from the economic damage done by the MNR, which has forced Mozambique to import from South Africa essential commodities such as electric power and clinker to make cement. Both were produced locally for export until the power lines and transport infrastructure were destroyed. The effect is the same as imposing economic sanctions.

The objective of continued support for destabilization seems to be to force the government into a coalition with the MNR, perhaps as an example for Angola. A complete overthrow of the present government would not seem to be in South Africa's interest, as Pretoria would then have to expend economic and military resources propping up a puppet regime, just when it is trying to extricate itself from the cost of doing that in Namibia.

Mozambican officials say they do not understand the reasons for continued destabilization or what it is that the South African authorities want from them. Mozambique seems to have regained the upper hand diplomatically since the Gorongosa revelations, but President Machel's animated visit to Washington in September 1985 and Mozambique's current cautious voting record at the U.N. General Assembly are a measure of the critical state of its affairs. When asked what his government would do about the "nonimplementation" of the Nkomati Accord, President Machel replied that there are three alternatives: to abrogate, to renegotiate the accord or to do nothing at all. The Mozambican government has since called upon world leaders to create a situation that will lead the South African government to "behave seriously and responsibly toward its assumed obligations" and has made detailed information available to the British and American governments, which it hopes will exert this influence.

On March 31, 1984, two weeks after the signing at Nkomati, the governments of South Africa and Swaziland revealed that they had signed an "agreement relating to security matters" two years earlier in which they undertook to "combat terrorism, insurgency and subversion individually and collectively." They agreed to respect each other's sovereignty and to maintain friendly relations, "not allowing any activities within their respective territories directed toward the commission of any act which involves a threat or use of force against each other's territorial integrity." The agreement forbids the presence of foreign military units or bases except in self-defense, and then "only after due notification to the other."

The content of the agreement was proposed in a letter from P. W. Botha to King Sobhuza II of Swaziland. In his reply dated February 17, 1982, Mabandla Fred Dlamini, then Prime Minister of Swaziland, quoted Botha's letter verbatim and signed it, saying that the exchange of letters would constitute an agreement between the two governments. The same date appears on a short note on headed paper over the signature of King Sobhuza, addressed to "My Dear Prime Minister," authorizing him to sign.

The intricacies of that arrangement may never be widely known, but there would seem to have been something in it for everyone—all advantageous to the South African government. Within four months of Dlamini's letter, South Africa announced its intention formally to cede to Swaziland two border regions to which King Sobhuza had historically laid claim. Although their inhabitants are ethnically related to the Swazis, the two areas in question—Kangwane on the northern border of Swaziland and Ingwavuma to the southeast—are designated ethnic "homeland" areas in South Africa (the latter is part of the KwaZulu homeland). The homeland leaders initiated a political and legal battle to prevent the transfer, keeping the issue in the courts until long after Sobhuza's death in August 1982. South African authorities publicly abandoned the plan in June 1984, three months after Nkomati.

The land deal would have given Swaziland an outlet to the sea but would have favored South Africa's ethnic homeland policy and provided a buffer zone along the southern border of Mozambique. However, the cost of administering the territories would have been transferred to Swaziland, outweighing any economic benefit, perhaps one reason why the then–prime minister, Prince Mabandla, opposed the deal.

Swaziland was already beset by economic problems, which have grown steadily worse through 1984 and 1985. Export earnings (especially for sugar, the country's main commodity export) have fallen and costs for imports such as oil have risen, with resulting high rates of inflation and unemployment. After the death of King Sobhuza, Swaziland moved even more firmly into the South African economic orbit,[2] and in late 1984 the governments of South Africa and Swaziland signed an agreement facilitating the exchange of trade representatives with full diplomatic status.

Swaziland had long served as a safe way station for refugees from South Africa, and it continued its policy of "polite tolerance" until about the time the security agreement was made public in March 1984. More than 300 ANC members were then deported, including, at year's end, the ANC's official representative. Twenty-three ANC members were threatened with deportation if they did not surrender to police, and seven others, whom Swazi police blamed for the assassination of a senior security officer, were arrested but later forcibly removed from prison. The ANC blamed South African agents, calling the whole affair a Pretoria-inspired provocation aimed at sabotaging ANC talks with Swaziland. Relations deteriorated further in 1985 with the expulsion from Swaziland of students and academics who are members of the ANC. Several ANC guerrillas and at least two Swazi policemen have been killed in recent incidents, and South African forces often cross the border in "hot pursuit," raiding villages and forcing villagers to report any ANC presence.

The accords with Mozambique and Swaziland increased pressure on other states in the region. Pik Botha told Parliament he was negotiating with neighboring countries in search of agreements that their territories would not be used as "springboards for subversion." He said that an agreement in principle had been reached with Botswana to allow each country's security forces to enter the other country in pursuit of terrorists, and that Pretoria was waiting to hear from Gaborone on how the accord could be implemented. The office of Botswanan President Quett Masire said it had "no knowledge of the negotiations, let alone the agreement in principle."

Subsequent economic pressure included a threatened renegotiation of the terms of the Southern African Customs Union (SACU) which links Botswana, Lesotho and Swaziland with South Africa. Payments under that agreement account for almost 40 percent of Botswana's revenue, about 60 percent of Swaziland's and more than 70 percent of Lesotho's. The South African finance minister ordered a review of the agreement, saying it "does not meet the needs of the eighties." And P. W. Botha said, "We see the customs union not in isolation as a revenue-sharing agreement, but as part of a comprehensive regional development strategy."

The Botswanan government assured South Africa that "subversive elements" would not be allowed to use its territory, but maintained its refusal to sign a formal security pact, giving as an example the MNR's continued infiltration of Mozambique despite the Nkomati Accord and saying it would be "difficult to have confidence in what [South Africa] says it will do." When President Masire met President Reagan at the White House in early 1984, he asked for Washington's support to prevent South Africa from forcing him to sign an agreement.

British and American behind-the-scenes pressure was credited with blunting South African insistence on a signed agreement. Instead, there was an agreed public statement "in which the foreign minister of South Africa said his government no longer required Botswana to sign an agreement because it accepted assurances that it does not allow use of its territory as a launching pad against South Africa. He said that South Africa also undertook not to allow its territory as a launching pad against Botswana."[3]

Relations deteriorated throughout 1985 with threats of "hot pursuit," more ministerial meetings and bomb blasts in Gaborone. On June 14 heavily armed South African commandos invaded Gaborone in the middle of the night, hitting ten separate targets and deeply shocking residents of the capital. South African authorities claimed that the raiders killed twelve "trained terrorists" and destroyed the "control centre of the ANC's Transvaal sabotage organization." But the targets had been private homes and an office block, and the victims caught asleep in their beds were all civilians—eight South Africans, two Botswanan citizens, a Dutch national and a six-year-old boy from Lesotho.

The attack seemed to be aimed at silencing a vocal community of South African exiles, as well as frightening and alienating the Botswanan community from the exile community, pressuring the Botswanan government to expel South African exiles, and generally boosting morale in South Africa itself by dramatizing the attack as a successful offensive against "terrorists." Botswanan officials said, however, that their nation would continue to receive refugees under the terms of the Geneva Convention.

In the first days of 1986, South Africa threatened Botswana again after land-mine explosions near their common border. Pik Botha said that he sent a message to Gaborone, "demanding an end to guerrilla attacks," and that South Africa would take appropriate measures to protect the lives of its citizens. The U.S. and British governments are reported to have intervened with Pretoria to counsel against possible military action. While threatening Botswana and Zimbabwe, attention was diverted from the action South Africa was taking against the most vulnerable independent country in the region, Lesotho.

The government of Lesotho had also refused to sign a security pact with Pretoria, saying that such an agreement would serve little purpose. For South Africa to sign accords with its neighbors instead of with its black population was "sidestepping the issue," Information Minister Desmond Sixishe had said. "The effect of a pact between us and South Africa would be to give them the right to intervene in our affairs with the excuse that we're not playing our part."

In early 1986, South Africa blockaded the tiny mountain kingdom by halting food, fuel and other essential imports at customs and undertaking lengthy searches of travelers and their vehicles at the border. A delegation from the country's 1,500-man paramilitary force went to Pretoria, as did five opposition politicians. Soon after they returned, the politicians were detained. Then the paramilitary staged a coup in the name of their commander, pledging loyalty to King Moshoeshoe II. Senior civil servants were ordered to work but government ministers remained at home waiting instructions. Prime Minister Leabua Jonathan said in a radio interview that if someone else wanted to try running the country, they should go ahead, but there were disturbing reports of South African troops rounding up ANC members. Subsequently Air Zimbabwe began airlifting ANC members out to Zambia, and South Africa ended its border restrictions.

Chief Jonathan won the preindependence election in

1965 with financial assistance from the South African government and became the first black leader of an independent country to visit South Africa. He lost the next election in 1970 but held on to power by suspending the constitution and declaring a state of emergency—with the assistance of the previous head of his paramilitary force, who was seconded from South Africa.

Jonathan then tried to distance himself from his powerful neighbor, and when his opponent, Ntsu Mokhele, formed a rebel group called the Lesotho Liberation Army (LLA), its guerrillas were given passage through South Africa. The LLA has operated from bases in South Africa and has always been more active when Pretoria has been displeased with Lesotho over ANC activities in the country. Like the MNR, its targets were economic as well as military, and there was some evidence that its operatives included ex-Rhodesians from the army of neighboring Transkei.

Although stoutly anticommunist, Jonathan reversed his earlier stance in order to court international credibility. He refused to recognize the Transkei homeland, and in May 1983 he toured five socialist countries, including the Soviet Union and China, and invited them to establish embassies in Maseru. When China and the Soviet Union accepted, South Africa retaliated with a food blockade.

Lesotho is a tiny, impoverished nation of 1.5 million people completely surrounded by South Africa. More than half of the adult male population works in mines, farms and industries across the border, and most rural households rely on income from the remittances of these migrant workers. All imports and exports pass through the republic, and Lesotho's shops and businesses are branches of the South African system, as is its railway. Ninety-five percent of its tourists, as well as most investment and all electricity, come from South Africa. As much as half of Lesotho's national budget is subsidized by foreign aid.

The blockade followed other, more direct South African interventions in Lesotho's affairs. In December 1982, South African troops, supported by helicopters and armored trucks, sped through border posts on the outskirts of Maseru and shot up several residences, including that of the ANC representative, leaving forty-two people dead. Information Minister Sixishe said it was a "traumatic" experience that "destabilized us psychologically." The U.N. Security Council appealed for $46 million in compensation, and more than a hundred ANC members were airlifted from Lesotho to Mozambique.

There was a rapprochement six months later when the foreign ministers of Lesotho and South Africa agreed that neither side would allow its soil to be used for attacks across the border. This agreement broke down almost immediately. The Lesothan government blamed South Africa for a new wave of LLA attacks, including the destruction of a military barracks near the Transkei border and a plot to assassinate the prime minister. South Africa accused Lesotho of turning a blind eye to ANC activities and imposed border restrictions, demanding the expulsion of 3,000 ANC members. In December 1983 a military aircraft on a different kind of mission landed at Maseru, carrying senior officials of the South African government, intelligence and defense forces for talks on "mutual security."

Initially South Africa withheld millions of rand in revenue due from the customs union, as well as helicopter spare parts, in an attempt to force Lesotho to renegotiate the union to include Transkei and Bophutatswana. In effect, that would have been a recognition of the homelands, and Jonathan's government refused. Lesotho was invited to join a regional development bank with the Bantustans, in the hope that recognition by one independent African country would lead to recognition by others. But Lesotho refused. In early 1984, South Africa exerted pressure to sign a security pact through continued border restrictions on Lesothan nationals and threats to cancel the Highland Water Scheme, a vast joint project for the sale of Lesotho's water to South Africa.

The pact Pretoria wanted Lesotho to sign was called a "security agreement" rather than a "nonaggression pact" and reportedly required Lesotho to notify South Africa of every refugee entering its territory and to provide for deportation or repatriation if Pretoria insisted.

Lesotho resisted the pressure to sign and in July 1984 accused South Africa of imposing sanctions by withholding a shipment of light arms from Britain. At the end of August, P. W. Botha again threatened to cancel the Highland Water Scheme, saying that Lesotho was unwilling to meet Pretoria's security needs. On October 1 Sixishe announced that the ANC had agreed to withdraw completely, and two days later the delayed shipment of weapons left Durban. A year later, Lesotho was under pressure again. South African commandos staged another raid on Maseru in December 1985, killing nine people, of whom six were South African. The republic imposed border restrictions that amounted to a blockade, and then occurred the military coup against Jonathan, the first such coup in southern Africa.

The South African Defense Force has had other adventures farther afield. For a time it gave sanctuary and training in Namibia to the Zambian antigovernment forces of Adamson Mushala. It made overtures to Ugandan rebels which were rejected by the major resistance movements.

It attempted a coup in the Seychelles that failed when weapons were discovered in false-bottomed suitcases at airport customs. Fronted by a mercenary force that hijacked a passenger plane back to Durban, the involvement of SADF and National Intelligence Service personnel in the Seychelles coup attempt was later admitted by P. W. Botha, who said it was "unauthorized." The weapons and communications equipment came from SADF stocks.

Zimbabwe seems to pose South Africa's main regional foreign policy dilemma, and destabilization, which began soon after independence in 1980, has come in several guises. South Africa's trade mission has the largest staff of any foreign mission in Harare, after Zimbabwe inherited Rhodesia's position as South Africa's main trading partner on the continent. But Prime Minister Robert Mugabe has, to Pretoria's great irritation, consistently refused to countenance ministerial-level contacts, and Zimbabwe's ministers and media continue to denounce apartheid.

Zimbabwe's central geographical position makes it key to any South African plan for regional cooperation, and also makes it vulnerable to pressure. But its inherited economic links ironically provide it with some defenses. South African businesses have large investments in mining and other sectors, owning about one-third of Zimbabwe's capital stock, and any move by South Africa to hamper trade would amount to shooting itself in the foot. An example is the preferential trade agreement which allows certain commodities into South Africa at favorable rates. Under constant threat of cancellation, the agreement continues to function in a kind of limbo, having been renegotiated but not formally approved. Zimbabwe has also tried to trim its trade dependence on its neighbor by seeking other markets: the share of Zimbabwe's total manufactured exports that was shipped to South Africa was down to 43 percent in late 1985 from 75 percent two years earlier.

Zimbabwe is vulnerable to a variety of economic and military pressures. Its traditional routes to the sea, which were blocked when Mozambique imposed sanctions against Rhodesia in 1976, were reopened in 1980, and Zimbabwe began to use these in preference to the longer and considerably more expensive routes through South Africa. However, sabotage of the railroad to Maputo has forced Zimbabwe to rely more heavily on the southern routes, and higher transportation costs have a ripple effect on the economy, increasing the prices of both imports and exports.

The pipeline from Beira to the border city of Mutare, which Zimbabwe depends upon for petroleum supplies, is also vulnerable. The destruction of a pumping station in late 1982 and the blowing up of the Beira oil storage tanks created a shortage that stretched emergency supplies and hampered transport, industry and tourism throughout that Christmas season. South African railways delayed alternative supplies, pleading a shortage of locomotives. From documents captured at MNR bases in Mozambique, it would appear that South African strategists were counting on their low-level destabilization in Zimbabwe's southwestern Matabeleland province (through supply of weapons to dissidents) to ensure that the Mugabe government would not commit troops to Mozambique. But the oil crisis had the opposite effect. Zimbabwe National Army contingents were stationed in central Mozambique for the first time to protect the railway, road and pipeline to Beira.

Zimbabwe is vulnerable to military incursion on all of its borders. The 800-mile border with Mozambique that was so porous to Mugabe's guerrillas during the Rhodesian liberation struggle has so far been crossed mainly by Mozambican refugees. But captured bandits have mentioned Zimbabweans operating with the MNR, suggesting the possibility of future cross-border incursions. Equally porous and almost as long is the Botswanan border on Zimbabwe's western flank, where dissidents from the Zimbabwe People's Revolutionary Army (ZPRA) take refuge. Some use it as a place to meet with contacts from the SADF for resupply of arms, ammunition and explosives.

The southern border with South Africa is the shortest, although no less vulnerable. After independence, military training camps were set up for recruits from the "private armies" of the previous "Zimbabwe-Rhodesia" leaders, Bishop Abel Muzorewa and Rev. Ndabaningi Sithole. Although South African authorities issue routine denials, as they do in the case of all of their covert operations, the Zimbabwean government has the names and locations of five camps in the Transvaal, three of them just south of the Limpopo River. The instructors are often ex-Rhodesian soldiers. Not all of the recruits return to Zimbabwe; some operate in Mozambique and Namibia as well as in various units of the South African military and intelligence services.

In Matabeleland, the South Africans have armed a force which they call "Super-ZAPU," mostly ex-ZPRA combatants who split with their colleagues over the question of collaboration with apartheid. The weapons they receive are not of South African origin but are usually East bloc weapons captured in neighboring countries or purchased on the international market. The South Africans can exert pressure on their surrogates in much the same way as they do on neighboring governments—by reducing or increasing the flow of weapons and ammunition, or maintaining the status quo.

South African interests have also been furthered in several respects by political developments inside Zimbabwe. These have included the bitter disappointment of Mugabe's rival, Joshua Nkomo, at losing the first election and failing to become prime minister, the subsequent purchase by Nkomo's allies of strategically placed farms where large quantities of arms were cached, Nkomo's dismissal from the Cabinet and the resultant attacks on development projects and infrastructure by armed Nkomo supporters. In addition, there are also criminal elements who have taken advantage of the situation for their personal gain, causing further turmoil and unrest.

As well as the economic infrastructure, major targets in Matabeleland have been officials of the ruling party, "sellouts" and white commercial farmers. In February 1984 South African security officials were summoned to Harare to meet their counterparts, who produced evidence of South African involvement with dissidents operating in southeastern and central Zimbabwe. To underscore the point, the Zimbabwean government officials provided details about the white farmers murdered by South African-trained and -armed dissidents. The question was obvious —was South Africa's objective to kill the whites of Zimbabwe?

After that meeting there were no attacks on white farmers for seventeen months and no infiltrations from South Africa until the beginning of August 1984, on the eve of the congress of the ruling party, the Zimbabwe African National Union (ZANU). Two groups of armed commandos, numbering about sixty, were seen crossing into Zimbabwe in the area where the borders of Zimbabwe, South Africa and Botswana meet. By the year's end, the security situation had begun to deteriorate sharply with the murder of two senators, one a member of ZANU and one a member of Nkomo's Zimbabwe African People's Union (ZAPU). Although the period of elections in June 1985

was relatively quiet, the murder of white farmers in Matabeleland resumed. The increase in such murders began
shortly after Zimbabwean military forces escalated their
role in Mozambique and seemed designed to reduce the
effectiveness of those forces by drawing them back to
southwestern Zimbabwe.

In the first three years of Zimbabwe's independence
there were several incidents of direct sabotage by South
African operatives—often ex-Rhodesians who remained
in the Zimbabwean military and security structures after
independence or who went south and joined the SADF
Special Forces. Armored vehicles were damaged by explosions at army headquarters, a large quantity of weapons
was stolen from another barracks and the main ammunition dump at Inkomo Barracks near Harare was sabo-
taged, causing the destruction of millions of dollars' worth
of weaponry. Captain Frank Gericke, an explosives expert
who was commander of the army engineers, was arrested,
but before questioning could be completed, he was sprung
from prison by a white police officer, and they and their
families escaped to South Africa. Sabotage at the main air
force base at Thornhill in the center of the country virtually wiped out Zimbabwe's strike and interception
capabilities, and a bomb at ZANU party headquarters in
Harare, timed to coincide with a meeting of the Central
Committee that was fortuitously postponed, killed shop-
pers on a busy commercial street.

The South Africans undoubtedly retain an extensive
espionage network in Zimbabwe, despite the breakup of a
spy ring of white operatives run by a member of the security detail assigned to the prime minister. But their tactics
have changed. In August 1982, three whites on a sabotage
mission were killed in the southeast corner of the country;
since that incident saboteurs have tended to be black and
to be sent only to areas where there is already military

activity (e.g., Matabeleland). Serious sabotage of the communications routes through Mozambique began in late 1982, at about the same time as "Super-ZAPU" made its appearance with more weapons and better coordinated actions than ZPRA.

Another area of destabilization is disinformation. "Radio Truth" beams to Zinbabwe from the SABC studios, purporting to be broadcast by dissident nationals but tending to toe the line of South African foreign policy and comment. Other disinformation readily traceable to Pretoria includes letters to embassies and ministries in Harare purporting to be from a ZPRA commander, mailings of leaflets to the same addresses from London, a smear campaign against senior white intelligence officers over the murder of a Malawian opposition leader and stories planted in the South African press.

Zimbabwe refuses to allow ANC bases or transit facilities on its territory, but the organization maintains a low-profile office in Harare. The first ANC representative assigned to Zimbabwe after the country's independence, Joe Nqabi, was assassinated at his residence by a South African hit squad which disappeared; two whites who did the initial reconnaissance were part of a South African espionage ring in Zimbabwe and are now in prison. The Zimbabwean government has never discussed or signed a security pact with South Africa, and from time to time the South Africans claim to have evidence of ANC infiltration. At the end of 1985 they massed troops on the border and threatened to invade Zimbabwe after land mines in the northern Transvaal killed several whites and damaged vehicles.

The People's Republic of Angola was one of the five areas of "regional conflict" chosen by the U.S. administration for discussion with the Soviet Union at the Reagan-Gorbachev summit in November 1985. However, in announcing this to the United Nations in October of that year, President Reagan omitted reference to the real regional protagonist, South Africa. Angola is the main external target for South Africa's "total strategy", and the transition from destabilization to diplomacy and back again has been so sudden that one South African magazine, the *Financial Mail,* likened it to a Transvaal thunderstorm.

Despite the Lusaka "understanding" in February 1984 and the much-publicized and -photographed "withdrawals" of men and equipment in early 1985, the SADF has maintained a powerful force on both sides of the Angola-Namibia border. By the end of 1985 they had openly come to the rescue of their surrogates and were again occupying parts of southern Angola.

South African forces have made twelve major incursions into Angola since they first entered the country in the second week of August 1975, and they have been in more than they have been out, occupying parts of the border area continuously since 1981. A description in *The Washington Post* that portrayed the country as a "physical and ideological battleground" since Portugal abruptly abandoned its 500-year colonial rule, seems appropriate.

Just before independence in November 1975, the People's Movement for the Liberation of Angola (MPLA), which was about to become the government in Luanda, called for Cuban assistance against a powerful South African force moving rapidly up the country toward the capital. The Cuban combat troops arrived just after independence and have been there ever since.[4] That offensive, called Operation Savannah, lasted several months and was the costliest SADF action in Angola, in terms of South African losses, until December 1983, when South African forces penetrated more than 150 miles into the country in Operation Askari. The Angolan army was well prepared for the latter attack, to Pretoria's surprise and dismay.

What had escaped South African military intelligence, or been ignored, was the reorganization of the Angolan defense forces and the appearance in the country of a considerable amount of new and sophisticated Soviet defense equipment, including helicopter gunships equipped with rockets and cannons, surface-to-air missiles for antiaircraft defense and a new radar system. This prevented the invaders from sending ground troops too far ahead or attacking by air. Ironically, according to American business and intelligence sources, Cuban troops not only were not involved in this fighting but had not fired on the South Africans since 1976. They are garrisoned in towns farther north and deployed to protect strategic installations, freeing Angolan soldiers for combat. Nonetheless, the issue of "linking" Cuban withdrawal to Namibian independence has dominated each stage of the negotiations of "constructive engagement," giving the process a higher profile in Washington and an acceptable face in Pretoria. To placate the United Nations, which regards the Cuban issue as interference in Angola's internal affairs, Secretary Crocker's forays into the region are usually conducted under the cover of Namibian negotiations.

At the same time as it was fostering accords with other Front-line states, the South African government was proposing to disengage from Angola. At the end of January 1984, P. W. Botha told Parliament that the SADF had begun a withdrawal as the first step in a hoped-for ceasefire. He said the cost of retaining Namibia had become too high. During the current financial year, he noted, "South Africa had made direct and indirect assistance available to the territory amounting to about 560 million rand [then

$450 million]," not including security spending of about $320–$400 million, and had further guaranteed loans of $550 million. "Our determination [to protect South-West Africa] has exacted a heavy price—in material, in international condemnation and in the lives of our young men," he said, declaring that "South Africa stands at the crossroads between confrontation and peace." A British newspaper, *The Guardian,* put it differently: "The iron fist of destabilization is now decorously clothed in the velvet glove of diplomacy."

The Reagan Administration, with its diplomatic and financial muscle, was standing by to perform its chosen role as broker. On February 16, 1984, an Angolan delegation led by the interior minister, Alexandre Rodrigues "Kito," met Crocker and Pik Botha in Lusaka. They set up a joint military commission which, over the next few months, monitored the hesitant South African withdrawal from Cuvelai, 120 miles north of the Namibian border, to Ngiva, twenty-five miles from the border, where it stalled. Almost a year later, in April 1985, South African forces withdrew across the border, amid much publicity, before reentering with a preemptive strike against the Angolan army, which was poised to overrun the border headquarters of antigovernment rebels.

Just one month after the SADF "withdrew" into Namibia, three white members of a SADF Special Forces unit were caught 1,400 miles further north, in the province of Cabinda, trying to sabotage the storage tanks at an oil installation jointly owned by the Angolan government and a U.S. company, Gulf Oil. Two of the intruders were killed and a substantial quantity of explosives and communications equipment recovered; the third was wounded and captured, and gave details of the operation. The nine-member unit had been landed by dinghy from an Israeli-built South African destroyer, he said, the same method used for other sabotage attacks in Angola and Mozambique.

The captured would-be saboteur was identified as the commander of the unit, Captain Wynand Petrus du Toit. He confirmed that the sabotage was to be attributed to the South African-backed National Union for the Total Independence of Angola (UNITA), and he gave details of another sabotage operation in the south in which he and others were landed by ship to destroy a railway bridge and which was also attributed to UNITA. He said that although these operations were to be claimed by UNITA, they used entirely SADF personnel, and he personally had never met anyone from UNITA. Du Toit said his unit was to leave a map and a Zaire currency note at the Cabinda site to make it appear the work of a UNITA group transiting Zaire. That was expected to disrupt Zaire's relations with Angola.

South African Defense Ministry officials at first denied any involvement in the incident; then, confronted with the evidence, they contradicted themselves, claiming the unit was searching for guerrillas belonging to the ANC and to the South-West Africa People's Organization (SWAPO). There are none in Cabinda.

Du Toit said there was more than one Special Forces unit operating in Angola, but he said they were not given details of each other's targets. These units may have been responsible for other sabotage attributed to UNITA, such as attacks on diamond mines, a dam and a pulp mill in 1983, and almost certainly for the destruction of two ships in Luanda harbor in 1984 as well as damage to the Cabinda oil pipeline and a railway workshop. After those and other incidents, and the seizure of more than a hundred foreign hostages, including British, Czech and Portuguese technicians, the UNITA leader, Jonas Savimbi, demanded direct negotiations and a coalition in Luanda. The Angolan government rejected Savimbi's demands and condemned his public appearance in Pretoria at the swearing in of P. W. Botha as state president.

Savimbi has highly placed friends in Washington and other capitals and receives financial and diplomatic encouragement for his operations despite his close alliance with South Africa. But UNITA was a subject pointedly avoided in the "constructive engagement" contacts with the Angolan government until 1985. These contacts moved into a new phase at midyear, when the U.S. Congress voted to overturn the Clark amendment, a nine-year-old ban on direct assistance to UNITA. The amendment had been passed in 1976 after disclosures of massive American involvement, through the Central Intelligence Agency, to try to prevent the MPLA from forming a government—an involvement that led to the South African invasion and the MPLA's appeal to Cuba for military support. The White House lauded the repeal of the troublesome amendment but maintained there were no immediate plans for funding UNITA.

By the end of the year, however, there was a public wrangle over the administration's proposal for as much as $200–300 million in covert aid to UNITA (to be administered by the CIA) and counterproposals by congressmen to authorize $27 million in overt "humanitarian" aid or the same amount of overt military aid. A few congressmen opposed any kind of aid to UNITA, arguing that it would increase Angola's dependence upon the Soviet Union. Secretary of State Shultz, who had publicly opposed any form of assistance, now spoke of supporting "people who fight for freedom . . . in a way that will be effective." The State Department seemed to be playing for time, squeezing every ounce of diplomatic mileage out of the threat to aid UNITA before moving on to the next stage, that of pursuing negotiations while covertly aiding UNITA in order to strengthen its position at the bargaining table without being seen openly as having a military entanglement in Angola.

A drawback for the administration is that aid to UNITA will probably be channeled through South Africa, further emphasizing the close U.S. links with Pretoria. The State Department would undoubtedly prefer to do this in private, as it would almost certainly damage relations in other parts of Africa. The large figures proposed for covert assistance have also raised concern in the region that more sophisticated military hardware will find its way into South Africa's arsenal, despite the U.N. arms embargo.

Just after the Clark amendment was repealed, $350 million worth of loan and export credits were approved for oil exploration in Angola, with one-third of the financing from the Export-Import Bank, a U.S. government agency. It marks the first time that American banks have participated in a major foreign oil exploration since the current oil glut began, and it indicated, among other things, that the multinational coalition of fifteen banks has confidence in Angola's ability to handle its balance of payments. State Department officials would argue that this financial package is consistent with their policy of "constructive engagement" because, in the case of Angola as in the case of South Africa, they are trying to change the politics, not damage the economy. Although the first Angolan government economic mission since independence was allowed to visit Washington in September 1985 to lobby investors, it still rings hollow beside the economic destruction caused throughout the region by deliberate South African destabilization.

The proposal for covert aid came from the CIA and the Defense Department shortly after a South African delegation visited Washington. It was promoted as a means of strengthening President Reagan's bargaining position at the summit with Gorbachev, and ultraconservative Republican groups also mooted the idea of a trade embargo against Angola. The U.S. government would have difficulty explaining why there should be such an embargo against Angola but not against South Africa. Since the United States is Angola's largest trading partner, this action would undoubtedly be harmful to the Angolan economy, but such a "signal" would not be without side effects. Angola is the third-largest U.S. trading partner in sub-Saharan Africa (after South Africa and Nigeria), with $1 billion in trade annually, including $600 million in oil purchases.

UNITA is often labeled "pro-Western" because it opposes a Marxist administration, but Western business interests operating in Angola say UNITA would be better described as "pro-Savimbi." They express doubts that he would settle for a minority share of power and feel he would be more difficult to deal with than the present government, which they have come to respect for its efficiency in business dealings despite the U.S. government's refusal to establish diplomatic relations. The fact that UNITA, which characterized itself as a "liberation movement," fought for a time in Angola alongside the Portuguese army that it purported to be fighting against, and received supplies from them to fight against the MPLA, does raise questions about its motives. Nonetheless, the State Department says it is a "matter of principle" to support UNITA's efforts to resist Soviet "designs" in Angola.

Angola is the rear base for the twenty-year-old war conducted by guerrillas of the South-West Africa People's Organization against South African rule in Namibia, and South African military incursions have, until recently, been in the guise of attacks on SWAPO guerrillas. When the South African government began talking to its other neighbors, it also made overtures to SWAPO through Zambian President Kenneth Kaunda. The most significant contact was an unpublicized meeting in Lusaka in early 1984 between senior SWAPO officials and a South African delegation from military intelligence, led by Gen. Westhuizen. Although nothing else came of this, South Africa released almost a hundred Angolan and Namibian prisoners, including Andimba Ja Toivo, a founder of SWAPO who was later elected secretary-general of the organization, effectively its number two position. If South Africa's intention was to divide SWAPO, it failed, but Toivo's release seemed to signal a dramatic step toward fulfilling one of the conditions of U.N. Security Council Resolution 435, which calls for the release of political prisoners.

SWAPO was enticed to a meeting in Lusaka with the internal Multi-Party Conference (MPC), cochaired by the Zambian president and the South African administrator-general of Namibia. SWAPO's position was strengthened by the defection of some key MPC leaders, and the meeting collapsed. But it brought into the open South Africa's intention to draw SWAPO away from Resolution 435 and a seven-month transition to elections and into protracted constitutional negotiations with the internal parties, which would have amounted to a cease-fire. Militarily curtailed by the Lusaka "understanding" which prevented infiltration through Angola's Cunene province, but politically strengthened by the defections to its ranks, SWAPO demurred. The MPC, having exposed their internal divisions, sent a delegation to Gabon, the Ivory Coast, Togo and Senegal, whose leaders tried unsuccessfully to arrange further meetings.

In June 1985 the administrator-general installed the MPC "transitional government" in Windhoek as a means of gaining time and exerting further pressure on SWAPO. The international community, as expected, refused to recognize it, as in the case of "Zimbabwe-Rhodesia." The lessons of Zimbabwe are not lost on the South African administration, which reluctantly realizes that SWAPO will win a "free and fair" election. There are, however, internal differences in South Africa over what to do about that. In the corridors of power there are three categories of opinion: (1) those opposed to any settlement involving SWAPO; (2) some who would accept such a settlement if the terms were right; and (3) those who believe that even a SWAPO government could be kept in line by its economic dependence. It is the latter group that is playing for time. Until the home front is more stable, the cost in political capital of handing over Namibia to a liberation movement would be too high. Meanwhile, the territory is used as a smuggling route for diamonds, ivory and teak from Angola, as well as a military staging ground, and certain sectors are working to ensure the post-independence economic dependence of this arid, desolate land, rich in minerals and sea coast.[5]

South African military incursions into southern Angola are now openly in support of UNITA. In September 1985 an Angolan offensive in the southeastern province of Kuando Kabango was met with a fierce South African counteroffensive, including preemptive air strikes behind the lines. Some of the new air force equipment was destroyed on the ground near Mavinga, more than 150 miles from the Namibian border. There are no SWAPO bases or infiltration routes in that area and the attack was openly in defense of UNITA as the Angolan army threatened to cut its supply routes to the rest of the country and overrun its headquarters at Jamba in the border area near the Caprivi Strip. It was no coincidence that the shift in tactics came a few weeks before the Reagan-Gorbachev summit and was designed to make political capital by giving the Soviet Union a "bloody nose" in Angola.

The South African strike amounted to open aggression against a sovereign state in an area where there is not a SWAPO guerrilla to be found, but where the Angolans say there are now combined South African–UNITA battalions. South African authorities subsequently admitted that a South African medical officer killed near Cazombo, 600 miles north of the border, was "assisting" UNITA.

Shortly after this preemptive strike, Gen. Malan admitted for the first time, after several years of denial, that South Africa was giving "moral, material and humanitarian aid" to UNITA. In an interview with the *Pretoria News* on October 4, 1985, he said other military considerations in Angola were the "limited" action against SWAPO and the "massive accumulation of sophisticated communist military material."

Angola's five-point bargaining position, including details of a phased withdrawal of 20,000 Cuban troops over three years, leaving 5,000 Cuban soldiers in the north to protect the capital and the Cabinda oilfields, was made public in November 1984 but remains on the table. Pretoria demanded the withdrawal of all Cubans over a period of twelve weeks, assurances that they would not be replaced by other foreign forces and limits on the number of Soviet-bloc advisers working in Angola. But the Frontline states regarded these demands as interference in Angola's internal affairs, and the Angolan government said it could not "make concessions which would be suicidal to its national integrity."

At the end of this process, more "linkages" had been identified. Angola cannot withdraw Cuban troops until South Africa stops supporting UNITA; South Africa will not do that until the Angolan government agrees to talk to Savimbi. On the other side, South Africa has refused to withdraw from southern Angola unless SWAPO is removed from the area and monitored; Angola cannot take that action until South Africa and SWAPO agree to a cease-fire.

Since then both countries have made military gains, but Angola has been scoring the economic points—for efficiency, good management and meeting international commitments. South Africa, in the depths of an economic crisis, stopped payment of $14 million in short-term debts for six months. When Secretary Crocker went off to Luanda again in January 1986, with his economic "carrot" of increased trade and financing for oil exploration and the military "stick" of threatened assistance to UNITA, Angolan President Eduardo dos Santos told him that the Angolan government does not understand whether to regard this as "a form of pressure on Angola or as a declaration of war by the United States." The Reagan administration's policy of "constructive engagement," publicly vaunted as a means of getting Cuban troops out of Angola, seems more likely designed to keep them there, at least in the foreseeable future.

Although it is difficult to determine whether the scenario was drafted in Washington or Pretoria, it must go something like this: Angola is not Mozambique and is too distant, too wealthy and too heavily armed by the Soviet Union to be drawn into South Africa's economic or security orbit or to be forced to abandon the ANC. Namibia is a liability and must be jettisoned in the foreseeable future with an internationally acceptable government (i.e.,

SWAPO). It is therefore necessary to weaken the present administration in Angola as much as possible before that happens, either by forcing it into negotiations with anticommunist groups or through economic influence, or both.

The Front for the National Liberation of Angola (FNLA), which was the third major contender for power in the struggle that followed the Portuguese withdrawal in 1975 and which once did Washington's bidding through Zaire, has disintegrated, although its various leaders still receive funding from right-wing groups in the U.S. UNITA is not cohesive, and some members of Savimbi's leadership have argued for rapprochement with Luanda. There are deep divisions within UNITA over South Africa's open support, which have resulted in several dismissals and disappearances and some defections. That leaves economic influence as the most seductive option for U.S. policymakers, coupled with Pretoria's short-term military action to destroy as much of the new armory as it can possibly reach before the border slips south.

As the protective colonial *laager* on South Africa's borders was collapsing from 1974 through 1980, a new set of Afrikaner administrators with military experience was taking power in Pretoria, in what has often been described as a "constitutional coup d'etat." These men believed themselves to be victims of the same colonial domination as the rest of the continent, having "liberated" their government from English-speaking control almost thirty years earlier. They had a paranoiac fear of socialism and the Soviet Union, which they saw manifest in most of their new neighbors, and would not countenance outside interference from anyone, even from their friends.

Taking advantage of a new array of circumstances that

presented themselves, they began to construct a different kind of *laager* that grew out of the dynamics of conflict within different sectors of their administration. The new *laager* is based, like the old one, on regional economic cooperation, mutual security and resistance to pressure from outsiders. But it uses military might beyond its borders to achieve political and economic ends.

Among the new circumstances that have influenced South Africa's regional "foreign policy" are the reorganization of the government and its security establishment since 1978, Zimbabwe's independence in 1980 and the change in the White House in 1981. Changes in the security establishment reflected in part a desire for long-term planning to replace the kind of ad hoc decision-making that caused the debacle in Angola in 1975, and in part a reaction to the kind of power wielded by individuals in the Vorster administration, such as General Hendrik van den Bergh, head of the powerful Bureau of State Security (BOSS).[6]

Since that time, different sectors of the leadership have drawn conflicting lessons from their experiences of international regional contacts—economic, military and political. Diplomats involved in negotiations in Europe, America and closer to home have learned that South Africa cannot rely totally on any Western government for support, and perhaps does not need to because of its own economic and military strength in the region. They have a better understanding of economic pressures used by and against South Africa and more knowledge about their immediate neighbors. Military leaders have learned from their regional campaigns and acts of sabotage that, although they are the military power in the region, the enemy hits back and South African financial and human losses may be heavier than expected. There is also a hard-line security sector which, reinforced by its experience in Namibia, still believes that suppression of black opposition remains the most effective tactic on South Africa's borders as well as at home, and that preparation must be made for a conventional military attack from the north.[7]

South African policy in the region is an amalgam of these points of view. Although still evolving, it is based on the belief that, in the long term, economic control is cheaper and more effective than military domination, but the latter must be used in the short term to achieve the former. General Constand Viljoen, on his retirement, spoke of the security forces' role in gaining time for the country to solve its political problems, and predicted that this dependency on the efficiency of the security forces would last for the "next few years, maybe even the next decade."

Viljoen's retirement after the Cabinda affair and the removal of the other two senior officials implicated in the Gorongosa documents is somewhat difficult to interpret. Both Louis Nel and Piet van der Westhuizen, whose posts were upgraded to State Security Council (SSC) "observer" status in 1982, would appear to have been promoted again. Nel became head of the new information bureau in the state president's office. He retained his rank as deputy minister, with special responsibility for projecting the government's image abroad, i.e. control of the foreign media, which the South African government holds responsible for the increase in international political and economic pressure. Westhuizen moved closer to the center of state power as secretary to the SSC, a post giving access to the most influential Cabinet committee in the land. The SSC agenda contains a far wider range of issues than the other three Cabinet committees, including relations with neighboring states, and its decisions are not automatically circulated or subject to confirmation by the full Cabinet. The SSC plays the role of "gatekeeper," getting input from all departments, conveying decisions from the Cabinet, and monitoring their implementation.

Although the predominance of apparently "hawkish" military decisions emanating from the SSC would seem to confirm the theory of militarization of the South African government, leading authorities on the South African body politic caution against simple assumptions. They argue that, "Given the common background and values of the [Afrikaner] participants, it would be misleading to suggest even a general sort of military dominance as the explanation for pre-emptive raids and support of anti-regime movements in southern Africa during the past few years. It is more likely that most SSC members thought this approach would be effective policy, and that SADF had little persuasion to do."[8] Viljoen's successor as SADF chief, Lieutenant General J. J. Geldenhuys, is a pragmatic soldier who prefers political accommodation to military stalemate.

The weakness of this integrated approach to conflict management is that "failure"—in Namibian fighting, in regional diplomacy, in the South African economy, in coping with urban black unrest—might bring perceptible basic divergencies among SSC participants. Failures, therefore, must be balanced by successes, even if that requires cross-border attacks.[9]

Another pillar of South African regional policy is that economic and security cooperation with neighboring states will rebuild the lost colonial *laager* in a neocolonial form. Third, the South African government would wish to destroy any belief in socialist ideology as a development strategy for the continent, and to show that free-enterprise capitalism is the logical development strategy. So much the better if, when it buries socialism, South Africa can show its own population that chaos is the result of majority rule. Another major goal is to limit the role and political influence of outside powers—including Western powers—in the region. In Namibia, for example, Pretoria has tried with some success to minimize U.N. involvement and limit the U.S. role of broker.

Throughout their history, Afrikaners have shown a strong instinct for survival. The last two years have brought home to their leaders the fragile nature of their economic dependencies: internationally, on overseas financial markets for the price of gold and the exchange rate of the U.S. dollar to the rand; regionally, on their neighbors for mutually lucrative business arrangements in preference to the high cost in money and lives of military intervention; internally, on the majority of their population, to whom they have denied basic human rights, whom they have forced to live in appalling social conditions and on whom they are ultimately most dependent for their prosperity and security.

The Afrikaners have also had the opportunity to scrutinize the power of their closest ally, the United States, as this power was used both to support them and to pressure them. It is a power they, as a regional superpower, would like to emulate. When Soviet officials summoned their South African counterparts to an unprecedented meeting at the United Nations in New York in November 1983 to warn them that "aggression cannot be left unpunished," South African leaders took it as a recognition of this role as regional superpower. Such status would ensure their survival through military and economic domination and would enhance their future ability to resist pressure, even from their allies.

NOTES

1. In a secret memo circulated in August 1983, South African Defense Minister Magnus Malan ordered all reference to the latter phrase eliminated.

2. Bids were tendered in 1983 for a cross-country rail link, to be plugged into South African railways at both ends, carrying traffic from the mining, industrial and agricultural areas of the eastern Transvaal to the port of Richards Bay in Natal. While this will contribute to Swaziland's revenue, it locks the country's transportation network into the South African system—instead of moving it away from it, as Swaziland's SADCC colleagues would prefer—and raises questions about South Africa's future plans for utilizing the port of Maputo.

3. Interview with Festus Mogae, permanent secretary to President Masire and head of the Botswanan civil service, *Financial Mail* (Johannesburg), July 12, 1985.

4. The authors were in Luanda at the time and have—as well as Angolan and South African versions of the dates at which the Cubans were summoned relative to the dates the South Africans invaded—a comparative version from the Portuguese military officers who were still in the country. In the face of irrefutable evidence that Cuban soldiers (there were a handful of military instructors present) were not requested or sent until after the South Africans entered Angola, the State Department finds that its version of the story, that the Cubans came first, better suits its purpose.

5. An official report compiled by a South African judge has accused the diamond monopoly of "uncontrolled stripping" of the richer ore bodies in Namibia and has recommended criminal proceedings against some members of the Diamond Board. See *The Observer* (London), November 3, 1985. South Africa is determined to hold onto Namibia's main port, a strategic enclave at Walvis Bay.

6. The former director-general of the Rhodesian Central Intelligence Organization, Ken Flower, has said that van den Bergh

refused to give the Rhodesians any assistance with the MNR
as it was against South African policy, and that they did not
receive any assistance until after the new regime took control
in 1978.
7. See Dean Geldenhuys, Kenneth W. Grundy and John Seiler,
"South Africa's Evolving State Security System," paper presented to the Study Group on Armed Forces and Society of
the International Political Science Association, West Berlin,
September 15, 1981.
8. Ibid.
9. A recent example of this is the South African attack on ANC
offices in Lusaka, Gaborone and Harare in May 1986, which
took place while Pretoria was negotiating with the Commonwealth Eminent Persons Group.

MORE ABOUT PENGUINS, PELICANS, PEREGRINES AND PUFFINS

For further information about books available from Penguins please write to Dept EP, Penguin Books Ltd, Harmondsworth, Middlesex UB7 0DA.

In the U.S.A.: For a complete list of books available from Penguins in the United States write to Dept DG, Penguin Books, 299 Murray Hill Parkway, East Rutherford, New Jersey 07073.

In Canada: For a complete list of books available from Penguins in Canada write to Penguin Books Canada Limited, 2801 John Street, Markham, Ontario L3R 1B4.

In Australia: For a complete list of books available from Penguins in Australia write to the Marketing Department, Penguin Books Australia Ltd, P.O. Box 257, Ringwood, Victoria 3134.

In New Zealand: For a complete list of books available from Penguins in New Zealand write to the Marketing Department, Penguin Books (N.Z.) Ltd, Private Bag, Takapuna, Auckland 9.

In India: For a complete list of books available from Penguins in India write to Penguin Overseas Ltd, 706 Eros Apartments, 56 Nehru Place, New Delhi 110019.

A CHOICE OF
PELICANS AND PEREGRINES

☐ **The Knight, the Lady and the Priest**
   Georges Duby   £6.95

The acclaimed study of the making of modern marriage in medieval France. 'He has traced this story – sometimes amusing, often horrifying, always startling – in a series of brilliant vignettes' – *Observer*

☐ **The Limits of Soviet Power** Jonathan Steele   £3.95

The Kremlin's foreign policy – Brezhnev to Chernenko, is discussed in this informed, informative 'wholly invaluable and extraordinarily timely study' – *Guardian*

☐ **Understanding Organizations** Charles B. Handy   £4.95

Third Edition. Designed as a practical source-book for managers, this Pelican looks at the concepts, key issues and current fashions in tackling organizational problems.

☐ **The Pelican Freud Library: Volume 12**   £5.95

Containing the major essays: *Civilization, Society and Religion, Group Psychology* and *Civilization and Its Discontents*, plus other works.

☐ **Windows on the Mind** Erich Harth   £4.95

Is there a physical explanation for the various phenomena that we call 'mind'? Professor Harth takes in age-old philosophers as well as the latest neuroscientific theories in his masterly study of memory, perception, free will, selfhood, sensation and other richly controversial fields.

☐ **The Pelican History of the World**
   J. M. Roberts   £5.95

'A stupendous achievement . . . This is the unrivalled World History for our day' – A. J. P. Taylor

A CHOICE OF
PELICANS AND PEREGRINES

☐ *A Question of Economics* **Peter Donaldson** £4.95

Twenty key issues – from the City and big business to trades unions – clarified and discussed by Peter Donaldson, author of *10 × Economics* and one of our greatest popularizers of economics.

☐ *Inside the Inner City* **Paul Harrison** £4.95

A report on urban poverty and conflict by the author of *Inside the Third World.* 'A major piece of evidence' – *Sunday Times.* 'A classic: it tells us what it is really like to be poor, and why' – *Time Out*

☐ *What Philosophy Is* **Anthony O'Hear** £4.95

What are human beings? How should people act? How do our thoughts and words relate to reality? Contemporary attitudes to these age-old questions are discussed in this new study, an eloquent and brilliant introduction to philosophy today.

☐ *The Arabs* **Peter Mansfield** £4.95

New Edition. 'Should be studied by anyone who wants to know about the Arab world and how the Arabs have become what they are today' – *Sunday Times*

☐ *Religion and the Rise of Capitalism*
 R. H. Tawney £3.95

The classic study of religious thought of social and economic issues from the later middle ages to the early eighteenth century.

☐ *The Mathematical Experience*
 Philip J. Davis and Reuben Hersh £7.95

Not since *Gödel, Escher, Bach* has such an entertaining book been written on the relationship of mathematics to the arts and sciences. 'It deserves to be read by everyone . . . an instant classic' – *New Scientist*

PENGUIN REFERENCE BOOKS

☐ **_The Penguin Map of the World_**   £2.95

Clear, colourful, crammed with information and fully up-to-date, this is a useful map to stick on your wall at home, at school or in the office.

☐ **_The Penguin Map of Europe_**   £2.95

Covers all land eastwards to the Urals, southwards to North Africa and up to Syria, Iraq and Iran * Scale = 1:5,500,000 * 4-colour artwork * Features main roads, railways, oil and gas pipelines, plus extra information including national flags, currencies and populations.

☐ **_The Penguin Map of the British Isles_**   £2.95

Including the Orkneys, the Shetlands, the Channel Islands and much of Normandy, this excellent map is ideal for planning routes and touring holidays, or as a study aid.

☐ **_The Penguin Dictionary of Quotations_**   £3.95

A treasure-trove of over 12,000 new gems and old favourites, from Aesop and Matthew Arnold to Xenophon and Zola.

☐ **_The Penguin Dictionary of Art and Artists_**   £3.95

Fifth Edition. 'A vast amount of information intelligently presented, carefully detailed, abreast of current thought and scholarship and easy to read' – _The Times Literary Supplement_

☐ **_The Penguin Pocket Thesaurus_**   £2.50

A pocket-sized version of Roget's classic, and an essential companion for all commuters, crossword addicts, students, journalists and the stuck-for-words.

PENGUIN REFERENCE BOOKS

☐ *The Penguin Dictionary of Troublesome Words*   £2.50

A witty, straightforward guide to the pitfalls and hotly disputed issues in standard written English, illustrated with examples and including a glossary of grammatical terms and an appendix on punctuation.

☐ *The Penguin Guide to the Law*   £8.95

This acclaimed reference book is designed for everyday use, and forms the most comprehensive handbook ever published on the law as it affects the individual.

☐ *The Penguin Dictionary of Religions*   £4.95

The rites, beliefs, gods and holy books of all the major religions throughout the world are covered in this book, which is illustrated with charts, maps and line drawings.

☐ *The Penguin Medical Encyclopedia*   £4.95

Covers the body and mind in sickness and in health, including drugs, surgery, history, institutions, medical vocabulary and many other aspects. Second Edition. 'Highly commendable' – *Journal of the Institute of Health Education*

☐ *The Penguin Dictionary of Physical Geography*   £4.95

This book discusses all the main terms used, in over 5,000 entries illustrated with diagrams and meticulously cross-referenced.

☐ *Roget's Thesaurus*   £3.50

Specially adapted for Penguins, Sue Lloyd's acclaimed new version of Roget's original will help you find the right words for your purposes. 'As normal a part of an intelligent household's library as the Bible, Shakespeare or a dictionary' – *Daily Telegraph*

A CHOICE OF PENGUINS

☐ *The Complete Penguin Stereo Record and Cassette Guide*
Greenfield, Layton and March £7.95

A new edition, now including information on compact discs. 'One of the few indispensables on the record collector's bookshelf' – *Gramophone*

☐ *Selected Letters of Malcolm Lowry*
Edited by Harvey Breit and Margerie Bonner Lowry £5.95

'Lowry emerges from these letters not only as an extremely interesting man, but also a lovable one' – Philip Toynbee

☐ *The First Day on the Somme*
Martin Middlebrook £3.95

1 July 1916 was the blackest day of slaughter in the history of the British Army. 'The soldiers receive the best service a historian can provide: their story told in their own words' – *Guardian*

☐ *A Better Class of Person* **John Osborne** £2.50

The playwright's autobiography, 1929–56. 'Splendidly enjoyable' – John Mortimer. 'One of the best, richest and most bitterly truthful autobiographies that I have ever read' – Melvyn Bragg

☐ *The Winning Streak* **Goldsmith and Clutterbuck** £2.95

Marks & Spencer, Saatchi & Saatchi, United Biscuits, GEC . . . The UK's top companies reveal their formulas for success, in an important and stimulating book that no British manager can afford to ignore.

☐ *The First World War* **A. J. P. Taylor** £4.95

'He manages in some 200 illustrated pages to say almost everything that is important . . . A special text . . . a remarkable collection of photographs' – *Observer*

A CHOICE OF PENGUINS

☐ *Man and the Natural World* **Keith Thomas** £4.95

Changing attitudes in England, 1500–1800. 'An encyclopedic study of man's relationship to animals and plants . . . a book to read again and again' – Paul Theroux, *Sunday Times* Books of the Year

☐ *Jean Rhys: Letters 1931–66*
‑**Edited by Francis Wyndham and Diana Melly** £4.95

'Eloquent and invaluable . . . her life emerges, and with it a portrait of an unexpectedly indomitable figure' – Marina Warner in the *Sunday Times*

☐ *The French Revolution* **Christopher Hibbert** £4.95

'One of the best accounts of the Revolution that I know . . . Mr Hibbert is outstanding' – J. H. Plumb in the *Sunday Telegraph*

☐ *Isak Dinesen* **Judith Thurman** £4.95

The acclaimed life of Karen Blixen, 'beautiful bride, disappointed wife, radiant lover, bereft and widowed woman, writer, sibyl, Scheherazade, child of Lucifer, Baroness; always a unique human being . . . an assiduously researched and finely narrated biography' – *Books & Bookmen*

☐ *The Amateur Naturalist*
Gerald Durrell with Lee Durrell £4.95

'Delight . . . on every page . . . packed with authoritative writing, learning without pomposity . . . it represents a real bargain' – *The Times Educational Supplement.* 'What treats are in store for the average British household' – *Daily Express*

☐ *When the Wind Blows* **Raymond Briggs** £2.95

'A visual parable against nuclear war: all the more chilling for being in the form of a strip cartoon' – *Sunday Times.* 'The most eloquent anti-Bomb statement you are likely to read' – *Daily Mail*